CONSCIENCE AND ITS RECOVERY

From the
Frankfurt School to
Feminism

GUYTON B. HAMMOND

CONSCIENCE AND ITS RECOVERY

From the Frankfurt School to Feminism

University Press of Virginia

Charlottesville and London

THE UNIVERSITY PRESS OF VIRGINIA
Copyright © 1993 by the Rector and Visitors
of the University of Virginia

First published 1993

Library of Congress Cataloging-in-Publication Data

Hammond, Guyton B., 1930–
    Conscience and its recovery : from the Frankfurt School to
feminism / Guyton B. Hammond.
        p.   cm. — (Studies in religion and culture)
    Includes bibliographical references and index.
    ISBN 0-8139-1446-9
    1. Conscience.   2. Self (Philosophy)   3. Ethics, Modern—20th
century.   I. Title.   II. Series: Studies in religion and culture
(Charlottesville, Va.)
    BJ1471.H36   1993
    170—dc20   93–9223
                                                                   CIP

Printed in the United States of America

For Mitchell

and his

generation

CONTENTS

PREFACE

THIS ESSAY had its inception in the early 1970s, when books by and about members of the Frankfurt School began appearing in English in increasing numbers. The treatment of the theme of authority and the family as a major philosophical issue by Max Horkheimer and his colleagues struck me at that time as immensely provocative. On the one hand these discussions gave me a new focus upon earlier studies I had made of Erich Fromm, Paul Tillich, Herbert Marcuse, and others. On the other hand they pointed forward to the newly emerging critique of patriarchy in the feminist literature. I was subsequently to discover in the works of Christopher Lasch similarly provocative considerations of the same theme.

I gradually came to see the critique of the patriarchal conscience as one continuing thread in this entire literature. I found here at once an entrée into a somewhat neglected aspect of Frankfurt School perspectives—their analysis of the formation of moral selves—and a valuable approach to contemporary issues of moral character. Whether I have succeeded in developing a clear and coherent position regarding these complex and many-sided issues remains for the reader to decide. This entire text may be viewed as a thought experiment—testing whether a particular way of thinking has constructive results.

In the first instance this study consists of a discussion of how to think about conscience, a subject regarding which we remain considerably muddled. But the debate about defining the nature of conscience is inseparable from the question of what it ought to be; inquiry into the conventional notion becomes a choice among alternative models. Ideas about conscience ultimately "cash out" as moral choices and lead into social policy. I shall be grateful if this essay makes even a small contribution to our thinking and choosing with respect to this intriguing subject.

I would like to thank friends and associates who read part or all of the manuscript (in one or another of its various stages) and made valuable comments: Frank Burch Brown, Catherine Snyder, Bob Stuart, George Telford, Bruce Hammond, and Stephen White. Our departmental secretary, Debbie Law, has been unfailingly helpful; I am grateful to her and to our departmental chairman, Charles A. Kennedy, for crucial assistance and support. Peter Laws generously assisted in computer use at a critical stage in the manuscript's preparation. Members of my family have very kindly refrained from asking me when I am going to finish; in this and in many other ways they have helped me persevere.

CONSCIENCE AND
ITS RECOVERY
From the
Frankfurt School to
Feminism

INTRODUCTION

ALMOST EVERYONE talks easily about conscience. Since many present-day disputes hinge on moral questions, references to conscience are frequent and impassioned. Yet, in spite of numerous studies of the subject, an uncertainty remains as to whether the term *conscience* has an actual referent or whether the concept is merely rhetorical. Is the idea of conscience sufficiently meaningful to play a significant role in current ethical discussions? This study will develop views that offer an affirmative answer to this question. But if the idea is to be viable, traditional and modern notions of conscience must be subjected to critique and reconstruction.[1]

To what experience, activity, or agency does the term refer? The proper starting point in attempting to answer this question is the notion of conscience as found in everyday usage. The term refers to a supposed agency in us "enjoining good acts";[2] it pronounces "judgment on our past moral performance" and "dictates what should be done in the future."[3] Thus conscience as the word is ordinarily used has to do with the activity of some agency of the self in self-judgment and idealization: one judges oneself in retrospect and models oneself in prospect in the light of one's ideal. Around this conventional notion and the experience of performing this activity, various interpretive theories and ideologies have gathered.

A case can be made that underlying many contemporary moral disputes is an often unacknowledged conflict between two sharply contrasting interpretations of conscience. Moral traditionalists, on the one hand, build a metaphysical psychology upon the conventional notion. Assuming that there is in each of us an agency that serves as a final court of appeal in making moral decisions, traditionalists view conscience as an inherent, God-given capacity for making moral judgments. If one acts contrary to its instruction, the pangs of a guilty conscience are expected to follow. This traditional conscience has a fixed and unchanging content, being in tune with the "law of God" or the "natural law." This view is defended both in naive and in more sophisticated ways in religious and philosophical contexts. On the other hand a contrary interpretation, with roots in twentieth-century social and psychological theory, has shaped antitraditionalist perspectives on conscience. The opinion has gained currency—especially since the wide dissemination of Sigmund Freud's psychological theories—that conscience derives from internalization in childhood of the admonitions of parents (and parental surrogates). This interpretation makes conscience dependent upon the interactions of parent and child in the family setting, an approach that, while giving conscience formation a certain inevitability, is taken to weaken or to destroy its compelling quality as unquestionable authority. If the dictates of conscience are viewed as deriving not from some inherent faculty of reason or God-given moral sense but from fallible parental instructions, its promptings come to be regarded as inhibitions rather than as guideposts, as something to be outgrown rather than conscientiously heeded. Thus, the first ideology regards conscience as something natural, as an authority built into the structure of selfhood. The second views it as an external imposition, as a form of domination that must be overcome in order for the individual to achieve self-fulfillment.

Neither of these dogmas about conscience seems to be in complete accord with contemporary experience. Many observers have noted a recent shift in the way moral character typically is formed. Earlier in American history the experience of a strict conscience was the norm: the voice of conscience was frequently heard. Indeed, all manner of therapies arose with the intent of freeing people from overstrict consciences. Today, however, the concern has arisen that young people are not developing consciences. Various critics question whether the proper social environment for the development of conscience is being provided. Evidence indicates that moral responsibility and maturity are being negatively affected. Not overbearing consciences but consciencelessness is now the problem.

If the foregoing describes present experience correctly, neither of the previously mentioned interpretations of conscience is adequate. If we observe historical-cultural change from too much conscience to too little, we can no longer postulate the existence of an internal agency with fixed and unchanging content. At the same time, if the absence of conscience is just as debilitating as an excessively rigid conscience, we cannot be satisfied with social trends that tend toward its elimination or with therapies that eradicate its last vestiges. If we reject interpretations that advocate either a rigid and absolutist conscience or a character without conscience, we are forced to look for some alternative understanding, beyond views that affirm dogmatic conscientiousness or conscienceless self-interestedness.

Some theorists sensitive to this situation argue that while absolutist claims for an agency of moral reasoning must be abandoned, conscience is still best understood as a mode of rational decision-making. This approach may acknowledge the multifarious influences that go into the shaping of morally mature character, but it nevertheless puts its emphasis upon the development of self-conscious reasoning in the realm of morality.[4] This account has considerable merit; it seems unlikely that any approach to well-developed conscience could separate it altogether from the process of reasoning. Nevertheless, the view I want to explore here has a different emphasis: it focuses upon aspects of the phenomenon of having a conscience that are neglected in this "rational" approach. Conscience has typically been experienced as the voice of an authoritative other with which the self identifies, such that the dictate of this other becomes the voice of one's best self. When asked why I am motivated to act or judge in a certain way, my answer is not to appeal to the rationality of the act or judgment but to assert that such an act or judgment is approved by my conscience. This approval by an ideal self who is in some sense other—this authoritativeness of conscience—needs further investigation to see if it can be affirmed after criticism.

This consideration leads back to the Freudian hypothesis that conscience originates in the relation of child to parent. I propose to pursue in this essay an analysis and critique of the parental aspect of conscience.[5] Freud assumed that the family found in nineteenth-century Europe was in its essentials a universal social

structure and consequently that the process of conscience formation was universally human. When this universalization of the
family is rejected, the family is relativized; parental authority
then mediates a particular social authority, and conscience is
thereby relativized and historicized. The perspective to be developed here is to accept this relativization but to explore the thesis
that there is nevertheless something in the parent-child relation
that is potentially universalizable. Is there a form of parental
authority that, when internalized, tends toward the development
of genuinely mature morality? This study will offer an affirmative
answer to that question. In Freudian terms we will explore the
constitution of the benign or beneficial superego along with critiques of pathological superegos; we will examine ways that morality can be parental without being authoritarian. The following
statement of Heinz Hartmann sets our task: "The much discussed
question of whether morals are, because of their origins, of necessity 'authoritarian' is, it seems to me, not always put the right way.
Every moral system has its origins in the relations of the child to
adults who are not only loved and hated but also persons in authority. However, the value systems evolving from these origins may
have an authoritarian, a nonauthoritarian, or an antiauthoritarian
character."[6] Our quest is for a possible authority without domination. What can be meant by a nonauthoritarian internalization of
authority?

There is a great deal of literature today criticizing Western individualism and pointing to the cruciality of "intersubjectivity" for
the most fulfilling type of self-formation.[7] While I agree with this
emphasis, my intent here is to urge that this intersubjectivity is in
part intergenerational and that an aspect of the self's internalization of or identification with the other is the internalization of
parental authority. The contention that beneficent conscience is
continuous with this internalization cannot be sustained until it
is subjected to rigorous critique. Contemporary objections to relationships of authority have their legitimacy, but the critique of
authority need not eventuate in the dissolution of all authority,
and the critique of conscience need not lead to its dissolution.

Parent-child interactions cannot be our whole story, however.
As will be later argued, it is the parental conscience with which
the child has to deal (whether through incorporation or resistance). And this conscience already has a cultural content (which
is to say, the existence of a human parent presupposes the existence of a moral tradition). The conscientious parent, not the

desiring child, is the true—even if problematical—starting point for moral culture. The internalization that creates conscience is an aspect of socialization. Parents stand between society and their offspring and play, at least in part, the role of mediators—representing and to a greater or lesser degree exemplifying societal-ideological commitments. (The extent to which parents are also autonomous sources of culture and morality formation is a disputed point to which we shall return.) Our study must give attention, therefore, to ideological as well as to psychological and familial factors. In the approach taken here, conscience is indeed a key point of intersection of the individual psyche (with its desires, wishes, aims), the parent (generating relations of both love and conflict), and society's norms, standards, and values.

Finally, our study raises the question whether conscience is capable of providing a point of transcendence. The Western religions have been in important respects familial religions; God has been viewed as the exalted father. Modernity knows, however, that the commandments of deity can be regarded as culturally relative: they are the rules and restrictions by means of which a particular culture organizes and channels human drives through the medium of the family. But the parental contribution does not consist simply of rules and restrictions. The parent also, in fact and in representation, offers love and nurturance. Conscience provides not only control and limit but also proffers vocation, meaning, an ideal self. A thesis to be explored here is whether there is (or can be) in conscience a utopian dimension—an intimation of an ideal community where the rules serve the end of human fulfillment. If so, conscience might provide a standpoint for ideology critique, a point of transcendence beyond culture.

It may be helpful to list here a number of assumptions that inform the analyses that follow:

1. The traditional view of conscience as a static and unchanging moral authority reproduced in each of us can no longer be upheld. Conscience did often seem permanent and even natural in earlier periods because a degree of stability in the moral sphere was achieved in spite of social and political changes. But we are now living in a time when this stability has disappeared.
2. Freud's account of the origin (not the end result) of conscience in the internalization of parental admonitions by the young is correct in its fundamentals. This discovery of the parent in the conscience is one of the great critical disillusionments of the

twentieth century. Yet there is a positive aspect to the thesis: it reveals more clearly the essential sociality of selfhood, the constitution of our selves, and in particular our moral sense in interaction with significant others. Conscience as monologue—the self as the only judge of itself—is a pathology of conscience.

3. Freud's assumption that the nuclear family is a natural unit transcending society and that therefore conscience formation in this family is everywhere the same is a view that must be rejected. Rather, the view found in the Marxian tradition (as well as elsewhere) must be endorsed, namely, that the family is historically variable and must be interpreted through its development. If the family varies historically, conscience will also vary.

4. Ideological factors, far from being mere reflections of other determinative social influences, may play a crucial role in individual character formation, as sociologists in the tradition of Max Weber have suggested. We must look not just at psychological patterns or at familial structures but also at ideological factors if we are to grasp the historical development of conscience.

5. Conscience took a distinctive form in the characters of individuals reared in the nuclear, bourgeois-Protestant families of the early modern West. Once one links conscience with particular types of family and ideology, it is no longer possible to deal with it in completely general or abstract terms.

6. We are threatened today with the loss of this conscience as a consequence of familial, ideological, and characterological changes.

7. In opposition to those who favor its dissolution, the viewpoint developed here is an attempt to recover the potential of conscience for transcendence and genuine authority. The disillusionment resulting from critique can be a prelude to the rescue and recovery of the valuable aspects of this traditional moral formation.

As these assumptions make clear, this study regards conscience as a complex phenomenon that requires a multidimensional approach; personal-psychological, familial, and ideological factors must all be kept in view. This kind of critique of conscience, attentive to familial and ideological-religious aspects and relating earlier historical periods to the present, was initiated in the past

generation by several members of the Frankfurt Institute for Social
Research: Max Horkheimer, Erich Fromm, Theodor Adorno, and
Herbert Marcuse (and continued in the contemporary work of
Juergen Habermas). Their searching inquiry into the forms taken
by the bourgeois-Protestant conscience in modern Western history and into its fate in the twentieth century deserves more
focused attention. Their approach in turn took shape as a synthesis of diverse intellectual currents. My attempt will be to retrace
the process of attaining this synthesis by first locating its key
elements in the thought of certain predecessors and then tracing
the development of this theme through the various texts written
by members of the Frankfurt School.

Ideologically speaking, the Frankfurt School literature concen-
trates on the Protestant conscience and its history (in an analysis
that is in effect a deconstruction of the Protestant ethic). An important dialogue partner with Frankfurt School members in dealing with these topics was the theologian Paul Tillich. Since Tillich
was a personal friend of key members of the Frankfurt School, was
nurtured in the same philosophical traditions as Frankfurt School
members, and was attuned to many of the same issues, I include a
discussion of Tillich's theory of conscience as well. Horkheimer
and his colleagues by no means ignored religious aspects of our
theme, but Tillich gave them fuller treatment, and he offered a
constructive proposal about conscience to which I return in my
own concluding reflections.

Horkheimer and his colleagues were hampered by the limited
amount of research on the history of the family that was available
to them. This gap in research has been filled to a considerable
extent in recent years, and critical and evaluative family studies
have taken advantage of this material. In a brief excursus I discuss
the implications of such studies for conscience critique, focusing
my attention on two contrasting views: Mark Poster's *Critical
Theory of the Family*, and Peter and Brigitte Berger's *The War over
the Family: Capturing the Middle Ground*. Conflicting accounts
of the family in its modern development pose a number of issues
that bear directly upon conscience interpretation.

The extended discussions of conscience in relation to family
and ideology found in the Frankfurt School literature have taken
on an added relevance since the rise of feminist theory in the
1970s. This new feminism has seen itself as antagonistic to the
culturally dominant ethic. As such, it has tended to be critical—
implicitly at least—of the Western conscience as well, viewing the

traditional ethic, its internalization, and its familial context as strongly patriarchal.[8] Because of their attacks on bourgeois-Protestant conscience formation, feminists have sometimes been accused of defending a liberation from conscientious constraints. Without an alternative approach to conscience, feminism has been susceptible to this charge. Most feminists regard the criticism of patriarchy as a basic, organizing theme with psychological, familial, and ideological aspects. I contend, and hope to show in this study, that it is useful to bring critiques of patriarchy and of conscience into close proximity, that indeed it is instructive to view patriarchy first and foremost as a type of conscience. An assessment of the ambiguous legacy of the patriarchal conscience is one of my main purposes here. I find in the Frankfurt School, in Tillich, and in feminism perspectives for a constructive critique of conscience that may point toward its renewal.

Some feminists have considered their criticism of patriarchy to be continuous with Frankfurt School themes. A group of "psychoanalytic" feminists (Juliet Mitchell, Dorothy Dinnerstein, Nancy Chodorow, Jessica Benjamin, and others) extend and amplify the critique initiated by the Frankfurt School while drawing also upon post-Freudian developments in psychoanalytic theory (I follow Chodorow and Benjamin in giving attention especially to the work of Melanie Klein and Janine Chasseguet-Smirgel).[9] My study pursues the implications of this feminist theory for conscience critique. Finally, I explore the debates between the feminists and the cultural historian Christopher Lasch, for, in certain respects, these disputes can be seen as conflicts between rival interpretations of the Frankfurt School heritage. An examination of Lasch's analysis of conscience leads toward the viewpoint developed here, since he gives attention to the characterological, the familial, and to a lesser extent the ideological-religious dimensions of the debates about the patriarchal conscience. In so doing, he brings Frankfurt School perspectives into ongoing dialogue with family theorists, with psychoanalytic feminists, and, at least by implication, with feminist theologians. I attempt to extend these dialogues further through an examination of Lasch's perspective.

Feminists make a convincing case that any renewal of conscience must be accomplished in a post-patriarchal framework. Psychoanalytic feminists describe the familial changes that are necessary. But changes in conscience are correlative not only with changes in the family but also with ideological-religious changes, as feminist theology has rightly emphasized. Any full inquiry into the possibility of a postpatriarchal conscience must deal with characterological, familial, and ideological development. This study attempts to keep all three in view.

I conclude that issues of great moment are at stake in these debates. The viability of any internalization of an authoritative value tradition is brought into question.[10] Is all internalization of socially legitimated authority a form of internalized domination, a denial of individual freedom and autonomy? Should the effort to preserve moral traditions be given up in favor of a pragmatic, present-oriented give and take, without deep, character-based value commitments? Or is life without internalized commitments and without linkage between generations a form of moral emptiness and decay? Are individuals more mature without an internalized conscience? Or does this condition lead to moral chaos?

These discussions move repeatedly from psychology through sociology to the level of basic value perspectives. They involve moral and moral-religious issues as well as social scientific issues. Moral philosophers and theologians as well as social scientists have an appropriate interest in these deliberations; descriptive and evaluative aspects of these problems cannot be separated. The interest of this study is finally moral-religious, that is, with ideological reconstruction. But this dimension is inseparable from the familial and the characterological dimensions.

Rather than advocating either the dissolution of conscience or resistance to its dissolution through the reassertion of traditional (patriarchal) authority, the literature referred to above suggests that the potential of conscience can be "rescued" (as Theodor Adorno once put it) through critique. In the view developed here, neither the dissolution of conscience nor the reaffirmation of it in its traditional form but the self-criticism of its pathologies is required by our present moral crisis. The reconstruction of morality does not entail the extrication of the self from the enchantment of the parental-societal voice by means of objectifying reflection but the actualizing of the potential for self-critique inherent in the moral tradition and its internalization.

As was suggested earlier, my approach to the recovery of conscience proposes that there is already in the earliest process of moral formation—in the early parent-child relation—an implicit moral ideal that is presupposed and sought: the ideal of perfected community. Parent-child relations are inherently moral (only the discarding of an infant as disposable waste puts the relationship outside the moral framework). These relations are moral but not symmetrical. The parent is in a position both to give and to require: ideally, the gift is nurturant love and the requirement has to do with contingent rules that structure a loving community. Inherent in the parent-child relation is the presupposition that nurturance and rules are for the child's good. The child, of course, may rebel against the imposed limits. But even in this rebellion is an implicit longing for a perfectly beneficent authority that provides the proper structure for an ideal community.[11] It is this presupposed utopia that provides the standpoint for critique.

Generally conscience is thought of as a conservative influence in the psyche: Freud called it a "garrison in a conquered city." By the same token it is often thought of as a force for preserving childish dependency—a backward-looking, past-oriented agency. But in the view defended here, conscience—potentially at least—has a future—as well as a past orientation. It looks at the self from the standpoint of an ideal future. As Hans Loewald has suggested: "Conscience . . . speaks to us, one might say, in the name of the inner future that envisages us as capable or incapable, as willing or unwilling to move toward it and encompass it, just as parents envisaged us in our potentialities and readiness for growth and development."[12] A renewed conscience can be not only the voice of the past, of tradition, of the unrecoverable parent, but also of the future, of humanity's completion in perfected community. Loss of this conscience is unacceptable because its loss entails the loss of the critical perspective (the utopian standpoint) and renders life "one-dimensional."

The Frankfurt School's approach to conscience took shape as a synthesis of themes from three great predecessors—Max Weber, Sigmund Freud, and Karl Marx. In Chapter 1, I extract from these predecessors' works certain key concepts that went into the distinctive approach to Western moral character developed by the Frankfurt Critical Theorists.[13] Also I refer to Wilhelm Reich, a transitional figure who began the synthesis that was brought to a kind of inconclusive conclusion by Erich Fromm, by Max Horkheimer, and in a different way by Paul Tillich.

1

ORIGINS OF THE
CRITICAL PERSPECTIVE
ON CONSCIENCE

THE CRITICAL THEORISTS regarded themselves as Marxists, so their version of Western Marxism might be our starting point. But Max Horkheimer and his colleagues rejected the Marxist "economism" that sought to reduce everything to the economic "base." Rather, they were prepared to take seriously the influence of ideological factors on socioeconomic development, and they were inclined to accord such institutions as the family and the political sphere a degree of autonomy vis-à-vis the economy.[1] Indeed, as many commentators have noted, the Frankfurt theorists returned in important ways to Marx's great predecessor, Hegel (and to the Hegelian elements in the early Marx), for their inspiration. Two themes from Hegel can be singled out as fundamental for critique as they understood it, and therefore as pivotal for our study as well.

Like Hegel, the members of the Frankfurt School saw consciousness (the realm of thought) in dialectical interaction with material and social reality (the objective realm). In this view, social institutions such as the family, the economy, government, and religion are human constructs (not something natural to humanity), even though at the same time these institutions reciprocally shape human consciousness. This Hegelian perspective prevents critical theory from turning either to positivism or to subjective idealism: neither the facts of existing social institutions nor the facts of consciousness can be regarded as fixed or final.

Secondly, the members of the Frankfurt School shared with Hegel the conviction that there is an emancipatory thrust to the entire historical process. They could not endorse Hegel's doctrine that an absolute Spirit actualizes itself in world history, but they nevertheless preserved remnants of the religiously inspired utopian quest, as indeed Marx did as well: mankind is engaged in a restless search for freedom in community. This utopian ideal functioned for Horkheimer and the others as a kind of negative theology; while not providing any positive content for belief, it served as a standpoint for critique of presently existing realities.[2]

Max Weber's Protestant Ethic

These Hegelian ideas undergirded the Western Marxism to which the Critical Theorists at least initially gave their allegiance. But distinctly Marxian ideas, with exceptions to be mentioned, were not in fact determinative for members of the Frankfurt School in the area under investigation here. Looming large on their intellectual horizons as a kind of counterweight to Marx was the great sociologist, Max Weber (1864–1920). Weber's seminal work, *The Protestant Ethic and the Spirit of Capitalism*, made the case that the Protestant ethic that emerged at the time of the Reformation constituted an essential basis for the rise of modern capitalism.[3] This "Weber thesis" became one component in the synthesis of the Frankfurt School and an important aspect of the school's approach to conscience. Certain themes from Weber thus become the starting point for this study. The problems of conflicting character types and views of conscience referred to in the Introduction can be reduced in Weber's terms to the questions: what were the implications of the Protestant ethic for human character, and what has happened to the Protestant ethic and the Protestant-Puritan character type in the twentieth century?

Weber offers a detailed analysis of the way this ethic—also described as the Puritan or work ethic—contributed to the development of modern Western civilization. His interest is not simply in capitalism narrowly conceived; he makes it clear that he finds in the Calvinist branch of Protestantism something that "made an indispensable contribution to the emergence of modern society."[4] With "a keen feeling for historical paradox," he defends the view that modern, commercial, secular culture has religious roots and determinants.[5]

In summary, Weber seeks to show that the general availability of persons of a particular character type was a prerequisite for early capitalism. Though by no means denying that economic forces also influence the development of character, he argues that the prototypical entrepreneurial type needed for capitalist enterprise could not simply be a product of the economic system; on the contrary, true capitalism in the modern sense developed only where this type was already present. What requires explaining is the rise of persons with a disciplined, self-controlled diligence that was quite out of keeping with traditional attitudes. In the outlook of an individual of this type, labor and its products are considered goods for reasons other than the pleasurable results for the worker. Weber contends that this view of work is explicable only in terms of a religious sense of vocation or calling to one's secular labors.[6] He explains the appearance of this new person by referring to the rise of the Calvinist ideology, which in this respect built upon but became more radical than Lutheranism. Calvinism encouraged a "this-worldly asceticism," which brought a monklike discipline and control to mundane activity.[7] Weber describes this pattern of living as a "rationalization" of life, in the sense that individuals base their actions upon consciously chosen, long-term purposes and calculations rather than upon momentary impulses or feelings.[8] Also emerging out of Calvinism was a sense that one can prove, as well as display, one's faith in worldly activity. Weber argues that out of this configuration of beliefs a new ethic, a new character type, and ultimately a new culture were born.

In Weber's eyes, however, this was a culture of a very peculiar sort. Each individual was understood to stand alone in the presence of God, apart from the commonalities of the group. One sought to scrutinize oneself, as it were, from the perspective of God. The "we-consciousness" of traditional culture was replaced by the "I-consciousness" of the Puritan-Protestant perspective. "Obeying God rather than men" meant obeying one's own conscience, understood as having divine authority, rather than obeying external authorities. Thus the Puritan conscience became one of the major sources of Western individualism. Though some interpreters have urged that the emphasis on the individual conscience was mitigated by participation in the Puritan church, Weber perceived the Protestant ethic as a major breach in the collectivism of traditionalist culture.

The interpretation of these patterns of this-worldly asceticism, rationalization, and individualization can take on a different coloration in different thought contexts. Weber uses Benjamin Frank-

lin as his prime example of the eventual characterological consequences of the Protestant work ethic. Franklin evokes images of
Yankee shrewdness, calculation, and common sense along with
conscientious discipline, an outlook that has been described as
"utilitarian individualism."[9] The initiative and productivity of
this type of person were admired by Weber, as they are generally in
Western culture to this day. European readers of Weber, however,
would be likely to recall Friedrich Nietzsche's biting attack on
bourgeois Protestant asceticism in such works as *Toward a Gene-
alogy of Morals* and *Twilight of the Idols*. Nietzsche regarded the
ascetic individual as dangerously powerful but ultimately life denying. Overtones of this perspective pervade Weber's work, in
uneasy combination with the more favorable view of the Protestant character.[10] Weber's ambivalence about the Protestant ethic
carries over into the Frankfurt School.

At least in his view of the final outcome of Western characterological development, Weber was pessimistic. In his famous conclusion to *The Protestant Ethic and the Spirit of Capitalism*, he
describes the emergence of "specialists without spirit; sensualists
without heart."[11] Perhaps this observation was a premonition of
Germany's descent into barbarism. Weber fears and warns against
the rise of a culture and a character type dominated by what has
aptly been called "conscienceless reason."[12] This critique of modern "rationalization" detached from underlying value commitments was carried forward by members of the Frankfurt School
and by Tillich.

Weber acknowledges that the development of his thesis about
Protestantism and the spirit of capitalism requires an understanding of "the manner in which ideas become effective forces in
history."[13] However, a gap in his analysis appears at just this point:
How did the Reformation doctrines come to have a formative
influence on the character structure of individuals? How did ideology become embedded in character? By what means did Lutheran
and Calvinist-Puritan ideas become internalized in the drives and
motivations of large numbers of individuals? Weber fails to deal
significantly with the process by means of which changes in ideology become incorporated into character structure. What is needed
is a kind of "historical psychology." The concepts needed for the
construction of this psychohistory were not available to Weber. It
remained for subsequent scholars to discover that such concepts
were emerging contemporaneously in the complex researches of
Sigmund Freud.[14]

The Freudian Superego

It was Sigmund Freud (1856–1939) who first taught the twentieth century how value systems are internalized into the psychic structure of individuals. Freud's treatment of "superego" formation quickly came to be regarded as basic to any discussion of this subject, even though many of the specifics of Freud's analysis continued to be vigorously debated (as we shall see in our own subsequent discussion). In Freud's account, internalization of cultural norms and standards takes place in the context of the family, as children interiorize this content as a result of extended and conflict-laden interactions with their parents. Furthermore, for Freud it is the father who is the pivotal figure of authority; it is he who represents cultural demand and restriction. In a controversial formulation, Freud systematizes the familial relationships into a universal "complex": the famous Oedipal triangle wherein the growing boy (Freud was primarily interested in male development), having recognized that he cannot rival or replace the father in the affections of the mother, opts instead for identification with the father, in the process internalizing paternal norms, prohibitions, and ideals. The resulting superego serves as monitor and judge of the rational ego as well as of instinct-dominated impulse (the id). In one account Freud describes the superego simply as the earliest part of the identifications that constitute the child's ego: "The ego is formed to a great extent out of identifications . . . ; the earliest of these identifications always fulfill a special office in the ego and stand apart from the rest of the ego in the form of a super-ego."[15]

Freud, in fact, exhibits some uncertainty as to whether both parents or only the father is involved in the formation of the superego. In *The Ego and the Id*, he states that the origin of the ego ideal (here equated with the superego) lies in "an individual's first and most important identification, his identification with the father in his own personal prehistory." In a footnote to this statement, he adds: "Perhaps it would be safer to say 'with the parents'; for before a child has arrived at a definite knowledge of the difference between the sexes, the lack of a penis, it does not distinguish in value between its father and its mother."[16] In the same work, addressing those who complain against the psychoanalytic theories that "there must surely be a higher nature in man," Freud responds: " 'Very true,' we can say, 'and here we have that higher nature in this ego ideal or super-ego, the representative of our relation to our parents. When we were little children we knew these higher natures, we admired them and feared them; and later we took them into ourselves.' "[17]

In subsequent passages Freud focuses exclusively on the father relation: "It is easy to show that the ego ideal answers to everything that is expected of the higher nature of man. As a substitute for a longing for the father, it contains the germ from which all religions have evolved."[18] Two considerations seem to lead Freud in the direction of associating the superego exclusively with the father. First is his conclusion that "religion and moral restraint were acquired" at least in the history of the human race "out of the father-complex . . . through the process of mastering the Oedipus complex."[19] Thus incestuous ties to the mother are broken and the Oedipal complex is overcome through internalization of the father's rules and prohibitions. A second reason that the superego is paternal for Freud lies in the nature of societal authority. The father is not simply another person separate from the mother; he represents socially legitimated authority. Freud states: "As a child grows up, the role of the father is carried on by teachers and others in authority; their injunctions and prohibitions remain powerful in the ego ideal and continue, in the form of conscience, to exercise moral censorship."[20] The "injunctions and prohibitions" of civilization, in Freud's view, are basically paternal, for culture itself is patriarchal.[21] Conscience, then, for Freud is also patriarchal.

Some Freudians preserve the interpretation that the superego derives from the child's early relations with both parents. Melanie Klein writes: "According to [Freud's] findings, which psychoanalytic practice has borne out in every instance, the person's conscience is a precipitate or representative of his early relation to his parents. He has in some sense internalized his parents—has taken them into himself. There they become a differentiated part of his ego—his super-ego—and an agency which advances against the rest of his ego certain requirements, reproaches, and admonitions, and which stands in opposition to his instinctual impulses."[22]

Klein maintains this reading of Freud by pushing the origins of the superego further back into early infancy than had Freud, to the stage when, as Freud said, the child "does not distinguish in value between its father and its mother." Klein's focus on early infancy and on the mother relation as a crucial context for character development has strongly influenced the feminist movement.

While Klein's reading of Freud minimizes the impact of the larger society and its ideologies upon formation of the superego,

Freud himself increasingly takes account of ideological factors and proceeds to qualify the simple thesis that conscience is reducible to parental instruction. In the following striking passage, Freud resists the idea that the formation of conscience can be reduced to the parental voice taken out of its social context, or that such formation can be reduced to more tangible external factors such as economic conditions; instead he emphasizes the role played by cultural tradition in conscience formation.

> Thus a child's super-ego is in fact constructed on the model not of its parents but of its parents' super-ego; the contents which fill it are the same and it becomes the vehicle of tradition and of all the time-resisting judgments of value which have propagated themselves in this manner from generation to generation. . . . It seems likely that what are known as materialistic views of history sin in under-estimating this factor. They brush it aside with the remark that human "ideologies" are nothing other than the product and super-structure of their contemporary economic conditions. That is true, but very probably not the whole truth. Mankind never lives entirely in the present. The past, the traditions of the race and of the people, lives on in the ideologies of the super-ego and yields only slowly to the influences of the present and to new changes; and so long as it operates through the super-ego it plays a powerful part in human life, independently of economic conditions.[23]

This version of Freud's superego theory—emphasizing its social and ideological dimensions—will occupy a central place in our study.

In the later work, *Civilization and Its Discontents* (1930), Freud constructs an all-encompassing social philosophy. Projecting the Oedipus complex back into a kind of "myth of origin," he postulates that civilization arose out of the process of internalizing the proscriptions of a primal father. In relation to this primal figure, and to other great leaders, a "cultural superego" is built up that consists of the prohibitions and constraints fundamental to epochs of civilization and is usually understood as the commandments of a deity.[24]

Freud could have focused his attention on the historical development of this cultural superego. (He did describe religious, metaphysical, and scientific stages of Western history in *The Future of an Illusion* [1927], and he might have discussed their different superegos.) But it is more consistent with the universality of the Oedipus complex to visualize superego formation as a repetitive structure required by all civilizations. Likewise the nuclear family is viewed more typically by Freud as in its essentials a universal human phenomenon. His sociohistorical theory is built upon a familial analogy—society is the family "written large." Therefore, even though ideologies may vary somewhat, in the end ideology and family reproduce a patriarchal superego. "Mother" represents precultural gratification, while "father" represents civilizing constraints. Attitudes toward religious and political authorities are in the Freudian scheme forever imprinted with "the law of the father." Ideologies with a strong motherly component—and cultures influenced by them—can only be regarded as regressive or infantile.[25]

Many Freudians have followed Freud in ignoring the potential for development of the cultural superego, thereby minimizing the role of the superego as "vehicle of tradition," not only in its conservative aspects but also in its liberal ones. This study will give more attention to this kind of development. In particular, the question will be raised whether there can be a progressive motherly element in culture. Freud cannot explicitly grant this; he assumes that reuniting, motherly tendencies can only be regressive and that only individualizing patriarchy is progressive. However, perhaps surprisingly, he concedes that the preeminent "task" of civilization is "one of uniting separate individuals into a community bound together by libidinal ties."[26] Toward this end, the cultural superego attempts to obviate the aggressiveness of individuals by the commandment to love one's neighbors as oneself. But this commandment, says Freud, is "impossible to fulfill."[27] Progressive unity is not simply a utopian ideal; it generates guilt since it cannot be accomplished. Freud concludes that it is best for us not to strive for an impossible goal. Motherly love ánd communal nurturance are supports we need but cannot have as adults.

These themes will be explored further at a later point. For the moment, our assertion is that Freud clarifies the mechanism by which ideologies are incorporated into character structure through the mediation of the family. The superego is conceived as a kind of social garrison within the individual. The process of superego formation is not a "natural" one, since enculturation is the imposition of a particular system of controls upon nature. But so long as the basic psychological structure of the family is universalized, so long as internalization is regarded as a repetitive pattern, there can be no explanation for the rise of a *new* conscience, as is entailed, at least implicitly, by Max Weber's discussion, as previously summarized. All culture is viewed as ascetic-repressive; the "work ethic" and the structuring of character in the patriarchal family are the foundations of civilization itself.

From the standpoint of our analysis, Freud supplies an essential ingredient missing in Weber, and vice versa. Weber does not recognize the crucial role played by the family in mediating an ethic to individuals, so he does not see that the character type he scrutinizes is as much shaped by the family as by the Protestant church.[28] Freud, on the other hand, fails to see that the conscience that he analyzed became a widespread phenomenon only in the "Protestant era." Interestingly, Freud in a late work (*Moses and Monotheism*) assigns to the prototypical Jewish character some of the traits that Weber associated with the Protestant-Calvinist, thus suggesting the origin of conscience in Judaism (a view not out of keeping with Weber, who perceived Protestantism as a return to certain Jewish perspectives). But before Freud's viewpoint can be reconciled and combined with that of Weber, another step must be taken, namely the "historicizing" not only of religion but also of the family. For recognition that the family has had a significant history, we must turn to another intellectual tradition.

Family Criticism in the Marxian Tradition

The thought of Karl Marx (1818–1883) and the Marxists provides an important framework for critical theory in some areas, but it is less crucial for the group's ideas about conscience. Other Marxian ideas will surface as we proceed, but for the moment only a statement regarding the Marxian view of the family is necessary, and briefer remarks about ideology and conscience in Marx will suffice. Reacting against the favorable view of the bourgeois family developed by Hegel, Marx comes to regard the family as a part of the superstructure of society that would be radically altered with the overthrow of the capitalist economic order. A year after Marx's death, *The Origin of the Family, Private Property, and the State*, by Friedrich Engels, Marx's close associate, was published. It drew in part upon unpublished notes of Marx. In this work Engels, referring to the anthropological researches of Lewis Henry Morgan and Johann Jakob Bachofen, theorizes that the patriarchal, monogamous, nuclear family arose as a derivative of private property interests on the part of men. Indeed, for Engels patriarchal monogamy is the "first class antagonism" and appeared at the dawn of civilization.[29] Engels follows the thesis of Bachofen that this sub-jugation of women replaced an earlier matriarchal period. Since this "world-historic defeat of the female sex," patriarchy has con-tinued with only minor modifications up to the bourgeois period.[30]

Although there is some disagreement within the basic Marxian texts regarding the issue of the fate of patriarchy in bourgeois culture, orthodox Marxism embraced the view that the patriarchal family contributes to exploitative capitalism and should be super-seded with the advent of "socialism."[31] Thus there exists in Marx-ism a tradition of family criticism and a basis for opposing the view that prevalent family forms are universal and dictated by nature. The family is shaped by historical forces rather than being a natural basis for history.

For Marxism, religion, like the family, is a part of the societal superstructure. Religious doctrines are ideologies that justify and defend the existing socioeconomic order. Protestantism, there-fore, is regarded as the ideology of emergent capitalism. Contra Max Weber, in the orthodox Marxist view the economic order is determinative and ideology is derivative.

A Marxist view of conscience can be developed by extrapolation, even though it is not the subject of extensive critique in the classic texts of Marxism. In the Marxian schema, "consciousness is a social product": the individual is a social creation. Bourgeois Prot-estant individuals "standing alone before God" and "governed by conscience" are actually produced in response to the needs of the capitalist economy. Their autonomy is an illusion; "behind their backs" they are controlled by impersonal market forces that serve the interests of the ruling classes. By implication, then, the bour-geois conscience speaks with the voice of the prevailing capitalist ideology. The separateness and isolation of bourgeois individuals, far from being an actualization of fuller humanity, is a state of alienation from mankind's essential sociality. This condition, which seems to be freedom, is actually a state of domination by alien interests disguised by ideology. God, father, and, implicitly, conscience are mystifications of class interests.[32]

Marxism offers no psychology of domination or analysis of char-acter types. It therefore contributes little to an understanding of the mechanism by which relations of authority are translated from objective economic conditions to the subjective perspectives and attitudes of individuals.[33] Most attention is focused on eco-nomic change; little analysis is provided of the process by means of which ideological change is effected.

The kind of analysis of conscience and moral character projected in the Introduction, one that is attentive to ideological and familial dimensions, becomes possible when elements of the Weberian, the Freudian, and the Marxian perspectives are brought into fruitful interaction. This synthesis was accomplished (not without continuing difficulties) by members of the Frankfurt School, in specific historical circumstances to which we will refer later. Eventually their work—spanning Europe and North America—resulted in a body of theory that has application not only to the context in which it appeared but also to contemporary debates about moral character.

Stated in a preliminary way, the Frankfurt theorists discovered that there was an underlying commonality in the critiques of bourgeois culture and character found in Weber, Freud, and Marx. All three point toward a characterization of bourgeois "man" (a masculine type is presupposed) in terms of ascetic, controlling domination. These critiques picture the modern middle-class individual as attempting to gain control over his own body and its instinctual drives, over the laboring class, over women, over nature itself. And for all three perspectives, the result is ambiguous, even tragic. On the one hand the ascetic character heightens individuality and moral responsibility; on the other hand its negative consequences are objectification, repression, and alienation. Critical theory develops this picture of bourgeois character in both its positive and negative aspects and initiates a discussion of how the negatives can be overcome. To use the terms set forth in the Introduction, these debates constitute a critique of the "conscientious" character type: How can the limitations of the Puritan, repressive character be overcome without lapsing into self-indulgent permissiveness? How can the deficiencies of the patriarchal character be overcome without losing individuality and moral responsibility? How can objectifying rationalization be overcome without forsaking rationality altogether?

Before we turn to the Frankfurt School proper, I first must consider one thinker who set the stage for its discussions; he achieved in part, but only in part, the requisite synthesis of the viewpoints mentioned above.

The Partial Synthesis of Wilhelm Reich

Marx, Freud, and Weber all were much discussed thinkers in post–World War I Germany, and interest in reconciling their partially contradictory perspectives was beginning to surface in many places by the 1920s. The synthesis of Marx and Weber attempted by Hungarian-born Georg Lukács (1885–1971), for example, influenced Horkheimer and Tillich.[34] But it was Wilhelm Reich who was the most immediate forerunner of the Frankfurt School in the analysis of character types.

Reich (1897–1957), a German psychoanalyst and younger associate of Freud, was for a time a member of the Communist party; later he reversed himself, migrated to the United States, and became a defender of Western democracy. Among the first to attempt a combination of the perspective of Marx-Engels with that of Freud, Reich made significant contributions to the problems we are pursuing, even though his later formulations became increasingly bizarre and unconvincing. One finds in Reich a struggle—never successfully resolved—to achieve an adequate view of the relation of ideology, family, and economy where all three are regarded as independent variables. The private economy, according to Reich, needs the patriarchal, monogamous family to perpetuate itself.[35] Reaffirming Engels's assertion that the domination of women by men in the patriarchal family was the first class division, Reich links the rise of capitalism with the rise of patriarchy. Primitive man tends toward communistic democracy and matriarchy. (Here Reich draws upon the anthropological research of Bronislaw Malinowski as Engels had drawn upon Bachofen and Morgan.) Capitalist and patriarchal patterns, along with monogamous marriage, are seen as originating at the dawn of civilization. In Reich's perspective, modern totalitarian movements have their roots in the repressive bourgeois family that has remained unchanged for millennia in spite of progress in the economic sphere.[36] Any fundamental change in the social order will require a change in the prevailing character type, necessitating an overthrow of the patriarchal family structure. Reich regards matriarchy as the "natural" family form and maintains that a return to matriarchy is essential to further progress.[37]

Reich never achieves complete clarity regarding the relation of the family to the economy, on the one hand, and to religious ideology, on the other. At times the change from "primitive work-democracy" to capitalist private property is given historical priority; at times the rise of the patriarchal-ascetic family is given precedence. More commonly, however, these "two inter-related processes" are viewed as parallel and simultaneous developments. "But if one starts from present-day economic and sexual organization and follows it backward, one eventually gets to a point where the economic and the sexual organizations flow into each other."[38] Similarly, Reich finds the patriarchal family and "patriarchal authoritarian mysticism" to be finally inseparable.[39] He accepts Freud's view that the concept of God in Western religion is an exalted father image, and he stresses to the point of exaggeration the basically Freudian assertion that religion "draws its power from the suppression of genital sexuality."[40] Consequently, he could see patriarchal religion and the patriarchal family as deriving from the same impulses. Not surprisingly, Reich also finds the same derivation for patriarchal-authoritarian governments: "Fascism is supposed to be a reversion to paganism and an archenemy of religion. Far from it—fascism is the supreme expression of religious mysticism. As such, it comes into being in peculiar social form. Fascism countenances that religiosity that stems from sexual perversion, and it transforms the masochistic character of the old patriarchal religion of suffering into a sadistic religion. In short, it transposes religion from the other-worldliness of the philosophy of suffering to the this-worldliness of sadistic murder."[41]

Reich's perspective makes the superego a key factor in the causal chain. Just as the family is the agency of society, so the superego is the agency of the family and religion that thwarts humanity's drive for wholeness and health. In all of Reich's alternative schematisms, it is patriarchy, not simply the family per se, that "mediates" between religion and the rise of capitalism, between ideology and economy. Because patriarchy has religious, politicoeconomic, and psychological dimensions, it can serve all of the purposes that Reich intended. In the last analysis, patriarchy is itself an ideology with implications for politics, economics, family, and individual character. In Reich's discussions, "ideology" refers not primarily to conscious ideas but to "the underlying, virtually unconscious aspirations of a people";[42] this concept in turn approximates what Freud called the "cultural superego." For Reich the patriarchal conscience is the internalization of the ideology of domination. His point is that internalized values are no longer strictly ideational; they are motivational as well. As Juliet Mitchell explains Reich's view, patriarchal ideology is reproduced in the internalized psychic structures of individuals; Mitchell follows Reich when she asserts that patriarchy is the prevailing ideology of human society.[43]

For Reich, then, patriarchy was the primordial structure of domination that continues without basic alteration in spite of the economic changes that have marked the modern period. The following passage summarizes many of the themes of Reich's Freudo-Marxism:

> The political ideology of the European Marxist parties was based on economic conditions that were confined to a period of some two hundred years, from about the seventeenth to the nineteenth century, during which the machine was developed. Twentieth-century fascism, on the other hand, raised the basic question of *man's character, human mysticism* and *craving for authority* which covered a *period of some four to six thousand years*. Here too, vulgar Marxism sought to run an elephant into a foxhole. The human structure with which sex-economic sociology is concerned did not evolve during the past two hundred years; on the contrary, it reflects a patriarchal authoritarian civilization that goes back thousands of years. Indeed, sex-economy goes so far as to say that the abominable excesses of the capitalist era of the past three thousand years (predatory imperialism, defraudation of the working man, racial subjugation, etc.) were possible only because the human structure of the untold masses who had endured all this had become totally dependent upon authority, incapable of freedom and extremely accessible to mysticism. That this structure is not native to man but was inculcated by social conditions and indoctrination does not alter its effects one bit; but it does point to a way out, namely *restructurization*.[44]

It should be clear why Reich is thought by feminists to be of contemporary relevance. He asserts in effect that there can be no fundamental change in Western society until its underlying patriarchy in family, ideology, economy, and government is removed. The passage quoted also reveals a fundamental limitation of Reich's analysis. Since the basic structure of patriarchy has remained static "for thousands of years," Reich cannot deal effectively with changes of character type, family, or ideology. Even the rise of fascism—interpreted by Reich as a change from otherworldly masochism to this-worldly sadism—involves no basic characterological or familial shifts. And, as Isaac Balbus and others have pointed out, the lessening of sexual repression typifying the contemporary period seems to have no appreciable effect upon capitalist values in the economic sphere, a fact that is inconsistent with the Reichian analysis.[45] Reich contributes, then, to the Marx-Freud synthesis and to debates about the patriarchal character of the Western conscience. He contributes only indirectly to our examination of the Protestant ethic as a distinctive culture-, family-, and character-forming ideology. Reich's approach could be applied to Protestantism, however. This was attempted by Erich Fromm, to whom we now turn.

2

FRANKFURT SCHOOL
PERSPECTIVES ON
CONSCIENCE

Erich Fromm and Max Horkheimer

Fromm's Path to the Weber-Freud-Marx Synthesis

WE HAVE SHOWN how patriarchy served in Reich's analysis as a
mediating category, linking ideology, family, character, economics, and politics. For Reich, as for Freud, advanced civilization has
heretofore been patriarchal; only within primitive societies have
alternative matriarchal social structures been found. However,
Reich followed Friedrich Engels in viewing repressive patriarchy
not as a universal structure of human culture but as a form of
domination that should be, and will be, replaced by a new society
organized on matriarchal principles. The thesis that patriarchy re-
emerged from the more matriarchal Middle Ages in the early
modern period, with the concomitant rise of modern capitalism
and the Protestant ideology, was first formulated by Erich Fromm
(1900–1980).

After an orthodox Jewish upbringing and after being schooled in
Marxian social theory and in psychoanalysis, Fromm in 1929 took
a position in the newly formed Frankfurt Psychoanalytic Institute.
There he joined forces with Max Horkheimer and his colleagues,
by 1930 as a member of the Frankfurt Institute for Social Research,
and launched a program of characterological studies. Fromm's
research and publications played an important role in giving early

shape and direction to critical theory, especially in the area of character analysis.[1]

It is Fromm who first brings together themes from Freud, Marx, and Weber in an analysis of Western character types; herein lies his originality rather than simply in the Marx-Freud synthesis. This complex intellectual construction (made to appear deceptively simple, perhaps, because of Fromm's talent for simplification) has been immensely provocative. But it contains a number of inner tensions, some of which we propose to examine here. The synthesis that emerges from these formulations has contemporary relevance, but the tensions within it remain also as contemporary controversies.

A brief excursus on how Fromm arrives at his threefold synthesis will shed light on the final formulation of his view of conscience and its relation to family and to ideology. In an essay published in 1930, "The Dogma of Christ," Fromm traces the development of the doctrines of Christ and of the trinity in early Christianity. Employing a Freudian view of religion, he seeks to show how changes in the socioeconomic situation of the Christian movement led to the evolution of doctrine. Describing this essay, Rainer Funk writes: "During the early thirties, Fromm's view of religion was a development of Freud's reductionist concept for Freud felt that religious phenomena were 'nothing but' libidinous fantasy satisfactions. Fromm interpreted both religious phenomena and psychic structure as reflections of the economic and social situation."[2] In his development of Freud's analysis of religion, Fromm finds a disguised content emerging in Catholic Christianity: "The strong, powerful father has become the sheltering and protective mother; the once rebellious, then suffering and passive son has become the small child. Under the guise of the fatherly God of the Jews, who in the struggle with the Near Eastern motherly divinities had gained dominance, the divine figure of the Great Mother emerges again, and becomes the dominating figure of medieval Christianity."[3] Fromm explains this change as an adjustment to changes in the socioeconomic situation. At the very end of the essay he refers to the rise of Protestantism in these words: "Only Protestantism turned back to the father-god. It stands at the beginning of a social epoch that permits an active attitude on the part of the masses in contrast to the passively infantile attitude of the Middle Ages."[4]

"The Dogma of Christ" makes no mention of the family as a mediating institution. While an intimate knowledge of early childhood experiences is crucial for successful analysis of the neurotic individual, when we turn to social psychology, Fromm asserts, knowledge of common psychic attitudes of normal adults can be gained from a comprehension of "the socially conditioned life pattern in which these people were situated after the early years of childhood."[5]

By 1932, when Fromm completed his paper, "The Method and Function of an Analytic Social Psychology," Fromm had discovered (as he believed) the mediating role of the family for all individuals. In the following important passage, Fromm sums up his conviction that the family is historically relative, a step that constitutes his first sharp break with Freud:

> Of course, the first critical influences on the growing child come from the family. But the family itself, all its typical internal emotional relationships and the educational ideals it embodies, are in turn conditioned by the social and class background of the family; in short, they are conditioned by the social structure in which it is rooted. (For example: the emotional relationships between father and son are quite different in the family that is part of a bourgeois, patriarchal society than they are in the family that is part of a matriarchal society.) The family is the medium through which the society or the social class stamps its specific structure on the child, and hence on the adult. *The family is the psychological agency of society.*[6]

This view of the family, involving a relativization even of the Oedipal complex, shows clear evidence of influence from Wilhelm Reich's formulations (an influence not observable in the earlier essay).[7] But Fromm is prepared to go further than Reich in historicizing the family and patriarchy, as can be seen in another essay written in the same year.

In "Psychoanalytic Characterology and Its Relevance for Social Psychology," Fromm summarizes what Freud had to say about character types, reviewing the so-called oral, anal, and genital types.[8] Discussing "characterological continuations" in adulthood of the child's developmental stages, Freud associated the following character traits with the anal character: orderliness, parsimony, obstinacy, punctuality, cleanliness, stinginess, love of accumulation, strong sense of privacy, zeal for work, devaluation of sexual pleasure. In the second half of his essay, Fromm proposes that psychoanalytic characterology can "serve as the starting point for

a social psychology that will show how the character traits common to most members of a society are conditioned by the distinctive nature of that society." The social influence on character
formation, he now asserts, "operates first and foremost through
the family."⁹ In an effort to illustrate this approach, he addresses
the "concrete sociological problem" of the "spirit of capitalism."
Drawing on the sociological literature (including Max Weber),
Fromm attempts to show that the bourgeois spirit and the anal
character display "a wide spectrum of agreement and correspon-
dence." Though Fromm in this essay does not attempt to document a connection between Protestantism and the bourgeois
spirit, he clearly assumes that a connection exists, and he contrasts medieval Catholic morality with that of the bourgeois-
Protestant world.¹⁰

In his 1934 essay, "The Theory of Mother Right and Its Relevance for Social Psychology," Fromm adds the final components to
his synthesis of Freud, Marx, and Weber. In the first part of the paper, Fromm introduces the theory of Johann Jakob Bachofen that a
period of matriarchy preceded patriarchy in the history of Western
culture. After showing how reactionary and progressive interpretations of Bachofen are permitted by ambivalences in the thought
of Bachofen himself and contending that the (socialist) progres-
sives looked forward to a revival of matriarchal principles on a
higher level, Fromm turns to a theoretical construction of two
"emotional complexes": the "patricentric" and the "matricentric"
complexes.¹¹ The patricentric character for Fromm combines
traits of Freud's anal and genital characters, differing from both in
that there is a corresponding patricentric culture (Freud did not
speak of an anal or genital culture and regarded all culture as
patricentric). Fromm sums up his description of the patricentric
individual: "A strict superego, guilt feelings, docile love for paternal authority, desire and pleasure at dominating weaker people,
acceptance of suffering as punishment for one's own guilt, and a
damaged capacity for happiness." He notes the similarity of the patricentric character to the anal character but remarks that the former typology, unlike the latter, "disregards the question of the
degree of maturity."¹²

The matricentric character and society, by contrast, are described as "characterized by a feeling of optimistic trust in mother's unconditional love, far fewer guilt feelings, a far weaker superego, and a greater capacity for pleasure and happiness . . . motherly
compassion and love for the weak and others in need of help." Here

Fromm notes that the "matricentric type *can be* an oral character" (hence immature). "But the matricentric type can also be a 'genital' character: i.e., psychically mature, active, not neurotic or arrested."[13] It is interesting that Fromm does not actually say that the patricentric type can be psychically mature, though it is implied. Fromm in fact has difficulties at this point; his final scheme is more congenial with a view of maturity as a return to matricentricity on a higher level (an issue to be discussed later). Consequently, a purely patricentric type could not be a "genital" character.

With the development of this typology Fromm prepares the ground for the introduction into his historical psychology of the "Weber thesis" about Protestantism.

> While both types [the patricentric and the matricentric] may well be found in any given society—depending primarily on the child's family constellation—it does seem that, as an average type, each is characteristic for a particular type of society. The patricentric type is probably dominant in bourgeois Protestant society, while the matricentric type would play a relatively major role in the Middle Ages and in southern European society today. This leads us to Weber's treatment of the connection between bourgeois capitalism and the Protestant work ethos, in contrast to the connection between Catholicism and the work ethos of Catholic countries. Whatever objections may be raised against specific theses of Weber, the fact of such a connection is now an assured part of scholarly knowledge. Weber himself treated the problem on the conscious and ideological level. But a complete understanding of the interrelationship can only be achieved by an analysis of the drive that serves as the basis for bourgeois-capitalism and the Protestant spirit.[14]

Having asserted these crucial connections, Fromm proceeds to describe Protestantism as especially patricentric, stressing the importance of the superego (or conscience) as internalized domination, replacing external coercion in the bourgeois economic order. Here the Protestant conscience is regarded as patriarchal and authoritarian. And Fromm closes the essay by expressing his anticipation that the matricentric principle will in time experience a renaissance.

Fromm's approach to conscience is in fact rich and complex and leaves open several avenues for further exploration. He follows Reich in putting more emphasis than Freud on the role of societal ideology, and correspondingly less on the instinctual physiological level, in the formation of conscience. Just as the family is viewed as the agency of society in creating the character types needed by the society, so the superego is viewed as the agency of the family within the psyches of individuals. But parents are effective in the task of character formation not simply by establishing "a garrison in a conquered city." The child—with an as yet unformed character—reacts to its parents with a mixture of fear, awe, hostility, admiration, and love. Therefore the parental prohibitions and admonitions—derived from the parental superegos rooted in ideology—come connected with a great many emotional overtones, thereby exerting a powerful influence on character formation. Indeed, the growing child to a considerable extent identifies his or her self with the parent and embraces the parental self-image as its own (even if this means rebelling against the actual parent). Thus ideas come to be incorporated into the individual's self-image.

All of this would be true if the two parents presented a united front. However, societal ideology (and to a certain extent actual experience) separates motherly and fatherly roles in conscience formation. Fromm departs from Freud in postulating that different ideologies give variable interpretations of "mother" and of "father" as role models. But he fails to explore different family types that would result from alternative ideologies of mothers and fathers (for example, he says very little about the difference between medieval and reformation families). Thus he initiates reflection regarding alternative superegos; but instead of pursuing further the idea of a matricentric superego, he soon returns to the Freudian postulate that the superego is invariably patricentric. By implication, a matricentric culture would move beyond the formation of the superego altogether.

Fromm's Evolutionary Scheme, Its Weakness and Its Merits

By the time of his 1941 work, the classic *Escape from Freedom*, Fromm had developed an evolutionary scheme for interpreting the rise of modernity. Fromm's philosophy of history can be interpreted as an expansion of Freud's suggestion of an analogy between the development of the individual and of the human race. Just as the individual gradually emerges from the tutelage of parents, so the "social character" (the character traits common to most members of a given society) becomes a more mature, or autonomous, character complex as history progresses.

Following Jacob Burckhardt and a number of other historians, Fromm in *Escape from Freedom* takes the position that in the late Middle Ages "a growing individualism was noticeable in all social classes and affected all spheres of human activity."[15] Fromm focuses his attention on this "emergence of the individual" (the title of Chapter 2) as a development with socioeconomic, ideological, and psychological dimensions and implications. Economically, this trend can be seen in the appearance of capitalistic tendencies; religiously, it is expressed in the rise of Protestantism; characterologically, fuller individuation requires a more pronounced internalization of societal-parental norms (in Freud's terms, superego formation). All of these developments are linked in what Fromm describes as the "patricentric complex," a multifaceted "mode of existence," similar in scope to the concept of patriarchy in Wilhelm Reich, and serving the same mediating functions.

Fromm's synthesis is similar to Reich's, but he applies Reich's account of the rise of civilization to "the Protestant era." By approaching modern Western civilization as a culture of "domination," Fromm is able, in the words of Douglas Kellner (describing the later use of the idea by Herbert Marcuse), to combine "Max Weber's theory of rationalization with Marx's critique of capitalism and a Freudo-Marxist notion of repression."[16] As Kellner urges, this composite idea of domination became a "key category" for critical theory. But Fromm, more specifically than other members of the Frankfurt School, focuses on patriarchal domination. In other words Fromm, like Reich, views patriarchy (or patricentricity) in its multidimensionality as the structure that mediates between the society and the individual. Ultimately, patriarchy is a cultural superego with multidimensional implications. Having historicized the rise (or the return) of patriarchy and repression, it was even more incumbent upon Fromm than Reich to answer the question: what caused the heightening of repression and the revival of patriarchy? In this and subsequent works Fromm develops his answer, which has to do with a problem inherent in the achievement of a new level of individuality. The decline of medieval institutions of authority, combined with individualizing economic forces and religious stress on the autonomy of individual conscience (each of these developments at least partially independent of the others) produced a new level of individuality but also led to "a feeling of powerless isolation and doubt."[17]

Fromm's account entails two contradictory functions of the superego. On the one hand strengthening of control by the superego contributes to autonomy by eliminating the necessity for external controls and submission to external authorities. If superego then gives way to ego, individuality is enhanced. On the other hand the internalization of a patriarchal ideology into the individual's psychic structure may result in an "authoritarian conscience." The latter is in fact regressive rather than progressive, becoming a new form of "submission to power." Fromm's accounts in *Escape from Freedom* and elsewhere blur the distinction between the positive and the negative results of internalization, and he never fully resolves the difficulty. In his approach patriarchy must be seen, in the last analysis, as a religious-ideological answer to the "problem of human existence," which is at heart the problem of lonely isolation.[18] It is a "flight" from the freedom and individualization seemingly made possible by bourgeois culture, a regressive return to dependency.

In a later section I will review Fromm's subsequent efforts to refine this analysis. The formulation just summarized has been widely influential, but Horkheimer and Adorno opposed it, for reasons to be examined shortly. One inherent difficulty in Fromm's Freud-Weber synthesis deserves mention here because not only did it haunt the Frommian perspective but it also limited the success of the Frankfurt School synthesis in general.

Fromm sees a close connection between the rise of modern capitalist tendencies, the appearance and successful propagation of the doctrines of Luther and Calvin, and a marked reversion to patriarchy (or patricentricity) after a period of relative matricentricity in the Middle Ages.[19] By contrast Max Weber views patriarchalism as one of the most basic forms of traditional domination; in order to understand the early modern period, it is the breaking of irrational patriarchal authority that requires explanation. All traditional authority is an extension of the authority of the father.[20] The point is summarized by one Weber scholar: "Protestantism itself contributed to the rationalization and secularization of culture. The ascetic sect broke with patriarchal and authoritarian rule and stressed the isolation of the individual before God. This, according to Weber, formed one of the most important foundations of modern individualism."[21] More incidentally, perhaps, but still significantly in our context, Weber explicitly rejects the theory of a "matriarchal" period (at least as a "legal" arrangement) preceding patriarchy. Weber sees the gradual weakening of "household authority" in the modern period. "In the course of cultural development, the internal and external determinants of the weakening of household authority gain ascendancy."[22] The individual gradually "has to break with tradition and subject himself to the relative insecurity of the impersonal urban market."[23]

It can be argued that the whole thrust of Weber's portrayal is that the modern individual becomes increasingly independent of familial ties and limitations. As far as the religious roots of this mentality are concerned, Weber finds them in the afamilial asceticism of the monastic movement in the Middle Ages that was transformed into a this-worldly asceticism by the Calvinists and the Puritans. Weber gives no special attention to the Protestant family except to stress its ascetic and rationalized qualities. "Of course every type of religious asceticism which is oriented toward the control of this world, and above all Puritanism, limits the legitimation of sexual expression to the aforementioned rational goal of reproduction."[24] Familial affections and interdependencies are, from the standpoint of the emerging bourgeois ethic, basically "irrational." Rationalization is not for Weber a familial function.

When the full implications of Weber's analysis of bourgeois-capitalist ethics are drawn out, it becomes clear that for him the bourgeois individual cannot be said to have deeply internalized a patriarchal culture. It can be argued on the contrary that the bourgeois as a pure type in Weber's terms is traditionless, hence cultureless, since he (the masculine pronoun is appropriate—Weber doesn't comment on the effect of the ethic on women) strives simply to be rational and goal oriented. Though Weber does not say so, the family was an anachronism for the prototypical bourgeois. Consequently, it is irrelevant to say that Weber should have added to his analysis the contribution of the bourgeois family to the rise of capitalism, a suggestion made by Peter and Brigitte Berger.[25] The family for Weber is a traditional institution, and we need an explanation of how traditionalism was disrupted in the early modern period.

From the Frommian standpoint, this view of the family poses questions. How can patriarchy result in a break with tradition? How can Weber's view of capitalism as highly individualistic be reconciled with Fromm's view of capitalism as patriarchal? If, as Fromm typically seems to suggest, the crucial ideological change was from matriarchal to patriarchal religion, why was individualization accentuated? If, on the other hand, the primary change leading to individualization was economic, was not the Weber thesis repudiated? The implication of Fromm's position is that a stronger internalization of the superego (a heightening of conscience) was the decisive change. Determining the causes for this change would necessitate a closer look at the bourgeois-Protestant family and its linking of asceticism with married life. Perhaps a different type of patriarchy, which could be understood to have an individualizing effect, might derive from a different type of family. But Fromm does not undertake the task of studying the bourgeois-Protestant family, perhaps because of his view that the family, as society's agency, tends to produce whatever character type the society wants. Fromm never attributes any independent role to the family; for him "mediation" is simply "transmission."[26]

Thus a case can be made that both Weber and Fromm should have given more attention to the process of internalization in the Protestant family, a turn that was uncongenial to them both. Before leaving Fromm, let us note certain merits of his schematism. When Fromm maintains that medieval culture and religion—hence the period's prevailing character structure—were significantly matricentric (in contrast to Reformation patricentricity), he relativizes not only fathers but also mothers. For Freud, the mother relation is precultural and essentially the same everywhere. Though Reich sees matriarchy as a historical possibility in a utopian future, he views this eventuality as a return to "nature."[27] Fromm occasionally associates mother with nature, and he views motherly love as a "biological necessity."[28] Even so, Fromm holds that mothering and the mother image vary in different societies; patricentric societies distort the "original" mother image. Furthermore (as Fromm would later argue) there can be regressive and progressive forms of matriarchalism. This tendency toward historicizing the mother-relation (along with Fromm's effort to describe an ideal type) raises questions that he never answers fully and that point deeply into contemporary debates.[29] For example, if mature mothering is a cultural achievement, is there a motherly conscience (in the form of a superego)? Does the mother represent cultural discipline (and not simply nurturance) for the growing child? In what way is matricentricity associated with repression (and sublimation)? We shall return to these points later. Even though Fromm's periodization of Western history may be of questionable merit, he opens up fruitful lines of inquiry. It may be, for example, that medieval religion developed matricentric aspects, even though the culture as a whole remained predominantly patriarchal. Unfortunately Fromm does not follow up his insights, and his contributions here remain fragmentary.

Max Horkheimer on the Bourgeois Family

Many of these same questions were debated by Max Horkheimer (1895–1973). Of secularized Jewish descent, Horkheimer was trained in academic psychology, economics, and philosophy, receiving a doctorate at the University of Frankfurt. After several years as a member of the Institute for Social Research, he was appointed its director in 1930, concomitantly being appointed to a new chair of social philosophy at the University of Frankfurt. He considered himself a Marxist of a nondoctrinaire sort, but his perspective, like that of his colleagues, was indebted to many nineteenth- and twentieth-century currents of thought. Remaining the institute's director through the years of exile in the United States and into the postwar years back in Frankfurt until his retirement in 1958, Horkheimer was the central figure in the creation of one of the most influential "schools" of thought in the twentieth century.[30]

Horkheimer in his inaugural lecture sets forth as the basic research project of the institute an investigation of the "connection between the economic life of society, the psychological development of its individuals and changes within specific areas of culture" (science, art, religion, law, customs, and the like).[31] Thus he visualizes a focus—to express the point in a Marxian way—on the interactions between the material base of society (its economy) and consciousness (shaped by ideology), and he sees this interaction mediated by the individual's psychological development. It is this same project that lies behind Fromm's linkage of concepts from Marx, Weber, and Freud that we described in the previous section.

Horkheimer proceeds to characterological studies partly under the influence of Fromm. But in the title essay of the large 1936 work that he edited, *Authority and the Family*, he gives more attention than did Fromm to the question of the family's role in the rise of modern culture.[32] For Horkheimer, as for Fromm, the family occupies a mediating position between the society's substructure (the economic order) and the superstructure (consciousness, the realm of ideology), in other words, the parent mediates consciousness to the child. Horkheimer accepts, against Freud, the Frommian relativization of the family. While Fromm largely contents himself with the assertion that the family is the agency of society without looking at developmental stages, Horkheimer in the 1936 work recognizes the need to look at the "developmental history of the family."[33] In fact, however, he accomplishes this only to a very limited degree.

Tensions among the Freudian, Marxian, and Weberian views of the family surface even in the question whether there was a distinctive bourgeois (or bourgeois-Protestant) family. Although in *Authority and the Family* Horkheimer proceeds to discuss characteristics of the bourgeois family and asserts that the family is the "germ cell" of bourgeois culture, he and his close associate Theodor Adorno have reservations about this that are later expressed explicitly. In the 1956 *Soziologische Exkurse* (translated as *Aspects of Sociology*, 1972) they write:

> The much-discussed crisis of the modern family did not fall from the sky. To understand it, one must become aware of the antagonisms with which the family has been shot through since the beginning of bourgeois society. In the midst of a total condition defined by exchange and therefore by rationality of simple individuals working for themselves, the family remains an essentially feudal institution, based on the principle of "blood," of natural relatedness. Therefore it has held fast to an irrational moment in the midst of an industrial society which aims at rationality, the exclusive domination of the principle that all relations must be calculable, and which will tolerate no other controls than those of supply and demand. As against that the bourgeois family was always, in a certain sense, an anachronism. . . . In the strict sense the "bourgeois family" does not exist at all.[34]

If the family is an "anachronism" in bourgeois society, however, it nevertheless serves an essential function in the structure of the society. When Horkheimer seeks to describe this function, he finds himself describing a distinctive and unique family form, and he has difficulty resolving this conceptual dilemma. Basically the problem is to reconcile Fromm and Weber: reconciling views of the family as a crucial link in the creation of a revolutionary new society (Fromm) and as a carryover of traditionalism (Weber). By looking at further details of Horkheimer's account, we can see that his resolution of the dilemma, namely, that a nonbourgeois institution plays a key role in the creation of bourgeois society, combines Weberian and Frommian insights.

In the 1936 work Horkheimer takes as the object of inquiry the "limited family of the patriarchal type" or the "limited bourgeois family." By "limited" he surely means what today is called the "nuclear" family. Horkheimer holds that this family, which like other cultural institutions interacts dynamically with the society as a whole, occupies a special place in the realm of character formation. Throughout his discussions Horkheimer persists in asserting two somewhat contrary theses concerning the bourgeois family. On the one hand he holds with Fromm that "the bourgeois child, unlike the child of ancient society, develops an authority-oriented character." Training for submission to authority, it is asserted, is one of the key functions of the bourgeois family. "The impulse of submission, however, is not a timeless drive, but a phenomenon emerging essentially from the limited bourgeois family."[35] Alongside this claim, on the other hand, Horkheimer asserts the opposing thesis that the bourgeois family could also serve as a seedbed for rebellion against the prevailing values to a certain extent: "The family not only educates for authority in bourgeois society; it also cultivates the dream of a better condition for mankind."[36]

In the course of his analysis Horkheimer throws out a number of observations that can be used to explain how the bourgeois family might serve both of these functions. He accepts Weber's thesis concerning the culture-forming influence of Protestantism and goes beyond Fromm in tracing the impact of Protestant ideology on the "Protestant conception of the family." While the father's unquestioned authority as God's representative provided the "first training for the bourgeois authority relationship," at the same time the traits of self-control, the disposition for work, consistency, and perseverance—traits instilled by this family—were regarded by Horkheimer as "indispensable" conditions of any genuinely progressive development.[37] He concludes that it is "impossible to separate rational and irrational elements" in the bourgeois-Protestant father-child relationship.[38]

In his account the mother's role in this family is decidedly ambiguous. Horkheimer, here in accord with later histories of the family, sees a greater degree of privacy and intimacy in the limited family, along with increased attention to child rearing.[39] In this context genuinely human relationships, and more specifically a relationship of love with the mother, can develop. Memories of such relations in early life may engender a life-long rebelliousness against the coldness of bourgeois society. In other respects, however, the role of the mother "strengthens the authority of the status quo." "Because the woman bows to the law of the patriarchal family, she becomes an instrument for maintaining authority in this society."[40]

For Horkheimer it is not patriarchy as such that makes the bourgeois-Protestant family unique. He rejects Fromm's thesis that Protestant patriarchy replaced medieval matriarchy. He inclines rather toward the view that civilization thus far has been characterized by patriarchy (after overthrowing a prehistorical, seemingly natural matriarchy).[41] But it is consistent with Horkheimer's premises to assert—here in accord with Fromm—that the phenomenon of "conscience" in the modern sense first became widespread in the Protestant era. The family had been and remained patriarchal, but the internalization of paternal authority came to be accentuated. In the intimacy of the nuclear family, this internalization was deeply personal in its childhood inception; although it becomes depersonalized in the later maturity of the individual, it remains exceptionally powerful.

Horkheimer's account of the authority of fathers in the early bourgeois family is also significantly ambivalent. Viewed from an instrumental, pragmatic standpoint, the father's authority to Horkheimer was "rational" insofar as in earlier bourgeois culture the father typically represented the demands of the culture and supplied the wherewithal for the child to survive and flourish in that culture. When in later periods the father's own autonomy was weakened, his authority became questionable, and his example was of limited utility. Elsewhere in Horkheimer's discussions, it is the father's representation of the moral ideal that constitutes his authoritativeness. When the force of ideological-religious ideals is seriously diminished or dissolved, paternal authority comes to be thought of simply as naked power.[42]

Conscience, Family, and Ideology in Horkheimer

At worst then, for Horkheimer, the bourgeois-Protestant conscience constitutes a form of domination that produces the "authority-oriented character." At best, it provides the individual strength to resist social control and an ideal standpoint from which to criticize the status quo. Horkheimer does not persistently pursue the question as to which conditions in the family or in the ideological sphere tend to lead toward one alternative rather than the other. His analysis tends in fact to refer to economic changes as the causal factors in characterological change, even though in principle he is committed to a model of interaction between ideological and economic factors.

Horkheimer and Fromm agree, then, in viewing the privatized bourgeois-Protestant family as the institutional context for the emergence of the modern individual. But while Fromm focuses on the growing capacity of the ego to resist superego domination, Horkheimer sees in the ideals of the superego a possible source of resistance to the actualities of the social situation. Thus, though both stress the formation of conscience in the bourgeois Protestant family, they differ in their interpretations of the role conscience plays in the process of individualization.

Horkheimer took note of a number of other developments affecting the family:

1. The destruction of the authority of the church hierarchy (in Protestant areas) led to the strengthening of the religious authority of fathers, who were given "an almost priestly consecration."[43]
2. The gradual defamilializing of government resulted in a more decisive severance of state and family, as family status came to have little influence on political power.
3. Increasing amounts of time and energy of mothers were devoted to child rearing which, combined with lowering mortality rates, contributed to a greater degree of child-centeredness, perhaps even extending to the "creation" of childhood as a distinct life period.
4. The higher evaluation of family life on the part of Protestants as a result of Luther's attack on monasticism led to a new climate of opinion regarding marriage.

Reference to other factors affecting the family can doubtless be found in Horkheimer's account, but enough has been said to attempt a summary sketch of the bourgeois family from his perspective. On the one hand, there was a significant continuity between bourgeois and prebourgeois families. The tradition-preserving aspect of the family stood in contrast with the radical changes that were taking place in other social institutions in the seventeenth century. In particular, the family had been, and remained, patriarchal. Hierarchy and coercion prevailed as structural relationships (husband-wife, parent-child) just as they had for millennia. At the same time there was room as there had always been for "love-patriarchalism," for relationships colored by tenderness and affection. In other words the familial relations were "irrational"— not determined by instrumental or contractual calculations—in contrast to the growing "rationality" of the economic sphere. The family tended not to partake in the "bourgeois principle"—society understood as a collection of social atoms related contractually rather than organically.

On the other hand, the family was significantly affected by tendencies of bourgeois-Protestant culture. The separation of family from state and economy accentuated its privatization, thereby making possible an increased intimacy and a greater focus on child rearing, especially on the part of women. Religiously speaking, with the decline of churchly authorities, the father was more directly identified as the representative of God (and thus his own authority was legitimated), but at the same time he was subordinated to the divine will that could overrule earthly wills; hence fatherly authority could be criticized from a moral standpoint. The father myth (belief in the fatherhood of God) contributed significantly to the content and to the imperative quality of conscience, while the deep internalization fostered by the bourgeois family intensified its impact.

The tensions in Horkheimer's account of the family are duplicated in his reflections about moral theory. In a 1933 essay, "Materialism and Morality," Horkheimer discusses the moral philosophy of Immanuel Kant, in which, he believes, "the moral conception of the bourgeoisie came to its purest expression."[44] Orthodox Marxian theory, it might be observed, had tended to be dismissive of bourgeois morality, viewing it as ideology in the pejorative sense, that is, as a way of rationalizing and justifying privileges for the ruling class. Horkheimer rejects this Marxian approach to morality. Though he agrees with the Marxian view that the claim of "eternal commandments" is an illusion, he contends that the bourgeois respect for the freedom and equality of all persons and the ideal of justice—all captured in Kant's concept of the categorical imperative—contain an implicit and permanently valid utopian dimension.[45] "The categorical imperative cannot be meaningfully realized in a society of isolated individuals. Its necessary implication is thus the transformation of this society." According to Horkheimer, Kant believed that duty and happiness can be reconciled in a better society.[46] Specific moral rules must indeed be seen as relative to a particular social order, and their absolutization retards social progress. But the "moral sentiment"—the universal aspect of morality—can find appropriate expression in present-day society in two forms: (1) in compassion for the suffering of others; and (2) in that politics which seeks to improve the lot of humanity.[47]

Thus Horkheimer finds arising within the relativities of the internalized superego a potential for universality and for criticism

of the present. However, just as his accounts of the familial relationships are too fragmentary to make clear under just which
circumstances the progressive conscience comes to predominate
over coercive and repressive aspects, so his moral theory winds up
with equivocation as to whether the bourgeois conscience can
play a constructive role. On the one hand "the appeal to morality
is more powerless than ever." On the other hand, "materialism
recognizes in compassion, as well as in progressive politics, productive forces historically related to bourgeois morality."[48] This
uncertain assessment of "bourgeois morality" characterized Horkheimer early and late. But he continues to look for something in
morality that transcends present-day culture. This transcending
"moment" in morality can be identified as an intimation of an
ideal community, a theme to which we shall return.

Horkheimer differs from Fromm in being willing to accord the
family a degree of autonomy in shaping the new bourgeois culture.
This is, however, a limited autonomy. In certain ways external
changes transformed the family's impact on its members; in other
ways the family preserved continuity with the past. One might say
that, having been changed by external forces, the family could
work in a partially autonomous way. Horkheimer's conclusions
can be summarized by saying that he winds up with a contradiction and a paradox. He finds two contradictory outcomes of the
bourgeois family: (1) the creation of individuals who have internalized coercion and who are therefore trained to submit to authority; and (2) the creation of individuals whose internalized
conscience gives them the strength to resist authority and to press
for the realization of ideals that they have made their own. At the
same time it is in a sense paradoxical, Horkheimer concludes, that
"rational" bourgeois society requires an "irrational" ethic, that the
separate, goal-oriented bourgeois individual requires a traditional
value system for his emergence. Bourgeois society is not built
simply upon biological individuals but upon conscientious, disciplined, ascetic individuals. Disciplined conscientiousness cannot
be derived from the premises of purely bourgeois values. The
familial relationships that produce the matrix required for the
generation of the disciplined character are not bourgeois, contractual relationships. But neither are they merely "natural." They
derive from a prebourgeois, traditional culture.

The paradox Horkheimer arrives at is basically Weberian, the
view that secular rationalized modernity required a certain traditional, nonrationalized institution for its appearance. While We-

ber emphasizes Protestant religion, Horkheimer sees the bourgeois-Protestant family in this role. This family, though built upon
traditional content, brings forth a new kind of patriarchy and a
new conscience: thus Fromm and Weber are reconciled, for the
new family is both patriarchal and revolutionary.

In Chapter 4 I will explore other themes developed by Fromm
and Horkheimer. Implicit in their accounts of the bourgeois-
Protestant family and of the rise of the modern individual are
differing evaluations of the Western conscience. Fromm in effect
relativizes it completely, and this leads him, as will appear in
Chapter 4, to look elsewhere for a point of transcendence beyond
cultural relativity. Horkheimer also acknowledges its relativity,
but he seeks nevertheless to find within it a standpoint from
which to criticize the present. This effort to recover the critical
function of conscience was to be articulated also by Adorno, as we
shall see.

Our focus thus far in reviewing the accounts of conscience given
by Fromm and Horkheimer has been upon psychosocial dimensions, upon conscience viewed as the internalization of parental
norms. "Ideological" factors have made their appearance, but in
secondary roles; history is seen as moving through economy and
family. Meanwhile religion, in the form of "Protestantism," too
often seems, in Fromm and Horkheimer, to be an ahistorical abstraction. For an account of these same issues that is more attentive to the history of Western religion, we turn to Paul Tillich.

3

PAUL TILLICH'S
CRITICAL THEOLOGY
AND ITS IMPLICATIONS
FOR CONSCIENCE

Tillich's Path to the Weber-Freud-Marx Synthesis

AFTER SERVING as a chaplain in the German army during World War I, Paul Tillich (1886–1965) taught theology and philosophy at several German universities, eventually assuming a professorship at the University of Frankfurt in 1929. From that date until his emigration from Germany to the United States in 1933, he was closely associated with Max Horkheimer and other members of the Frankfurt Institute for Social Research. Later, in New York City, they had close ties as well. Though Tillich was more influenced by the tradition of Christian theology than were Horkheimer and the others by Jewish thought, the influence of the "prophetic" tradition upon all of them was considerable. Tillich's analyses of father religion, of vocation, and of the Protestant ethic and conscience—all closely in touch with Frankfurt School perspectives during the 1930s and 1940s—contribute further dimensions to our investigation of these topics.[1]

As early as his 1926 work, *The Religious Situation*, Tillich was already attempting to synthesize insights from the three traditions that also influenced the Frankfurt School—the Weberian, the Marxian, and the Freudian—incorporating them into a broader theological context.[2] As Ronald Stone has noted, *The Religious*

Situation builds its central argument upon Weberian categories.[3] Tillich pursues a critique of "the spirit of capitalist society," using the phrase in Weber's sense; like Weber, he is interested in bourgeois character as well as in bourgeois culture. While Tillich follows Weber in seeing an integral connection between Protestantism and capitalism, he is more interested than Weber in pursuing the theme that there was an original spiritual substance, or content, that was later eroded in bourgeois culture, a content derived at least partially from Protestantism. He also goes beyond Weber in examining ways the "churches" (Catholicism, Judaism, and Protestantism) have interacted with the spirit of bourgeois culture.[4] At the same time Tillich builds upon the reconciliation of Weber and Marx already accomplished by Georg Lukács and others.[5] Tillich employs the Marxian and Weberian critiques when he criticizes the "self-sufficient finitude" of capitalist culture that tends toward the exclusion of all sense of ultimate meaning or purpose in life. He faults Marxian orthodoxy for ignoring the fact that original Marxism, like the original bourgeois perspective, had a religious content—a substance that Tillich and others in the 1920s were attempting to recover through religious socialism. This content was lost in so-called scientific Marxist materialism under the impact of bourgeois ideas and the spirit of capitalism.

In *The Religious Situation,* Tillich also assigns considerable importance to the new psychoanalytic method (which "became effective [that is, influential] after 1900"), viewing it as a method that breaks through the "rationalistic, atomistic conception of nature" and recovers the depth dimension of existence.[6] At this time Tillich approaches psychoanalysis as a therapy that can assist in overcoming the repressive dominance of consciousness (ego) over the rest of the psyche. In particular Tillich sees it contributing to the development of a new, less repressive ethic of sexual relations.[7]

In 1926, however, Tillich was not yet using the categories of Freudian family theory in his Weberian-Marxian critique of the capitalist spirit. He takes this step in his 1933 essay, *The Socialist Decision.*[8] There he offers a critique of the bourgeois "principle" from the standpoint of the socialist "principle" and of prophetic religion, and his use of father themes suggests an effort to combine the approaches of Weber and Fromm to Protestantism and patriarchy. In the process he proposes two different types of ideological-religious patriarchy with different cultural and characterological consequences. The first type characterizes traditional cultures.

All such cultures, according to Tillich, find meaning in terms of myths of origin, some of which deal with the significance of the mother, but father myths predominate. Father traditions hark back to a primeval law that "shapes the unconscious."[9] As long as consciousness is bound to a myth of origin, "nothing new can happen"; cyclic patterns of thought and behavior prevail.[10]

There is in the tie to the father, however, not only a tradition-preserving aspect but also potential for a reformatory aspect. According to Tillich, it was the uniqueness of prophetic religion (patriarchal Judaism) to realize a second type of patriarchy, a potential latent in all father myth: to absolutize its demanding character until it turns against itself. "On the basis of a powerful social myth of origin, Jewish prophetism radicalized the social imperative to the point of freeing itself from the bond of origin."[11] Instead of repetition, father demand elevated into religious unconditionality looks toward the fulfillment of the origin in the goal of being. Here religion becomes ethical; mere being is overruled by "oughtness." Expressed differently, nostalgia for a golden age in the past (the age of the founding fathers) gives way to expectation of future consummation. What is most distinctive about prophetic Judaism for Tillich is that in it "bondage to the myth of origin" is broken, but a tie to the origin is preserved: "The father, understood as origin, remains also for the prophetic consciousness as bearer of the demand, as ruler of history, and as creator of the new."[12]

This second type of patriarchy emphasizes future orientation, ranking time above space, openness to the future over ties to soil, familial ancestry, nation. At the same time it risks the emptiness of a life cut off from the meaning-giving empowerment of these linkages. In Tillich's account, origin is ambiguous: viewed merely as source, it can be limiting and confining; but viewed as creation, it has a progressive thrust. The latter is possible only when "what is" (the present fact) is seen as incomplete and a partial distortion of true being. The "whither" must be seen as predominating over the "whence," but as the being's true fulfillment, not as something imposed and alien.[13] The drive of being toward a utopian consummation, here explicit in Tillich, is implicit in all the Frankfurt School texts.

This analysis of prophetic religion is applied by Tillich to the relation between Protestantism and bourgeois society. In his view Protestantism, especially Calvinism, constituted a renewal of prophetic religion, hence of progressivist patriarchy. (Lutheranism preserved more of the traditionalist father content.) As such, Calvinism became one of the major roots of modern bourgeois society, which arose as the result of a decisive break with the "bond of origin." The influence of Calvinism was combined with a second source of severance from the past: Renaissance and Enlightenment humanism, the roots of which lie in Greek thought rather than in Judaism.[14] In an essay written during his Frankfurt years, Tillich describes bourgeois consciousness as follows: "In place of the mythic consciousness bound to powers of origin, to 'Mothers' and 'Fathers,' appears the assurance of standing in a calculable, explainable, and therefore controllable reality. Also demand loses the character of otherworldliness and makes reference to progressive analyses and transformation of the encountered reality. The rational system arises whose bearer is bourgeois society and in which the myth of origin echoes only as a dream and as something necessary for the feelings, without reality and sustaining power."[15] In prophetism and Protestantism, on the other hand, myth remains, but it is broken by unconditional ethical demand: "The prophetic expectation of a coming righteousness tears consciousness loose from orientation toward the ancient and holy origin. Transcendence remains, but it is a transcendence of the Whither and not the Whence. Myth remains, but it is broken by ethic."[16] Tillich's description of the whither of human being as a goal that is not alien or imposed but fulfilling of that being can be interpreted as a more religiously committed version of Weber's theme of vocation.[17] Vocation calls one out of ties to the past and repetition, toward a divinely ordained mission. Like Weber, Tillich finds the Calvinist sense of vocation in one's worldly calling and the renewal among Puritans of the Judaic "belief that they were God's chosen people" to be important Protestant contributions to bourgeois culture.[18] Tillich regards the Puritans' disciplined effort to fulfill their vocation both individually and collectively to be a religious substance that is crucial to bourgeois culture and that is not fostered or renewed by bourgeois culture itself.

In a more theologically affirmative sense than Weber, Tillich views vocation as a divine gift or promise as well as a task. This theme of gracious gift in Tillich's understanding of Protestantism introduces an important qualification of the demand aspect, a point to be discussed later.[19] As destiny, vocation is constitutive of one's being; it belongs to what one is. The command to be oneself is not heteronomous, not an alien law. Yet one can fail to fulfill one's calling; the opportunity for fulfillment may be missed. In striving to fulfill one's vocation, one gives meaning to the temporal sequence of events. This idea surely can be linked to Tillich's theme of *kairos*, "the moment of time filled with unconditioned meaning and demand." In a kairic moment "the holy that is given and the holy that is demanded meet."[20] The concept of expectation (found in several essays collected in *Political Expectation* and in *The Socialist Decision*) also contains this combination of "already" and "not yet," of promise and demand.[21] As an example of Tillich's thinking, it seems clear that his appeal for a "socialist decision" in 1933 was a proclamation of a fated kairic moment when a specific type of decision was required of and given to German Protestants—a vocation that they could fulfill or miss.[22]

In *The Socialist Decision* Tillich uses his distinction between traditionalist religion and prophetic, ethical religion to lay the foundation for a philosophy-theology of history that draws themes from Weber, Marx, and Freud among others. In his perspective, it is ethical father religion (thus Judaism and Protestantism) that draws individuals out of childish and idolatrous dependencies. The agency within the psyche that works for psychic and spiritual maturity is the moral conscience. Tillich refers to this moral conscience as "unconditional (moral) demand."[23] In postulating this third element in the psyche—distinguishable from "being" and "consciousness"—Tillich combines themes from Freud, Marx, and Immanuel Kant.[24] He understands morality with Kant as a categorical imperative but finds the roots of moral demand in the father relation;[25] and he argues that the moral demand, to be legitimate, must finally come, not from some alien source, but from human nature, from our own essence (a theme that Tillich may well have gleaned from the early Marx).[26] It seems quite possible that this effort to link Freud, Marx, and Kant may have derived from Tillich's conversations with Horkheimer. They take similar approaches to morality in this respect.

In giving primacy to "ought" over "is"—to demand over origin— Tillich breaks with deterministic materialism, whether Marxian or Freudian. At the same time he rejects domination by the ego or consciousness, which to Tillich had come to mean objectification and rationalization (following Weber). This opposition to ego domination would appear to point in an anti-Freudian direction. But Tillich instead interprets psychoanalysis as a methodology that "dethrones consciousness and shatters faith in its supremacy."[27] It seems odd that in this context he does not see psychoanalysis as dethroning conscience also. Tillich's critique of conscience takes a different turn. He seeks to go beyond the moral conscience rather than collapsing it into ego.

Another of Tillich's triads contains closely related themes. Tillich's reflections about the relation of Protestantism to bourgeois culture lead him to the employment of three terms that describe types of culture: autonomy, heteronomy, and theonomy.[28] For Tillich these types of culture are also character types; he has in view the relation of individual cultures or characters to traditional authority. The autonomous culture or character breaks its ties with such authority and stands alone; in the process, however, it loses meaningful content and sense of purpose. Heteronomy arises in reaction to "anxiety . . . in the face of autonomy."[29] It consists of submission to external authority that imposes meanings from without. Theonomy, in Tillich's sense, describes a culture or character in which meaning (for Tillich this implies a sense of "ultimacy") is not alien to autonomous development but represents fulfillment or completion. Both autonomy and heteronomy emerge out of archaic (or by implication infantile) theonomy; both are unsatisfying and evoke quests for a new theonomy. But the latter is viewed by Tillich as something given rather than something achieved. Tillich's discussions of autonomy and heteronomy are very much in touch with Frankfurt School analyses of the tragedy of autonomy and the rise of authoritarian heteronomies. As we shall see in the next chapter, Fromm and Marcuse seek different solutions to the tragedy of autonomy.

Tillich on Family, Ideology, and Conscience

What are the implications of Tillich's formulations for our discussions of family, ideology, and conscience? As we have seen, his interest is in familial myths rather than in the family as such—in familial relations transposed into the ideological sphere. In referring to the radicalizing of father demand until it turns against itself, Tillich is thinking of the way conscience, while originating with parental ideals, may cause an individual to break with a parent or even with a parental ideal, on the basis of a heightening of that very ideal. For example, some American Southerners broke with their parents over the issue of segregation on the basis of a heightening of the parents' own ideals of equality. Thus conscience maintains a connection with the father even while criticizing the father. It draws upon the power of tradition while rejecting its claim to finality or absoluteness. In Tillich's view, critique without rootedness is powerless, just as protest without affirmation is merely negative and impotent. Here the mythic father provides a standpoint for criticizing all earthly fathers.

In these earlier discussions, Tillich stresses the patriarchal nature of tradition and critique, though acknowledging secondarily
the possibility of a matriarchal dimension in tradition as well. In
this emphasis he remains in accord with Weber's interpretation of
traditionalism. In later essays Tillich tends toward the view that
the content or substance of tradition is motherly rather than fatherly, at times using Catholicism to illustrate the motherly nature of tradition. In a 1941 essay, "The Abiding Meaning of the
Catholic Church for Protestantism," Tillich writes: "Catholicism
represents the truth of the fact that the 'holiness of being' must
precede the holiness of the 'ought' and that without the 'Mother,'
the priestly-sacramental church, the 'Father,' the prophetic-
eschatological movement, would be rootless."[30] In this expression
Tillich emphasizes the motherly more than the fatherly aspect of
tradition and traditional religion. One may well detect here a turn
from a Weberian to a Frommian position regarding tradition and
Catholicism. Although the father "predominates," the mother
"precedes," just as gift precedes demand and being precedes oughtness. In the later Tillich, where prophetic religion becomes the
religion of grace, and the goal—New Being—is gift as well as
task, one can recognize the perhaps surreptitious reappearance of
mother religion within the progressive religion of demand. "[New
Being] is the reality of that which the law commands, the reunion
with one's true being, and this means reunion with oneself, with
others, and with the ground of one's self and others. Where there is
New Being, there is grace, and vice versa. Autonomous or heteronomous morality is without ultimate moral motivating power.
Only love or Spiritual Presence can motivate by giving what it
demands."[31] This later turn affects Tillich's approach to God as
well. The Calvinistic God was sternly patriarchal. But in one late
essay Tillich writes: "One can say that psychotherapy has replaced the emphasis on the demanding yet remote God by an
emphasis on his self-giving nearness. . . . If I were permitted to
express a bold suggestion, I would say that psychotherapy and the
experience of pastoral counseling have helped to reintroduce the
female element, so conspicuously lacking in most Protestantism,
into the idea of God."[32]

In summary, then, the early Tillich regards classic Calvinism
and Puritanism as patriarchal in the second sense we have indi-
cated: father demand heightened until it turns upon itself, thereby
breaking its bondage to, but retaining connection with, the tradition in which it was first nourished. This description of Calvinist

Protestantism has very personal overtones for Tillich: it describes his relationship to his own puritanical father. In Protestantism, patriarchy actualizes its potential for its own critique. Here patriarchy, which generally, as Weber maintains, is the core of traditionalism, becomes revolutionary. The later Tillich is inclined to put more emphasis on the motherly content in tradition. Perhaps it can be suggested that in his final position (in his development of the doctrines of creation and of the New Being), he implicitly finds both parents in origin and goal. Since Calvinists became more future oriented and broke more fully with tradition than did Lutherans, Calvinists and Puritans were enabled more fully to achieve what Tillich called "religious personality" (to which we will turn in a moment), but at the same time this achievement was more fragile and easily eroded.

While traditional society and Protestantism tend to be patriarchal (with an implicitly matriarchal element), bourgeois society in Tillich's perspective tends to be nonpatriarchal and nonmatriarchal. Protestantism, along with Renaissance humanism, contributed to the rise of bourgeois autonomy; early bourgeois society carried over mythic meanings and content from Calvinist utopian and humanist universalist sources. But the bourgeois principle of self-sufficient finitude is itself empty of any ultimate meanings, whether patricentric or matricentric in symbolic content. Though Tillich does not express the point exactly this way, bourgeois culture is in a sense no culture at all, since in his view "religion is the substance of culture." Tillich sums up the contrast between Protestantism and the capitalist spirit in these words:

> Indeed, the popular exaggeration of Max Weber's thesis about the significance of Calvinism for the rise of the capitalist spirit often makes it appear as though Protestantism itself were nothing but the capitalist spirit. On the contrary it may be asserted that original Protestantism was the sharpest protest it is possible to think of against the spirit of self-sufficient finitude, in its ecclesiastical and hierarchical as well as in its humanistic and rationalistic form. Luther raised his protest against both of these with dynamic, prophetic force in the name of that which is absolutely beyond, of the divine reality which prevails over all human reality.[33]

Losing both father myth and mother myth, bourgeois society tends to dissolve all ultimate meanings. By preserving father myth, Protestantism retains its link with ultimacy. Only in the contemporary period have overt attempts been made to restore mother myth to religion in the West.

Corresponding to these analyses of Protestantism and bourgeois society, Tillich distinguishes Protestant and bourgeois character types, though his characterizations remain fragmentary. Protestant types are discussed by Tillich under two headings: (1) the development of religious personality in the Calvinist churches; and (2) the development of "transmoral conscience" on the basis of Luther's doctrine. I turn to his discussion of Calvinist types first because his analysis is more Weberian and grows more directly out of the themes just summarized.

Tillich finds in Calvinism the heightening of conscience that overcomes bondage to tradition and leads to further individualization. In traditional society the group has a sacral power that serves to subordinate the individual to the community. Medieval monasticism began the process of dissolving the sacral power of the group by locating the holy, or ultimate meaning, in "the center of ethical personality." The monk, if not holy in his person, at least symbolized or represented holiness. Protestantism finds the possibility of a new religious form "by laicizing the monastic ideal of interior discipline." The ascetic life-style per se (withdrawal from the world into a separate community) is rejected as another objectification of the holy; it is the interior discipline that counts, not the external form. Prophetic protest is directed against any claim of holiness or ultimacy on the part of any finite reality. Thus the holy is seemingly subjectivized in personality or character. But the Protestant knows that he/she is not holy either; instead, he/she is forgiven. The state of being accepted is indeed an objective grace (the gift of faith), with the authority that comes from objectivity and givenness; however, it is easily dissolved into an ethical act or a subjective feeling. The holy is present only as judgment— a negation of existing reality—and as faith, not as something existing.[34]

Tillich finds a new personality emerging from the Protestant critique, which he terms the "heroic personality": "The heroic personality is aware of the boundary situation of man and always subjects himself to prophetic as well as to ethical rational criticism. His seriousness, his dignity, his great majesty—to use a term often applied to Calvin—is based on the fact that he refuses to allow the depths of prophetic criticism to be covered over and hidden by any objective form of grace."[35] Tillich here describes the religious critique of religion, the fatherly critique of the father: no finite reality is holy, only God is God. He terms this the "Protestant principle"; it arises from the absolutization of father demand, which, becoming self-critical, relativizes all authorities except the ultimate, or perfection itself. This critique preserves a link with the "givenness" of meaningful content, with fatherly expectation and vocation, a link that is lacking in purely autonomous critique.

Tillich holds that the greatness of Calvinist Protestantism—its creative principle—lies in its cultivation of the interior ethical and spiritual life of the individual. By implication this means its cultivation of conscience. But this is also its tragedy. By criticizing all objective embodiments of the holy and depending upon the subjective conscience, the Calvinist character tends toward secularization and the loss of meaning. The tendency toward "a self-enclosed and self-sufficient autonomous culture" has its correlate in a personality that is cut off from all meaningful contents. Through criticism of sanctified meanings one becomes "cut off from one's own psychic depths and from the supportive powers of the community." This kind of Protestantism, says Tillich, must overcome its individualistic personalism without neglecting its central truth that "the center of the personality . . . remains a focal point in the religious relationship, the relationship to the Unconditional."[36]

Tillich can be interpreted here as giving a favorable account of the classic Calvinist-Puritan conscience so long as it remained "prophetic" and Protestant. Acceptance of the judgment of God in one's conscience, along with God's forgiveness, frees one from all other, relative judgments and enables one to find meaningful vocation without debilitating guilt. Traditionalist patriarchy may be characterized as "submission to power," but Tillich disputes Erich Fromm's claim that the Calvinist conscience can be thus described. Its key difficulty is not so much authoritarianism as it is secularization and the consequent loss of meaningful content.

In his interpretations of Luther, Tillich develops a second terminology for describing the Protestant character. Luther is said by Tillich to have pointed toward a new conscience, a "transmoral conscience."[37] Luther experienced judgment and condemnation in his traditional patriarchal conscience that was heightened in the monastic community. To escape this guilty conscience, he turned not to his own efforts but to divine grace as proclaimed in the Christian gospel. For Luther, the message of grace is beyond morality, not in morality per se. The moral conscience plays an essential function: it accentuates self-awareness, individualization, and the sense of personal responsibility. But it must be transcended, thus requiring the presence of the divine, that is, it requires overcoming the separation of guilt with the reconciling acceptance that comes from God.[38]

Tillich sees in Luther not the abject, submissive appeal for mercy to the arbitrary authority of God—the image of Luther that led Fromm and others to identify him as authoritarian—but rather Luther's rebellion against a religion of law or commandment. Luther's struggles to allay the anxieties of his conscience led him not to a religion of moral conscience but to a critique of this conscience from a standpoint beyond it. Monasticism was a religion of moral conscience; Luther's Protestantism was a religion of transmoral conscience. The latter in Tillich's description is the "joyful" conscience that "accepts one's acceptance" as a gift from God.[39]

Tillich admits that this perspective is morally "dangerous"; it implicitly recognizes the relativity or provisional validity of the commands of conscience.[40] The Lutheran claim that salvation is a gift becomes for Tillich the claim that ultimate meaning or validity is given, not simply demanded or sought. Grace or transcendent meaning does appear in the finite realm, though here as a new conscience. The transmoral conscience involves the experience of a new reality—the state of being forgiven and reconciled—rather than the experience of new moral commands.

In using the term *conscience,* a process of internalization is suggested. In spite of this Tillich does not pursue the question how this presumably nonpaternal conscience is internalized or what sort of superego would result. It is unclear what a new conscience would be if it is not simply beliefs concerning some external reality. Since Tillich himself continually relates theological concepts to psychological processes, a psychological interpretation of the transmoral conscience is possible and desirable. It is plausible to suppose that it is the motherly conscience that Luther and Tillich discover "beyond the father." It may be suggested that Tillich's concept entails a mother relationship, a recovery of nurturance after autonomy. One can only speculate why Tillich did not draw this connection explicitly. After he reaches, in his later work, the conception that the goal of life is the New Being, the way is prepared for an association of goal with mother, since mother is connected with "being" rather than with "oughtness."[41] His earlier association of mother with nature and origin seemingly prevents him from developing this symbolization.

If, as Tillich suggests, the moral conscience derives from the radicalization of father demand to the extent that fatherly norms are perceived as God's law, the transmoral conscience can be understood to derive from motherly acceptance and nurturance perceived as unconditional and holy. When this conscience appears, the conviction develops that one is accepted in spite of feelings of unworthiness. This transmutation of parental relations into a mythic worldview is accomplished socially in the religion of the group. It can be argued that for internalized norms to become conscience, this kind of transmutation is necessary. If one adopts the view that moral imperatives are "categorical" (unconditional), morality requires that no such imperative can issue from a "conditional" (finite or relative) authority. From the moral point of view the individual cannot perceive his/her own father's commands as unconditional, nor can acceptance by one's own mother be regarded as unconditional. It is the unconditionality of the deliverances of conscience that makes them moral (for Tillich, moral-religious). The process of mythicizing the parents parallels the process of absolutizing the moral notions. They are two sides of the same process. According to this perspective Kant's notion of the categorical imperative would be, in Tillich's words, a "halfway demythologizing" of morality. By the same token complete secularization and demythologization—the dissolution of father and mother myth and the de-absolutization of the moral notions—would mean the dissolution of conscience.

Tillich's discussions of conscience can be drawn together by combining his analysis of Calvinism with his analysis of Luther. Calvinism as seen by Tillich made a greater contribution to the cultivation of the individualizing function of conscience—the development of individual moral responsibility. Tillich associates the moral conscience very closely with the achievement of selfhood. He contends that "ego-self and conscience grow in mutual dependence" and "the self discovers itself in the experience of a split between what it is and what it ought to be."[42] If so, Calvinism contributed greatly to the fuller realization of moral selfhood. Luther also emphasized the role of the anguished conscience, but his original contribution was in charting the path toward reunion beyond separation: the transmoral conscience. The Protestant "heroic personality" as described by Tillich was more Calvinistic than Lutheran, characterized more by the moral conscience. Luther's transmoral conscience has a unifying rather than a separating function. Tillich suggests that the unifying conscience discovered by Luther was soon lost by Protestants, and both Calvinists and Lutherans were susceptible to secularization. The bourgeois character—more akin to Calvinism—cuts its ties to father and mother. Gaining autonomy and becoming rationalized (in Weber's sense), this individual tends to lose connection with the ultimacy of meaning-giving tradition and experiences the loss of the vocational sense as well as the sense of unifying acceptance. According to Tillich's analysis, this autonomy becomes increasingly sterile and empty.

Clearly Tillich's view of conscience as I have constructed it here—as instrument of individualization and as bearer of empowering origin and meaning-giving goal—is a largely favorable account; even the negative features (the repressive and punitive superego as described by Reich, Fromm, and others) are regarded by Tillich as beneficial when combined with the reconciling conscience. His critique of conscience does not consist of demythologizing or secularizing conscience; instead, it involves supplementing and correcting father myth with mother myth. (Tillich's ontology can be regarded, however, as a halfway demythologizing of the myth.) For Tillich, the conscience that combines moral and transmoral components possesses theonomous, rather than heteronomous, authority.

Put into the wider context of our study, Tillich especially helps us to see the impact of Protestant ideologies on conscience formation. Although he uses familial symbols, he does not focus special attention on the family per se. He does not explore the thesis suggested by Horkheimer that the heightened conscience was mediated to individuals through the bourgeois-Protestant family. Tillich draws a direct line from Protestant doctrine and the Puritan church to the individual conscience. This approach is basically Weberian and suffers the same limitation: it does not deal adequately with the process of internalization. Early Puritanism was collectivistic and even the Puritan vocational sense was collective.[43] Horkheimer is surely correct that it was the Puritan family that translated collective ideals and goals into individual ideals and goals, thus creating the individualizing conscience. It was the combination of Protestant religion and the bourgeois-Protestant family that produced the modern conscience. Tillich neglects the family as Horkheimer to some extent neglects Protestant religion.

The analyses of conscience found in Fromm, Horkheimer, and Tillich can be viewed as complementary, adding detail relative to the bourgeois family, Protestant ideology, and the social psychology of internalization. Interestingly, there are ambivalences in all three thinkers regarding each of our three dimensions: (1) the bourgeois family viewed as oppressor of the individual versus the bourgeois family as liberator of the individual; (2) Protestant religion as authoritarianism versus Protestant religion as individualism; (3) the superego as internalized domination versus the superego as a source of individualization and moral autonomy. Modifying a phrase coined by Paul Connerton, I suggest that we have arrived at what might be termed the tragedy of individualization: the achievement of greater individual moral responsibility and autonomy entails new forms of domination and/or loss of meaningful content.[44] Or, as Tillich would express it, heightened individualization involves loss of participation. The efforts of these writers to unravel the liberating and oppressing aspects of the bourgeois family, Protestant religion, and the individualizing conscience were only partially successful. Theodor Adorno, in the last major work of the first-generation Critical Theorists, concludes—as I shall show in the next chapter—that as far as conscience is concerned, the negative and the positive aspects cannot be separated.

In the 1950s and 1960s Tillich turned his attention to the elaboration of a "systematic theology," the study of which lies beyond the scope of this essay.[45] Fromm and Horkheimer continued to investigate the themes in question here. And Marcuse, Adorno, and Habermas also made contributions. To these further explorations we now turn.

4

LATER DEVELOPMENTS
IN CRITICAL THEORY

Fascism, Democracy, and Conscience

THE ANALYSES of character types developed within the Frankfurt School emerged in a specific context: the effort to account for the rise of right-wing (fascist) movements in central and southern Europe in the 1920s and 1930s. The issue was given its most pointed formulation by neo-Marxists, who wished to determine why the masses had given their support to a reactionary ideology at a time when economic conditions were favorable for a progressive democratic-socialist revolution. Wilhelm Reich poses the Marxian problematic: "The reality of the situation showed that the economic crisis which, according to [Marxist] expectations, was supposed to entail a development to the Left in the ideology of the masses, had led to an extreme development to the Right in the ideology of the proletarian strata of the population. The result was cleavage between the economic basis, which developed to the Left, and the ideology of broad layers of society, which developed to the Right."[1]

Reich not only enunciates the problem; he also attempts an explanation of these developments. As we have already seen, Reich criticizes his fellow Marxists for not discovering that patriarchal domination was embedded more deeply in the Western psyche than was economic oppression. Efforts to eliminate the latter without rooting out the former were doomed to futility. In the end, however, Reich has no explanation for Naziism per se. His emphasis is on the continuity between fascism and earlier stages of patriarchy. Fascism is simply a particularly virulent form of the same disease that has afflicted Western culture since its inception.

Fromm follows Reich's analysis of Naziism with certain qualifications. In particular, he rejects Reich's exclusive focus on the repression of sexuality as the source of most human ills. As we have seen, however, Reich at times explains this repression as a result of the "fear of freedom," and this idea is given a central place in the Frommian scheme of things. Fromm revises Reich by linking Protestantism with Naziism and describes both in terms of the "authoritarian character." In *Escape from Freedom* (1941), he sums up his description of the fascist character structure:

> For a great part of the lower middle class in Germany and other European countries, the sado-masochistic character is typical, and, as will be shown later, it is a kind of character structure to which the Nazi ideology had its strongest appeal. Since the term "sado-masochistic" is associated with ideas of perversion and neurosis, I prefer to speak instead of the sado-masochistic character, especially when not the neurotic but the normal person is meant, of the "authoritarian character." This terminology is justified because the sado-masochistic person is always characterized by his attitude toward authority. He admires authority and tends to submit to it, but at the same time he wants to be an authority himself and have others submit to him. . . . By the term "authoritarian character" we imply that it represents the personality structure which is the human basis of Fascism.[2]

Since Fromm earlier in the same work describes Luther and his followers as essentially authoritarian, it is clear that he is asserting a direct line of continuity between the prototypical Protestant and the Nazi.[3] Protestants are described by Fromm as especially patriarchal or "patricentric," so by implication it would follow that fascism would also be regarded as patriarchal. In his actual descriptions of Naziism, Fromm reverts to the terms *sadism* and *masochism*, perhaps intending the implication of perversion. He employs *authoritarian* and *patricentric* to describe the more normal character typical of Western European culture in the nineteenth and early twentieth centuries. Indeed, these terms come to signify the type of character produced by the internalization of parental norms into a superego through the mechanism of the Oedipus complex, that is, Freudian normality. The substitution of internal for external authority is regarded by Fromm as a modern development initiated in large part by the Protestant Reformation. But this internalized domination or conscience (superego) "rules with a harshness as great as external authorities" and can be even more severe, "since the individual feels its orders to be his own; how can he rebel against himself?"[4] As the later *Man for Himself* (1947) was to make clear, the "normal" Western conscience is regarded by Fromm as authoritarian.[5] The Nazi character was simply a more extreme version of the bourgeois-Protestant character.

This more extreme authoritarianism cannot, Fromm concludes, be linked to a more extreme familial authority. He finds in fact that the German middle-class family was weakened in the period between the wars. Indeed, Fromm contends that all traditional authorities such as the state (and the monarchy) had been weakened; economic collapse, among other factors, contributed to the erosion of the influence of all authorities.[6]

While the erosion of the strength of traditional authorities has occurred throughout the Western world, Fromm detects two different types of response to this situation, one in fascist countries, the other in the democracies. Fascism as a nationalistic ideology is responsive to a "craving for submission as well as for domination" found especially in the lower middle class of such countries as Germany.[7] Here the führer becomes a father-substitute and the nation serves a meaning-giving function, as an object of devotion. By implication it is the absence of the father in the family situation that leads to the frantic search for an authoritative father figure in place of actual paternal influence. A kind of puzzle or inconsistency appears in Fromm's analysis at this point: both the strong, domineering father and the weak or absent father lead to the authoritarian character. Fascist authoritarianism could derive from either strong or weak paternal authority.[8]

In the democratic countries Fromm sees another pattern emerging, that of "anonymous authority." In this pattern the authority of conscience "has been replaced by the anonymous authority of common sense and public opinion as instruments of conformity."[9] While in the 1941 work this character type is referred to as "fertile soil for the political purposes of Fascism," by 1955, in *The Sane Society*, the type is associated only with the conformist democracies.[10] Fromm at that point contends that the new character type has "a new kind of superego" not constructed "in the image of an authoritarian father. Virtue is to be adjusted and to be like the rest. Vice, to be different."[11] Notably, this type of individual tends to lose the sense of individual selfhood. Rather than being a repressive authority against which the ego struggles, anonymous authority offers nothing against which the ego can test and thereby form itself. "As long as there was overt authority, there was conflict, and there was rebellion—against irrational authority. In the fight with the commands of one's conscience, in the fight against irrational authority, the personality developed—specifically the sense of self developed. . . . But if I am not aware of submitting or rebelling, if I am ruled by an anonymous authority, I lose the sense of self, I become a 'one,' a part of the 'It.' "[12]

As we saw in Chapter 2, Fromm in *Escape from Freedom* is emphasizing the emergence of the individual in the modern period. This development came about primarily through the break with traditional religious authorities (associated with the Reformation) and the strong internalization of authority in the superego (so that external authorities were replaced by an internal authority). The latter development would seem to require a relative strengthening and intensification of familial relationships. Fromm, however, puts more stress on ideological factors, thus emphasizing societal rather than familial patriarchy. The family merely transmits the Protestant ideology of dominance by a patriarchal God. It was the bourgeois-Protestant ideology that produced the seemingly autonomous but actually lonely and anxious modern individual. Twentieth-century individuals are more lonely and isolated than ever, according to Fromm's analysis, and it is the concomitant fear of freedom and longing for lost authority that provoke the turn to the fascist systems. But whereas patriarchal Protestantism combined with early capitalism tended to produce the modern individual (through the instrumentality of the bourgeois-Protestant family), fascist authoritarianism represents a flight from individuality. What is the difference, in Fromm's terms, between Calvinist and fascist authoritarianism? One answer seems to be that in the case of fascism internalization has failed, and authority remains external. Adorno develops this approach in his 1950 work, *The Authoritarian Personality*. This answer, however, seems to suggest that the patriarchal family was of decreasing importance as a causal factor in the decline of individuality and the correlated rise of fascism. Fromm never explicitly revised his estimate of the bourgeois family; he leaves standing his Reichian criticism of its patriarchal-repressive character. In his analysis of democratic conformism, another view of the family is suggested, but it remains undeveloped. For more clear-cut signs of a reversal on the issue of the family, we must turn to Max Horkheimer.

As we saw earlier, Horkheimer is more prepared than Fromm to acknowledge positive as well as negative consequences of the bourgeois familial structure and its impact on individuals. He recognized that the family's structure and function varied in different time periods. Does he consider the family to be a training ground for fascism? As is the case with Fromm, Horkheimer finds evidence that the influence of the family on individuals is eroding rather than increasing in the twentieth century. Because of his perception of the dual nature of the family, he is more prepared than Fromm for the view that it is the weakening, rather than the strengthening, of the German family that contributed to the rise of Hitler. As the point was formulated in an essay he prepared at the Frankfurt Institute in the 1950s: totalitarian government appears as a "substitute for the no longer existing authority of the family" rather than as a "continuation of such an authority."[13]

While Horkheimer equivocates somewhat on the question of a continuity between the bourgeois family and totalitarian regimes, he persists in asserting a link between the bourgeois-capitalist socioeconomic system and the rise of fascism. Instead of maintaining that the family functions by providing whatever character type is demanded by the socioeconomic or ideological order, Horkheimer continues to hold that bourgeois-capitalist society tends to dissolve all traditional institutions and values, including the family. However, he does not contend that authority per se is dissolved; becoming "abstract," authority is all the more "inhuman and relentless."[14] This view—and the correlative conclusion that in late industrial society persons more and more become "social atoms"—accords well with the Marxian view of the alienating trends of capitalist society and with the Weberian emphasis on the continuing elimination of traditional elements in bourgeois society ("rationalization"). What remains unclear is the sense in which the society could still be termed patriarchal (the Freudian component) with "the transference of paternal authority to the collective." Horkheimer notes that the implications of this transference for authority structures remain unclear.[15]

In a 1949 essay, Horkheimer elaborates his position further.[16] He first notes a growing consensus in both analytic and nonanalytic psychology that repression is bad, that "the external repression of

impulses . . . is a major cause in the development of hateful character." This insight has led to a "new conception of education," an
approach that uses as little coercion as possible, for "coercion
leads the pupil to seek destructive outlets in hatred of other individuals and groups."[17] Thus, "in short, educational psychology
maintains that authoritarian education is the basic evil."[18]

Horkheimer acknowledges that there is merit in these points,
but he suggests that psychological analysis must be supplemented
and corrected by social analysis. To illustrate his argument, he
offers a capsule history of "the father-relationship so central to
Freudian theory." The Victorian family (probably for Horkheimer
a synonym for the bourgeois family) in which the sons "had genuine reason and opportunity to identify themselves with the father as with the responsible head of the family," has now disappeared. Now the individual must adjust to constantly changing
economic circumstances, and the father's example is not helpful.
The son may no longer fear and respect the father when very little
of value and interest can be transmitted from the older generation
to the younger. This does not mean, however, that all "images of
authority" are eliminated. Though Horkheimer continues to in-
sist that these images "are, in the last analysis, derived from the
pattern of the father-son relationship . . . these authoritarian patterns today seem to consist much more of powerful collectives
than of a superior individuality as it appeared in the traditional
filial relationships to the father." This change does not fundamentally alter the individual's "belief in authority." "What is affected
is . . . the formation of an integrated, continuously functioning
superego. The consistent ego and superego, the essential traits of
the traditional middle-class idea of the individual, are necessarily
undermined in modern society."[19] This conclusion—that one detrimental effect of contemporary society is a decline in superego
formation—represents an important shift of emphasis in Horkheimer's version of critical theory.

This theory about the decline of the superego poses difficulties
for the Weber-Freud-Marx synthesis. How is the Freudian thesis
that the heightening of repression accompanies the progressive
development of civilization to be reconciled with the Weberian
thesis regarding the erosion of familial influence? If the family is
weakened, is repression inevitably lessened? Horkheimer's effort
to interpret the totalitarian state as a substitute for the absent
father can be seen as responsive to these problems. In this discussion, however, the question of the nature of patriarchy is reopened.

On the presumption that familial patriarchy is predominant, the decline of the patriarchal family would herald the demise of patriarchy. If instead patriarchy is civilizational or societal, the decline of familial influence will only lead to a change in the form of patriarchy, not to its disappearance. Was Freud correct in his contention that human acculturation requires a strong father figure for the growing infant?

According to Horkheimer's reading of the situation, patriarchy reasserts itself even as superego formation declines. The capitalist economy, the bourgeois family, and Protestant religion conspired to create autonomous, self-regulated individuals who developed strong individual consciences. But if the strong family and Protestant religion disappear, this construction collapses; the fascist state then becomes a father substitute. Does this mean that a psychological need overrides the need of the capitalist economy for autonomous individuals? Or is late capitalism no longer interested in autonomy, so that behind our backs, as it were, the economic system is bringing the era of the individual to a close (and Weber's "iron cage" is taking over)? Horkheimer tends toward the latter view.

Whether fascism is seen as regressive or simply as a further extension of capitalism, the bourgeois-Protestant family now appears to be the creator and protector of individuals, the only alternative to the totalitarian state. In this view, which contradicts earlier perspectives of the Frankfurt School, the family is valued for its contribution to the rise of individual conscience, and the decline of the family constitutes a threat to individualization. Adorno was to discuss these themes further in the 1950s.

Theodor Adorno (1903–1969), a close associate of Horkheimer throughout their careers, pursues these discussions in terms of the "failure of internalization." In a 1951 essay he formulates a Freudian analysis of the fascist mentality in which he distinguishes between the father image resulting from Oedipal processes and a pre-Oedipal primal father that is more of a group ideal. Freud referred to the latter in his discussion of hypnosis, where he interpreted the group mentality as "a retrogression of individuals to the relation between primal horde and primal father."[20] Adorno argues that fascists have "collectivized the hypnotic spell," thus reproducing the relation to the pre-Oedipal primal father. This means that the group ideal replaces the introjected image of the child's own father, and the individual becomes willing to yield unquestioningly to powerful external, collective agencies instead of developing a secure individual superego.[21]

Adorno and others pursue this idea further in *The Authoritarian Personality* (1950) in terms of the distinction between internalized and externalized conscience.[22] Adorno and his coworkers speak of an externalized conscience in cases where the individual has failed "to build up a consistent and enduring set of moral values within the personality"; in this situation the individual is forced "to seek some organizing and coordinating agency outside of himself" to which he submits in making moral decisions.[23] According to this theory, the failure to establish an internalized, integrated superego results in a weakness of the integrating capacity of the ego, a failure of individualization as well as of moral development. On the one hand, Adorno grants that individuals with strict internalized consciences may be either authoritarian or antiauthoritarian.[24] On the other, he contends that failure of internalization may contribute to the authoritarian character.[25] It was this uncertain outcome regarding the evaluation of superego-conscience formation that, more than anything else, brought into question the usefulness of the book's conclusions.

Thus Horkheimer and Adorno come increasingly to be critical of the view that the authoritarian family and the superego (characterized as internalized domination) were the seedbed of fascism. Rather, it is the child's search for "a more powerful father than the real one . . . a superfather, as it were" that provides its psychological basis.[26] By the same token they come increasingly to the defense of superego formation as a constructive aspect of selfhood. Failure of internalization, they conclude, leads to a lack of consistent identity and to a susceptibility to the collectivized ego ideal offered by totalitarian groups, a view that contrasts with Fromm, who continues to interpret fascism in terms of internalized domination.

From the standpoint of our study, the second thoughts of Horkheimer and Adorno about the superego must be considered significant, even though these considerations prevented them from bringing the theory of the "authoritarian personality" into sharper focus. As we shall see shortly, Adorno in *Negative Dialectics* (1966) gives final form to the view that restrictive and liberating aspects of conscience cannot be separated; he rejects the possibility of a utopian solution, while at the same time affirming the legitimacy of conscience. Meanwhile Fromm and Herbert Marcuse both construct affirmative visions of utopian societies "beyond domination." The next section investigates the implications of these visions for our study of conscience.

Criticism and Affirmation in Fromm and Marcuse

In the 1950s and 1960s, Fromm pursued further the implications of the rise of the isolated ego. In his view the Protestant conscience contributed to the emergence of the individual in the early modern period. Given a sort of freedom by the decline of traditional authorities (political, social, and religious), given impetus by capitalist encouragement of private initiative, and finding it possible to rebel against overt familial domination, the individual ego began to come into its own. This individual freedom, however, was lonely and frightening. It was, says Fromm, only a negative freedom, a "freedom from" that was also an alienation—from nature, from other people, even from one's own natural existence. The openness that allowed the individual to be "for himself" was intimidating, and modern individuals therefore tended to shrink back into time-honored dependencies.

Similarly for Fromm, on the societal level patriarchal morality and religion (represented preeminently by ancient Judaism and early modern Protestantism) have fostered individualization and control (self-control and control of nature). This is an important stage in human development, but not the final stage.[27] And if mature solutions to the problem of individualization are not found (if patriarchy remains when it should have been outgrown), patriarchal structures become regressive and authoritarian.

What then is a progressive solution to the problem of the loneliness and anxiety of individualization? Basically for Fromm it is the recovery of unity after separation. In Fromm's description it is positive freedom ("freedom to"), in which the individual moves forward to a "new relatedness" based on the progressive relations of love, reason, and creative work. The mature character type is also termed a "productive" character (a more cultural-ideological rendering of Freud's "genital" character).[28]

Fromm insists on the correlation of culture and character. While Freud holds that the genital (mature) character is possible in patriarchal culture, Fromm regards the productive character as requiring a postpatriarchal culture for its full actualization. What form should conscience take in a postpatriarchal context? Fromm postulates that in a mature (sane) society the inner voice of oneself "present in every human being and independent of external sanctions and rewards" could be heard by the self.[29] This voice (in contrast to the internalized voice of authority) is termed "humanistic conscience" by Fromm. His appeal here is to the healthy and mature natural self that is realized after the development of consciousness and rationality rather than the self that is socially dominated. However, in correlation with this subjective inner self on the objective side is the "amazing agreement" in the ethical wisdom of the human race: "The human race, in the last five or six thousand years of its cultural development, has formulated ethical norms in its religious and philosophical systems toward which the conscience of every individual must be orientated, if he is not to start from the beginning . . . the common elements in these teachings are more important than their differences."[30] Fromm is able to arrive at ethical absolutes through this postulated coordination of subjective and objective content; yet in the end the coordination is assumed rather than demonstrated.

These affirmations of traditional values seemed to some of Fromm's colleagues and other liberals to lose the critical element in critical theory. But it is possible to argue that another aspect of his approach to postpatriarchal conscience—the thrust toward the recovery of a repressed matricentricity—did conserve the critical perspective. In *The Sane Society*, Fromm asserts that in addition to the fatherly conscience recognized by Freud there is a motherly conscience, the internalization of the mother's voice.[31] Although the claim in this passage is that all consciences have this component, the clear implication elsewhere in the work is that capitalist society stifles and represses the motherly content.[32] Though Fromm does not explicitly link the humanistic conscience and the motherly conscience, it seems clear that they are closely related concepts. The full realization of the humanistic conscience will await the transformation of culture in postpatriarchal directions. Development beyond patriarchy requires "a dialectical progression to a higher form of matriarchalism."[33] Progressive development is a "blending of the positive aspect of both patriarchal and matriarchal spirit."[34] The mature conscience, then, includes "reason, discipline . . . individualism" (the positive aspects of patriarchy), as well as love and forgiveness (the positive aspects of matriarchy).[35] Full human development moves from a primary mother orientation through father orientation to a combination of the two. But "in the process of maturing, the conscience becomes more and more independent from these original father and mother figures; *we become,* as it were, *our own father and our own mother.*"[36] Humanistic conscience thus requires the recovery of the motherly aspect of conscience.

Fromm's analysis makes possible two partially conflicting views of bourgeois-capitalist patriarchal culture. As a culture that cultivates the isolated ego (enabling individuals to rebel against traditional authorities), bourgeois culture can be termed progressive, but still immature and characterized by alienation. Insofar as it fosters a dominating, punitive superego, however, it is regressive. Fromm occasionally approaches the two as historical stages: high bourgeois culture in the nineteenth century can be termed progressive but immature; the fascist period in Europe would qualify as regressive, as would the "anonymous authority" of democratic conformism. There is a continuing lack of clarity in his references to bourgeois-Protestant character and culture because these alternative interpretations are not clearly distinguished. For example, if the positive aspect of the Lutheran Reformation were being stressed, the resulting character could be termed individualist but alienated; when stressing the negative aspect, Fromm describes the same character as authoritarian.

In his later work Fromm shows an increasing interest in, and positive evaluation of, religious mysticism. Correlatively he expresses doubt as to whether the accomplishment of a well-defined sense of a separate ego is a proper humanistic goal. He notes that the great religions teach a "forgetting of one's ego" or "giving up craving for possessions of any kind, including one's own ego."[37] These observations lead him to view present-day "other-directedness" in a more positive light; since they are less alienated, other-directed personality types (described by Fromm as "marketing" types) may be better able to move toward a new model of sharing, loving productivity that is not preoccupied with preserving ego separation.[38] Oddly enough, those drawn to mystical religion share with the other-directed a lessening of egocentricity. It is difficult to reconcile this emphasis with Fromm's earlier celebration of the ego's emergence.

Unfortunately, Fromm does not explore the implications of the motherly conscience: whether, for example, this requires a different status for the mother vis-à-vis the larger society. A case can be made that Fromm's failure to explore the further implications of recovering the repressed motherly content severely limits the success of his critique of conscience. As we shall see, this task has recently been taken up by a group of psychoanalytic feminists.[39]

In the 1950s Herbert Marcuse (1898–1979), building upon the perspective developed earlier by Horkheimer and Adorno, published an alternative vision of the good society and in the process attacked Fromm's formulations vigorously (although, as Martin Jay has suggested, the differences between the two were not as great as might be supposed from the tone of the exchange).[40] In *Eros and Civilization* (1955) and in subsequent essays, Marcuse offers an interpretation of ego and superego that he finds to be implicit in the earlier works of critical theory. He pursues the implications of the idea put forward by Horkheimer and Adorno (especially in *Dialectic of Enlightenment*) that, in Marcuse's words, "the introjection of the master" is the "dynamic of civilization."[41] Marcuse emphasizes that the Western ego (not simply the superego) is essentially connected with the structure of domination. Thus while the early Fromm and others see the path to maturity in replacing superego controls with ego controls, Marcuse attacks the model of ego domination as itself basically repressive and hence inimical to full human actualization. His complaint about ego domination is similar to Fromm's later, more negative view of ego control and his defense of mysticism. It is a radicalizing of the view that society as a whole is patriarchal. The distinctive step taken by Marcuse (though he was anticipated in part by Reich and even by Fromm), is the hypothesis that domination of the instincts by the ego is characteristic of a specific form of civilization, not of civilization as such. His approach relativizes not only the patriarchal superego but also the ego and its grasp upon reality, including empirical science and even sense perception. The way the ego relates to reality is determined by a culture of domination. The individual ego that seeks its own self-preservation through control of itself, of nature, and of other persons is not simply natural or presocial; it is the product of a culture that has this kind of individualism as its inner principle, that is, bourgeois culture.[42] Patriarchy, then, is civilizational, rather than just familial, but it is not inevitable.

Marcuse approaches this topic through a discussion of Freud's theme of the reality principle. Freud maintains that the ego is the agency within the psyche that attempts to cope with reality as it actually is. Unlike the superego or the id, the ego is governed by the reality principle.[43] To Marcuse, however, reality is a matter of social definition. Western civilization imposes its particular view of reality (and the relation of ego to reality) through the socialization process. Summarizing Marcuse, Kellner states: "For Marcuse,

the reality principle enforces the totality of society's requirements, norms and prohibitions which are imposed upon the individual from 'outside.' This process constitutes for him a thoroughgoing domination of the individual by society which shapes
thought and behavior, desires and needs, language and consciousness."[44] The reality principle of modern Western civilization is the
"performance principle," in which nature "is experienced as raw
material to be mastered" and the ego is viewed "as an aggressive,
offensive subject, fighting and striving to conquer the resistant
world." Reason is understood as repressive, seeking "to tame instinctual drives for pleasure and enjoyment."[45]

According to Marcuse's analysis the ego as a whole (including
the superego as one of its aspects) results from internalization and
serves the function of control that conscience is understood to
serve in standard interpretations of Freud. Perhaps surprisingly,
this approach enables Marcuse to view the emergence of a sharply
delineated superego in the high bourgeois period as one of the
liberating aspects of bourgeois culture. When the father in the
bourgeois family was "the paradigmatic representative of the reality principle," the struggle between father and son had the effect of
strengthening the (male) ego for resistance to other authorities and
gave persons criteria against which other authorities could be
measured;[46] thus individualization was fostered.[47] The paternal
conscience was not simply arbitrary domination but contained
emancipatory ideals—the utopian ideals of bourgeois society.[48]
Without a developed conscience, individuals fall prey more easily
to external authorities.[49]

According to Marcuse, however, the forming of the superego as a
distinct agency within the psyche—a function of the bourgeois
family—was a temporary phenomenon that in the twentieth century is being supplanted by more direct social domination. The
relative freedom and autonomy given by bourgeois society to the
family and through the family to individuals can also be taken
away by bourgeois society. Fascism was a form of bourgeois society
that took away this freedom, but advanced industrial society is
accomplishing the same end in a more conformist fashion. "Now,
however, under the rule of economic, political, and cultural mo-
nopolies, the formation of the mature superego seems to skip the
stage of individualization: the generic atom becomes directly a
social atom."[50]

Rather than advocating the recovery of conscience (which still
would exist within civilization as domination), Marcuse proposes a

more radical solution. For him the only alternative to domination now is an entirely new, nonrepressive type of civilization. Technological progress has made possible "a qualitatively different, non-repressive reality principle."[51] The new reality principle will be unifying rather than separating and erotic rather than repressive.[52] A new synthesizing rationality will be required. Although the movement to totally new forms will be a subversion of the old and in part a regression behind "the institutions of society in which the reality ego exists," it is a regression "*after* culture had done its work and created the mankind and the world that could be free . . . in the light of mature consciousness and guided by a new rationality."[53] Marcuse is convinced that repression can be abolished while "the achievements of repression would be preserved."[54]

It seems clear that the superego as such would not play a significant role in Marcuse's utopia. The implication is that this utopia becomes possible only after the achievement of individuality. How individuals maintain individualization in a fully nonrepressive culture remains unclear. The culture that Marcuse seeks to escape is a culture "bound up with the father." Nonrepressive culture " 'recalls' the maternal phase of the history of the human race." His effort is to determine "whether the Narcissistic-maternal attitude toward reality cannot 'return' in less primordial, less devouring forms under the power of the mature ego and in a mature civilization."[55] Thus only a mother-oriented conscience could have a place in this society. One can doubt whether the term *conscience* would be appropriate even here, however. Marcuse's perspective in describing this alternative culture, as Chodorow has argued, is that of the male child, while parental values are neglected. In Marcuse's vision, women are "symbols of alternative principles of civilization" and the objects of drive gratification rather than persons in interaction with whom one might experience restriction or limitation.[56]

Although Fromm (like Tillich) speaks from the male perspective of the recovery of matricentric qualities, his theme of the return to matricentricity at a higher level of development and his reference to the internalization of the maternal voice both give more weight to the maternal point of view than is found in Marcuse. Marcuse in fact faults Fromm for retaining an idealistic and hence repressive "image of the woman as mother"; what is "at stake is rather the ascent of Eros [a broadened love-concept, but rooted in sexuality] over aggression."[57] Fromm accuses Marcuse of being mired in a "nineteenth century bourgeois materialism" that tries unsuccessfully to reduce all human needs to the level of instinct.[58] Both look toward the restoration of the unitive tendency in culture and conscience. Both view this as occurring after individualization; the "achievements of repression" must be preserved. What form will the mature conscience take in this imagined future? Marcuse is no more explicit than Fromm.

It remains significant that Horkheimer, Adorno, Tillich, Fromm, and Marcuse all issue a call for the recovery of feminine, motherly values in order to overcome the ills of patriarchy. It seems fair to suggest that giving this idea further explication and specificity, which all failed to do, had to await society's development toward the further liberation of women. This theme in their writings anticipates contemporary feminist discussions that will be reviewed in a later section of this study.

The Later Adorno and Habermas on the Critique of Conscience

The later Adorno, in his *Negative Dialectics*, returns to the theme of the critique of conscience in the form of a lengthy analysis of Immanuel Kant's concept of freedom (autonomy).[59] Through a discussion of Kant, he seeks to uncover "the heteronomous admixture in the inner composition of autonomy."[60] (Here *heteronomous* is the equivalent of *authoritarian*.) By selecting Kant's thought as his focal point, Adorno centers upon a representative of Enlightenment humanism and therefore upon a view that bases conscience upon reason and natural moral law, rather than upon divine commandment or revelation. Kant's religion was Deist rather than Calvinist. Nevertheless, Adorno's critique of Kant's enlightened man of conscience takes the same point of departure as Fromm's critique of the Lutheran or Calvinist: external, patriarchal authority has been internalized in a repressive superego. Kant, in taking the coercive conscience as a categorical absolute not to be criticized, has failed to follow through the Enlightenment project of gaining liberation from heteronomous authorities.[61]

Adorno's assessment of the Kantian ethic thus builds upon the Frommian synthesis: Kant is seen as presenting an ethic of the bourgeois class built upon repression (internalized domination). At two important points Adorno's position differs from that of Fromm. First, he views the distinction between ego and superego as provisional and insubstantial. "The separation of ego and superego, which the analytical topology insists upon, is a dubious affair;

genetically, both of them lead equally to the internalization of the father-image."[62] For Adorno, as for Marcuse and even at times for Horkheimer, it is the ego that serves as the agency of civilization within the psyche.[63] This view is distinctly different from Fromm's position that the superego is the agency of civilization while the ego is the stronghold of the individual. Thus while Fromm's attacks were focused on the "authoritarian conscience," Adorno holds that critiques of the superego soon extend to the ego as well. He writes: "The analytical theories about the super-ego, however bold their beginnings, will therefore flag in short order, lest they be obliged to spread to the coddled ego."[64]

Secondly, then, rather than viewing the lonely ego, as Fromm does, as the point where the individual transcends the society, Adorno finds a point of transcendence in the content of conscience. Adorno holds that in addition to the component of coercion (derived from the particularities of the internalized parental superego) there is a universalistic, utopian component: "the idea of a solidarity transcending the divergent individual interests." Conscience is not reducible to particularistic coercion; but its universality is not separable from its particularity. The liberation effected by conscience is inseparable from domination. Only in a reconciled utopian condition—fully actualized individuals in a perfected society—would it be possible to separate freedom and repression. In a society that is not free, it is not possible to differentiate beneficent and harmful parts of conscience so that negative features could be criticized, leaving a healthy superego intact.[65] For the present there remains only the continuation of critique that, beginning with the Freudian discovery of the father in the superego, spreads to the ego and to the society. But the potential for this critique can be found in conscience itself. Adorno's description of this process leads him to one of the most affirmative conclusions reached in his version of critical theory: "But freedom need not remain what it was, and what it arose from. Ripening, rather, in the internalization of social coercion into conscience, with the resistance to social authority which critically measures that authority by its own principles, is a potential that would rid men of coercion. In the critique of conscience, the rescue of this potential is envisioned . . . not in the psychological realm, however, but in the objectivity of a reconciled life of the free. . . . Conscience is the mark of shame of an unfree society."[66]

In these passages Adorno achieves a summation of what he and Horkheimer want to say about conscience. The result is a fragment; the critique is not completed. It will be my contention later that psychoanalytic feminism provides avenues for continuation of the critique. But Adorno's assertion is an important one: that there is a point of transcendence in conscience—even if we understand the origins of conscience in Freudian terms—and that this point of transcendence lies in the intimation of an ideal community. Conscience does indeed involve the acknowledgment of rules. But transcendence consists not in submission to rules imposed arbitrarily but in their acceptance as the discipline of a loving community. In such a community the partially arbitrary character of the rules does not generate resistance but is acceded to in the interest of and in solidarity with the whole. The particularities of conscience are a part of vocation: an individual can identify his or her own duties in particular circumstances, and these duties have a moral ultimacy in spite of their relativity.

Horkheimer and Adorno have been criticized for affirming the superego, an agency that in Freud's account at least draws its energy from redirected aggression and requires repression and the threat of violence for its construction. Two responses may be made to this criticism. On the one hand the critical aspect of conscience may indeed be related to sublimated aggression, or to what has been called "creative destruction."[67] Moral autonomy arises when parental values are questioned and subjected to critique. The weapons for this challenge of parental authority are fashioned out of aggression and out of insistence on the parental ideal over actual parental behavior.[68] On the other hand the capacity to challenge the parent, as Horkheimer and Adorno saw, stems in the end from a deeper relation of regard and affection. In the psychodynamics of the psyche, the superego draws upon the energies of both love and aggression.[69]

Thus for Horkheimer and Adorno the bourgeois conscience is inextricably connected with the bourgeois family, interpreted as a community of discipline and love. Hegel, the great nineteenth-century progenitor of Marx, interpreted the actual bourgeois family as a kind of not-yet-rational embodiment of the ideal society. Horkheimer and Adorno know better: the often brutal reality belies this claim. But the ideal of the bourgeois family, incorporated into the consciences of its members, is an anticipation of the ideal society. More specifically, the ideal of the bourgeois mother, say Horkheimer and Adorno, is more than simply an ideological cover for the exploitation of women. It gives genuine vocational dignity and legitimation to selfless generosity and fosters the idea of equality. "If. . . those who in reality were oppressed and forced to make sacrifices were provided with the halo of voluntary selflessness and goodness, then this was not merely lip-service for the subjugated, but endowed them with an idea of dignity, which ultimately as human dignity, worked toward emancipation; in it the idea of the equality of human beings, of real humanism, became concretized."[70]

A truly liberating family cannot be actualized in an unfree society, but "in a free world a family in freedom is readily conceivable . . . a form of close and joyous cohabitation of individuals, protected from barbarity and yet without doing violence to that nature which is both preserved and resolved [aufgehoben = transcended: GBH] in it."[71] Horkheimer and Adorno conclude that the bourgeois concept of the family contradicts its actuality and therefore "contain[s] the presuppositions for its own critique."[72] This can be interpreted to mean that the bourgeois conscience and its distance from the actual is given structure by the image of an ideal community that is remembered and anticipated.

This analysis of the bourgeois family found in Horkheimer and Adorno is similar in one important respect to Tillich's analysis of prophetic-Protestant religion. There is something in each institution's self-understanding that drives it beyond its own present actuality; each "contains the presuppositions for its own critique." In fact the two analyses belong together. Tillich failed to acknowledge how key aspects of Protestant religion were linked with the bourgeois-Protestant family. A strong case can be made that the two institutions in concert created the prototypical conscientious individual. (Again, the claim is not that this is the only way to create such individuals.)

In spite of the affirmations we have just examined, Horkheimer and Adorno conclude pessimistically. The family served a liberating function in earlier generations. But that age is now past, and they see no substitute for the weakened family in the present. Conscience is once again dissolved into direct social control. Marcuse's phrase, "one-dimensional man," applies to the individual who has no inner duality between ego and conscience. Adorno's affirmation of conscience is overwhelmed by negation. Critical theory concludes with what Weber termed the "iron cage" of bureaucracy (Horkheimer's "administered society") rather than with Marx's revolution, Freud's stoical individualism, or Tillich's quest for a new theonomy.

One perspective on the thought of Juergen Habermas, the most important of the second-generation Critical Theorists, is to see in his work an effort to find an alternative to internalized domination. Without attempting a detailed treatment of Habermas, the next section describes his approach to "sociation without repression."[73] A case can be made that Habermas found the ideal community that was missing in Horkheimer and Adorno in the "ideal speech situation" presupposed in every speech act (the presupposition of a utopian community of communication).

Habermas sees a basic transition taking place in the authorization or legitimation of morality. In the past, morality has been legitimized by "naturelike" traditions that were internalized in conscience and supported by interpretive worldviews. These traditions are, he states, irretrievably a thing of the past. In the absence of religious-ideological motivations, "purposive-rational" (instrumental) decisions, based on self-preservation, tend to prevail. Still, Habermas claims that moral progress is possible in a posttraditional context. Norms can now be justified on the basis of "intersubjectively conceived principles of pure practical reason."[74] In looking for an alternative to traditional authority, Habermas turns away from childhood internalization to the stage of adolescence. It is in and through interaction in a peer group that a communicative ethic, as distinguished from an authority-based ethic, can be developed. Joel Whitebook, tracing the background of Habermas's thought, notes Jean Piaget's view that "true autonomy can only be learned in reciprocal interaction between peers."[75] In this vein Habermas focuses on peer interaction with his emphasis on the validation of ethical claims through "uncoerced discourse." According to Habermas, cultural traditions remain potent as long as they are propagated in an unreflective, not-to-be-questioned manner. Criticism destroys unquestionable authority. "Once their unquestionable character has been destroyed, the stabilization of validity claims can succeed only through discourse."[76] Habermas suggests that the crisis of tradition-oriented propagation of moral values offers an opportunity for new modes of autonomy and creates new dangers of moral disintegration.[77]

In the concluding pages of *The Theory of Communicative Action*, volume 2, Habermas compares the traditional mode of socialization with a new mode now making its appearance. In the traditional mode, as interpreted by critical theory (in which Freud's Oedipus complex is "interpreted sociologically"), the family served as the agency of society in establishing the imperatives of the socioeconomic order in the "superego structures of the dominant social character." Today, says Habermas, with "the leveling out of parental authority," some contend (he seems to have Marcuse in mind) that the larger society ("systemic imperatives") can more directly determine character and conduct. But Habermas holds that this may be a misreading of the situation: "In egalitarian patterns of relationship, in individuated forms of intercourse, and in liberalized child-rearing practices, some of the potential for rationality ingrained in communicative action is *also* released." Rather than being a mere conduit for societally based imperatives, the contemporary nuclear family may be growing more autonomous. "Communicative infrastructures are developing that have freed themselves from latent entanglements in systemic dependencies."[78]

This latter interpretation is suggested to Habermas by two emerging developments: "the diminishing significance of the Oedipal problematic and the growing significance of adolescent crises." Regarding the first, Habermas cites Christopher Lasch's work (to which I will refer in detail later) to document the shift from problems rooted in the "internalization of societal repression" to difficulties of intrafamilial communication growing out of such situations as "instabilities in parental behavior." In other words, the freeing of communications in the family from hierarchical rigidities and from blind conformity to societal norms offers opportunity for greater autonomy, but it also generates new difficulties. As for the second development, if systemic imperatives have not been internalized into "systematically distorted communication," the growing child socialized in the family setting may achieve a degree of autonomy but may find it more difficult to adjust to "the functional requirements of adult roles." This means that it becomes difficult "for the coming generation to connect up with the preceding one."[79]

Instead of attempting to preserve or restore traditional authority as the basis for legitimizing moral judgments and actions, Habermas offers the process of coming to an understanding through uncoerced discourse. The liberating community sought by Horkheimer and Adorno is placed by Habermas in a transcendental location: it is a presupposition of all discourse. "The utopian perspective of reconciliation and freedom is ingrained in the conditions for the communicative sociation of individuals; it is built into the linguistic mechanism of the reproduction of the species."[80] Adorno followed Freud by providing a critique of the isolated Cartesian ego, showing that "ego-identity—takes shape only in forms of an intact intersubjectivity." The child gains identity in the Freudian view only through interactions with parents and caretakers. But Habermas postulates the possibility of a form of intersubjectivity that permits "a mutual and constraint-free understanding among individuals in their dealings with one another—sociation without repression."[81]

Would individuals socialized in this way develop an internalized conscience? In recent essays, Habermas has sought to address this question. In the "post-conventional" situation, when the authority of tradition-oriented norms has been questioned, distinction must be made between "fundamental moral conceptions" and "culturally habituated empirical motives." One must learn to be motivated to moral action by "principled moral judgments." To accomplish this in the absence of authoritarian restrictions, internalization must be limited to "a few highly abstract and universal principles."[82] In an earlier essay, Habermas alludes to the same issue when he advocates a type of internalization wherein "the principle of the justification of possible principles (that is, the readiness to engage in discursive clarification of practical questions) [is] alone internalized."[83]

Habermas seems to suggest that it is not norms but the principle of intersubjectivity that must be internalized. We must acknowledge that we are "creatures that are individuated through socialization." The fundamental moral imperative grows out of the fact that "the identity of the individual and that of the collective are interdependent; they form and maintain themselves together."[84] In the last analysis, it is language itself, along with its presuppositions, that alone should be internalized.

Habermas concedes that there must be a correlative development in the institutions of socialization if this type of postconventional morality is to survive and flourish. "There has to be a modicum of congruence between morality and the practices of socialization and education. The latter must promote the requisite internalization of superego controls and the abstractness of ego identities [detachment of the ego from specific social roles, i.e., the capacity for abstraction and universalization]."[85] To this extent, but only to this extent, Habermas admits the need for the internalization of moral tradition. This approach entails endorsement of the distinction between morality in the strict sense and ideas concerning the good life. While the former lends itself to universalization, the latter can be debated only within a specific cultural context.[86]

With these complex reflections, Habermas raises a number of issues germane to our topic. His stance suggests a determination on his part to minimize internalization and the authority of moral tradition. By the same token, he seeks to minimize the impact of the family and of ideology on the formation of the fully moral individual.[87] Our analysis, shaped by certain feminist concerns summarized in later chapters, leads us to question the direction taken by Habermas regarding these issues.

In the Introduction I suggested that a critique of conscience must include a critique of the family. Members of the Frankfurt School tended to generalize about the family without much detailed analysis of family history. Recent studies of the modern history of the family should enable us to give more specificity to the generalizations of critical theory. In the next chapter I examine a work that attempts to do just that: to develop a critical theory of the family. By way of contrast I also consider a work that undertakes to defend the bourgeois family against "critical" attacks. In the view developed here, both works are seriously flawed. But by setting them into juxtaposition, we can identify several important issues of family interpretation as they have a bearing on conscience formation.

5

FAMILY STUDIES
AND CONSCIENCE

A Brief Excursus

STUDIES of the family began to reappear within social and political theory in the 1970s, stimulated in part by feminist concerns, in part by substantial research on the history of the family, and indeed in part by the work of the Frankfurt School itself.[1] In this chapter I examine two such studies that offer conflicting analyses of the bourgeois family. Consideration of issues raised by these accounts will assist us in evaluating the Frankfurt School's legacy in the field of family studies.

Mark Poster's Critical Theory of the Family

Mark Poster's *Critical Theory of the Family* was published in 1978 in an effort to advance "radical social theory" (63) by constructing upon Frankfurt School foundations a more adequate family theory than he found in the writings of its proponents.[2] Poster proposes to conceptualize the family "as an emotional structure, with relative autonomy, which constitutes hierarchies of age and sex in psychological forms" (155), and he finds the Freudian psychology best suited for this purpose. In constructing a critical theory, however, the Freudian categories must be combined with Marxian critique, the critique of domination (see, for example, xix, 164–65). Poster concludes that Freud accurately described the psyche and the familial structure of the bourgeoisie, but the bourgeois family must be understood as dependent upon its specific social context.

Critique presupposes that family structures are variable, that no one pattern is simply natural. Indeed, Freud's assumption that the bourgeois family is a natural form must be considered ideological (xiv–xv). All presently existing institutional forms must be criticized from the standpoint of emancipation. Critical theory, according to Poster, is normative in seeking reform toward the end of human liberation (xix). Thus Poster follows the Frankfurt School in its synthesis of Freud and Marx and in its critique of domination.

From this Freudo-Marxist perspective Poster provides a valuable sketch of the characteristics of the bourgeois family with detail largely lacking in Fromm's and Horkheimer's discussions. A summary of the characteristics found by Poster will be useful here (see 167–78):

1. Familial relations take on a new emotional intensity and depth.
2. There is a systematic effort to delay sexual gratification.
3. Women and children are viewed as asexual.
4. Sexual activity is viewed as "the model of impulsive, incautious action" (169).
5. Strict sex-role divisions are enforced, and women are confined to the home.
6. A high degree of privacy is cultivated.
7. Home is viewed as a place of leisure, not of production.
8. Authority of parents over children is heightened.
9. "Norms for family relations no longer [are] set in the context of community traditions" (171).
10. A pattern of love-hate relations between parent and offspring develops; the child is pulled between the desires of the body and parental love.

An important consequence of this familial structure, according to Poster, is that a new type of individuality is created. The deep internalization of parental rules enables the individual to function independently of external authorities. The bourgeois family generated "a modern citizen who needed no external sanctions or supports but was self-motivated to confront a competitive world, make independent decisions and battle for capital" (175). The feeling of autonomy, however, is an illusion: "Individuality is gained

at the price of unconsciously incorporating parental norms" (178).
Bourgeois types see themselves as "captains of their own souls,"
but they are actually bound by age and sex hierarchies and behave
in ways that "promote the interests of the new dominant class"
(177).

Poster's discussions of family structure and the formation of the
superego draw him inevitably into a critique of ideology, and here
his perspective is exclusively Marxian. Notable from the standpoint of the present study is the absence of the Weberian corrective
of Marx, or, more accurately, of Marxism. In spite of granting a
partial autonomy to the family (141), Poster's approach is largely
reductive and economistic. In his account the bourgeois ideology
of the family serves the interests of the economically dominant
class; in no way does it exert an independent influence upon the
formation of character and culture. Although Poster presupposes
certain Weberian categories for describing bourgeois culture such
as rationalization and this-worldly asceticism, he fails to consider
their ideological roots in Calvinism. And he ignores the vocational
sense that Weber considered so important for the bourgeois character. Socioeconomic factors predominate as causal influences.

It can be argued that in his failure to recognize ideological influence, Poster has interpolated elements of the twentieth-century
situation into his descriptions of the eighteenth and nineteenth
centuries. His treatment of the superego makes this especially
clear. For Poster, the superego consists simply and solely of internalized parental rules, though as with Freud the superego is fueled
by the individual's anger redirected toward the self. "The important result of the child's drama of ambivalence was that it internalized deeply a pattern of rules which summed up its authority-
love relation with its parents" (175). Having maintained that in the
bourgeois period the family gains independence from all external
authorities (171), Poster seemingly is left with the merely arbitrary
authority of the parents. This treatment of superego formation
reduces it to a power struggle between parent and offspring without any admixture of that universality to which Adorno refers.
Without a dimension of transcendence transmitted from the parental superego to the child's superego, nothing is left but a power
struggle that is somewhat mitigated by affection. Without this
dimension, conscience loses any legitimacy as moral arbiter. It is
not surprising that Poster seems to view internalized authority as
entirely expendable.

Poster's neglect of the ideological factor also limits his account of bourgeois women. Although Poster does not attempt to describe the detailed characteristics of bourgeois men and women separately—and cannot be faulted for not having done so—it can still be maintained that his general picture of bourgeois women is flawed by his failure to recognize the ideology of motherhood as a causal factor. With the privatization of the family and its increasing separation from the economic sphere, women were to some extent cloistered in the home, a point often noted. This permitted and encouraged the development of a Protestant ethic for women. Higher moral-religious expectations for women as mothers surfaced, comparable to the "counsels of perfection" for the cloister in the Middle Ages. Men who had been tainted by the world could withdraw to the hearth, where women were to create a morally purer realm.

To be sure this ethic was, as Poster insists, repressive for women, calling upon them to live sacrificially in a way not expected of men. But like the Calvinist heroic character, assumed to be male, there was as well a certain greatness—flawed though it clearly was—about this motherly character. Central to this ideological structure was motherhood not simply as natural instinct, nor as medium of capitalist domination, but as vocation. Motherly nurturance provided not only a haven in a heartless world, but also an implicit and at times explicit criticism of that world. As Horkheimer urged, there was a utopian element (though mixed with repression) in the motherly love fostered in the bourgeois family. Poster overlooks this utopian dimension in the ideal of the bourgeois family.

When Poster makes his own attempt at a utopian model of the family, it is clear that he finds no place for the inculcation of transgenerational value traditions. For him the goals are to "diminish hierarchy and augment individual development" (204). Toward this end the intensity of bourgeois parent-child relations ought to be lessened, and children ought to be encouraged to identify with a wide range of adults, as in the Israeli kibbutz (204). "Parents can share affection and love with their children without intruding upon the independent psychic life of the younger generation" (205). Here the cultivation of individual responsibility through deep internalization of a parental superego gives way to the quest for self-realization in interaction with one's peers. Thus Poster does not mourn the passing of the bourgeois individual; he seems in fact to celebrate the appearance of the other-directed individual.

Poster's book, then, can be taken as representative of those thinkers, including certain feminists, who blame the Western nuclear family for a variety of modern problems and who favor societal evolution away from this familial model. My contention is that this approach to a critical theory is one-sided and in need of correction through an account of the contributions of the bourgeois family. Such an account is found in Peter Berger and Brigitte Berger, *The War over the Family.*

Brigitte and Peter Berger's The War over the Family

With Brigitte and Peter Berger's *The War over the Family* we are in a thought-world informed much more by Weber than by Marx and Freud.[3] Here we find a spirited defense of the bourgeois family as the most viable option "for the raising of children who will have a good chance of becoming responsible and autonomous individuals" (167). The Bergers try to find the middle ground between the critical camp, which they associate closely with feminism, and the neo-traditionalist camp, "which must be seen as essentially a backlash phenomenon" (28). The Bergers contend that the nuclear, bourgeois family, far from being a consequence of modernization, is one of the preconditions for modernization (87). "The most dramatic way of putting this," they claim with acknowledged overstatement, "would be to say that modernity did not produce the nuclear family but, on the contrary, the nuclear family produced modernity" (91). Seeing a continual decline of patriarchal dominance in this family (93, 96, 102), they maintain that patriarchy is not essential to it but is simply a holdover from the past.

On the other hand the connection of Protestantism and the bourgeois family is viewed as essential. No effort is made in this work to separate the Puritan and the bourgeois families; secularization heralds the beginning of the end for both (117). The authors attempt to extend the Weber thesis to cover the family: "We agree with Weber in his understanding of the role of Protestantism in the genesis of modern capitalism—though Weber could not have known the equally important role of the family, as uncovered by recent research" (98).[4]

The Bergers follow Weber in linking rationalization and individualization to the Calvinist worldview. Calvinism gave birth to this "social-psychological constellation for peculiar religious reasons," but it did so through the instrumentality of the family: "The anti-magical, radically transcendent orientation of Protestant faith had

the consequence of freeing the world from supernatural interven-
tions . . . and thus laying it open first to the rational inquiries of the
scientist and then to the imposition of rational controls by both
the engineer and the entrepreneur. Further, the peculiar solitude of
the Protestant religious experience . . . fostered an austere individualism . . . . These virtues were built into the socialization process
as it was established in the bourgeois family in Protestant countries" (109).

The Bergers do not share the neo-Marxian ambivalence about
the repressive basis for bourgeois individualization. In their classic
forms the bourgeois-Protestant virtues contributed to the realization of genuine individuality and autonomy (109). The Puritan
character typically was strong and resolute, revolutionary and
antitraditional. The Bergers see no reason to regard this character
as authoritarian or excessively repressed (111, 116). Nor do they
share Max Weber's conviction that rationalization, though essential to modernity, inevitably becomes a new form of domination.

The claim of Weber that ascetic rationalization leads inexorably
to the iron cage of "mechanized petrifaction" in fact undergoes an
interesting transmutation in the Bergers' account.[5] On the one
hand, rather than conceding that bourgeois civilization petrifies
the human spirit, the Bergers maintain that this civilization is a
magnificent achievement, well worth fighting to preserve. More
specifically, the bourgeois family must be preserved. On the other
hand, however, certain characteristics internal to bourgeois culture threaten to become hypertrophic "to the point where the
earlier fabric of modern bourgeois society can no longer contain
them" (118). This radicalization of modern tendencies the Bergers
term hypermodernity, and this is divided into two subcategories,
hyperrationality and hyperindividualism (118). Under the latter
two rubrics the Bergers place many of the negative features of
modern bourgeois culture described by Weber and the Frankfurt
School. With the argument that "hyper-modern developments
often show considerable affinity with counter-modern ones" (118),
they are able to adopt a stance in defense of modernity against
those forces, whether radical or reactionary, that seek to dissolve
it. True bourgeois culture respects rationality; science and technology have increasingly freed us from bondage to the forces of
nature. But hyperrationality, extending scientific-technological
control "into every aspect of life, including the family," is experienced as oppressive and dehumanizing (118–19). Likewise, true
bourgeois culture fosters individuality, but hyperindividualism in

an unwarranted way brings about "an increasing emphasis on the individual over against every collective entity, including the family itself" (120).

In this connection the Bergers launch what must be regarded as a bitter attack on contemporary feminism, approaching it as a prime example of hyperindividualism. "The individual woman is now emphasized over against every communal context in which she may find herself—a redefinition of her situation that breaks not only the community between the spouses but (more fundamentally) the mother-child dyad, which if anthropologists are correct, is the most basic human community of all. Thus the search for individual identity in isolation from all communal definitions becomes a central concern of life" (120).

The Bergers find the roots of the feminist attack on the bourgeois nuclear family in Marxism, especially in Engels's *The Origin of the Family, Private Property and the State* (1884). They consider the Frankfurt School to be an important link between Marxism and contemporary feminism (172–73). The work especially mentioned in this connection is Adorno, et al., *The Authoritarian Personality*. Oddly the Bergers do not see the ambivalences and uncertainties regarding the family and character structure that pervade this large volume. In a sweeping summary of a work consisting of some 990 pages, they write: "The argument here is that (right-wing) authoritarianism has its roots in the type of family produced by bourgeois-capitalist society" (173). Ignoring the fact that Horkheimer and Adorno defend the bourgeois family in terms not unlike their own, the Bergers associate Adorno with the stronger attack on the family found in Wilhelm Reich and give the impression that all of the neo-Marxists "look upon the bourgeois family as the major obstacle to healthy and non-repressed individuals" (173). For Horkheimer and Adorno, at least, this account is entirely inaccurate.

The Bergers make a strong case for the idea that one of the basic functions of the family is conserving and propagating meaning and values. Acknowledging that the bourgeois ethos has important roots in religion and that it receives continuing support and legitimation from business, government, and other institutions, nevertheless, they argue, the family has played a unique role in "instilling basic moral values" (176).

Middle-class institutions and values have been weakened since the 1960s, and cultural revitalization is needed, the Bergers contend. But this process requires the development of self-reliant and responsible individuals; for this purpose no alternative to the bourgeois family has been found (182). The Bergers are aware that the prototypical family stands frequently in contrast with "the empirical differences between the many forms of family arrangements in contemporary society" (185); what is of crucial importance, however, is the ideal, which still exerts considerable formative power, pointing to "a central value set that permits the maintenance of a democratic consensus" (185).

Having launched broadside attacks on feminism throughout earlier sections of the book, the Bergers make rather large concessions to feminists in the closing pages. "There is a wide range of feminist issues—that is, dealing with women's rights—that command very wide support in Western societies and that would command even wider support if they were not perceived as, intentionally or unintentionally, opposed to the family. It seems to us that the recognition and enhancement of women's rights should be on the agenda of every decent society today" (205). Having argued convincingly that the family plays a very large role in the construction of meanings and values (especially in the area of gender roles), it is difficult to see how the changes in attitude that the Bergers endorse relative to women could be effected without some reformatory changes in the bourgeois family.

The Bergers can be faulted for adopting a defensive posture vis-à-vis the ideology of the bourgeois family rather than contributing to the critique of ideology. Unlike Horkheimer and Tillich, they do not find in either the family or religion "the presuppositions for their own critique." Rather, they associate the Jewish and Christian traditions with the "old normative definition" of the family. By and large they maintain that empirical data confirm the merits of this family form. What they do not acknowledge is the effort by feminists and others to reform the familial ideology without breaking with core values of the Western tradition. When the Bergers assert that their defense of the bourgeois family is based on its contribution to autonomy and freedom (192), they are not sufficiently attentive to the feminist contention that this has been much less true for women than for men.

A comparison of comments made by Poster and by the Bergers regarding the method of child rearing found in the Israeli kibbutz is instructive from the standpoint of our study.[6] Their contrasting evaluations of the kibbutzim provide insight into their conflicting assessments of the bourgeois family. Both understand the method of child rearing found in that context to be one that lessens the intensity of identification of child with parents; given the presence in the kibbutz of a variety of adult authority figures, identification becomes more diffuse.[7] But in Poster's account the result of these practices is "to diminish hierarchy and augment individual development," while the Bergers conclude that the personalities developed in the kibbutz are "emphatically collectivistic and conformist."[8] Thus we find opposing assessments of the same phenomenon—a "loosening of parent-child relations."[9] Can ways be found to mediate this dispute?[10]

Consideration of Bruno Bettelheim's more detailed analysis of character structure in the kibbutz (found in his work, *The Children of the Dream*) offers us a sharpened perspective on these matters. Bettelheim suggests that the superegos developed in the kibbutz and in the Western bourgeois family are different. He postulates that in the former context a kind of "collective superego"—the internalized voice of the group—emerges.[11] Bettelheim sees both positive and negative features of alternative types of internalization. "The source of the kibbutz superego is less powerful and awesome than for the child growing up in an authoritarian, middle-class family. But the commands are more inescapable because there is nowhere a dissenting voice to support one's own doubts or dissent."[12] In the bourgeois family the child is clearly subordinate to the parent; the resulting superego contributes to a "morality of constraint." "In the kibbutz, from the very beginning, relations between child and adult are not unilateral, and the peer group is much more important—when conscience develops in the kibbutz it is founded less on constraint and more on cooperation."[13]

Bettelheim theorizes that American society may also be evolving toward a "morality of cooperation," as parents become "less and less domineering in the child's life" and the peer groups become "more important—much sooner in life."[14] But he contends that in the rise of Western individualism, "it was precisely the personal superego (or moral demand) that asserted itself." The individual conscience of the Protestant Reformation (including, we might add, of Puritanism) was characteristically able to speak against prevailing community mores. This could come about because the superego resulted from the internalization of "some very particular and highly personalized figures, chiefly the parents."[15] (We might be inclined to add, though Bettelheim does not, that insofar as the parental superego was a religious conscience, a utopian aspect was also present—providing internalized ideals that offer a perspective for social critique).

Returning, then, to Poster and the Bergers, we can see that Poster chooses to highlight the freeing of children from domination by parents, while favoring the achievement of a morality of cooperation. He clearly favors the reduction of internalization to the bare minimum required for the child to become a functioning adult. In taking this position, he has affinities with the view of Habermas discussed in the preceding chapter. Poster puts little weight on the superego's contribution either to individualization or to moral responsibility. Stressing the sociality of the ego, he downplays the value of bourgeois individuality and the morality of the anguished conscience. He places no importance on the deep internalization of ideals as a positive motive for moral behavior. Nor does he stress the value of linkage to traditions. Poster's individual seems to grow up in the present without historic memory, simply realizing his or her own "independent psychic life" without vocation or inherited meaning. With peer orientation replacing age hierarchies, the description of this character as "other directed" would seem to be apt. Poster attacks Marcuse and Horkheimer for their individualism, but he does not successfully answer Marcuse's claim, echoed by the Bergers, that in the absence of strong families and developed superegos individuals are more than ever dominated by the larger society.[16] Poster's viewpoint is attractive to feminists because he takes a strong stand against familial patriarchy, but he does this by seeking to eliminate all authority and all participation in meaningful tradition.

The Bergers take the opposite tack, focusing on the capacity of the bourgeois conscience to resist conformist peer pressures, a capacity thought to be lacking among the kibbutzim. In consequence, they seek "ways to reassert the emotional and moral primacy of the family."[17] The family, they hold, is essential to the preservation and re-creation of personal autonomy and democratic values. They stress the contribution of strong superego formation to moral character, and view that formation as a product of the exclusivity and intensity of parent-child relations in the traditional family. They make a convincing case for the view that the bourgeois family was closely integrated with Protestant religion and that each had a formative influence upon the other. The family became itself a quasi-religious institution, as Protestantism became in important respects a family religion. In this setting, conscience was a religious-familial agency within the individual psyche. If, as the Bergers suggest, secularization threatens the bourgeois-Protestant ethos and the bourgeois family, it threatens to dissolve conscience as well.

An important aspect of their emphasis on the integration of religion, family, and conscience is the implication that the individualizing agency—the guilty conscience—has communal roots and assumes a transcendent point of reference. In important respects the individual is the creation not just of the nuclear family but of the ideological community. This fact sets limits to the individualism of bourgeois culture and provides a basis for social integration. The Bergers write: "Only by accepting a higher force located outside the individual, the family, and society as a whole, could there be a perceived unity between individual, family, and societal interests. Especially the fine balance between individualism and voluntary cooperation, which was particularly important in America (as Alexis de Tocqueville saw so clearly), required powerful religious underpinnings."[18]

Thus for the Bergers the bourgeois family was integrated with the whole society by means of its integration with bourgeois-Protestant religion. In connection with this ideology, conscience and even gender roles were given social and religious legitimation and invested with religious meaning. The Bergers' account of the strengths of the bourgeois family has merit, but their contention that it can be preserved intact in the present cultural context and only needs defending against hypertrophies must be rejected. It is the severance of the family from larger, meaning-giving communities and its failure to achieve its own egalitarian ideals that have brought questions of justice to the fore. The Bergers mistakenly assert that the demands of women for greater vocational dignity and greater equality are based on hyperindividualism.[19] It is the utopia at the heart of bourgeois culture—"with liberty and justice for all"—that more than anything else fires the feminist protest. Thus feminism represents an extension of critical theory; at its best it fosters a vision of individuals-in-community as a goal of but never attained by bourgeois culture. The Bergers seem blind to these dimensions of the feminist protest.

To arrive at tentative conclusions here, I would argue that Horkheimer's ambivalences about the bourgeois family, as discussed in Chapter 2, provide in the end a more balanced perspective than either of the two more single-minded studies surveyed above. Both Poster and the Bergers acknowledge the important role of the bourgeois family in creating a new type of individualization through the instrumentality of internalized conscience. Poster argues, however, that the consequent sense of autonomy is largely illusory, being based upon the internalization of age, sex, and class hierarchies. The Bergers endorse bourgeois individualization unreservedly, while criticizing only that hyperindividualism that derogates all community, even the bourgeois family itself. Disagreeing with both, I hold with Horkheimer and Adorno that, on the one hand, bourgeois individualization and the conscience integral to it were genuine moral accomplishments, while, on the other hand, I hold that this autonomy was deeply flawed, being built upon a largely coercive authority. This latter position leads not to some form of afamilial neo-collectivism or to an unqualified reaffirmation of the bourgeois family but to critique and reform of family and ideology in the direction of a more genuinely liberating authority and conscience.

Do these reflections provide any useful perspective on the problems confronting the contemporary nuclear family? Should greater efforts be made to defend the bourgeois family, or do current developments toward more plurality in living arrangements dictate that we abandon the quest for a normative pattern? No global answer to this question can be attempted here. But perhaps Horkheimer's ambivalences point the way toward a provisional approach. On the one hand, any effort to recover the kind of authority accorded parents in the early modern period is both impractical and undesirable. In our more open and fluid society, children find many role models; to a certain extent nurturance and discipline can be derived from nonfamilial sources. Nuclearity can lead to claustrophobic isolation; the thoroughgoing privatization of the family often leads to social and moral isolation as well. And in such families the danger of authoritarianism is real. Our study makes a case for "de-privatizing" nurturance as well as moral discipline. Social institutions other than the family (including the state) must share in the functions of mothering and fathering. As Sidney Callahan suggests: "Fortunate children and families will have access to intact neighborhood institutions, such as churches, civic organizations, unions, youth groups, and so on, where moral discourse and moral evaluation of the day's events are still a part of life. The larger political arena and the media . . . can also be a source of moral discourse. . . . [The school also must take up] its moral responsibility for engendering and encouraging conscience development."[20]

On the other hand, we should avoid the supposition that intimate and secure relations with parental figures are easily dispensable, or that traditional familial ties can without detriment be replaced by contractual relationships. The notion that a society would function successfully without some means of fostering its own normative standards of behavior is surely chimerical. The Bergers are correct in asserting that no satisfactory substitute has been found for the family in providing moral structure for the lives of children. While it may be true that American families are evolving away from the predominance of one standard model to a much more pluralistic situation, this tendency by no means suggests the disappearance of life in families per se. Critique of the bourgeois family is in order; but along with critique must come reconstruction and the quest for a corrected normative model.

The conclusion of Jean Bethke Elshtain seems warranted, that contemporary challenges "push toward a loosening but not a wholesale negation in our normative endorsement of intergenerational family life." Alternative life-styles must be granted not only the right to exist but also the recognition that they foster countercultural values that contribute a richness to culture that otherwise would be lacking. However, the nuclear intergenerational family can, as Elshtain insists, be privileged as "central and critical in nurturing recognitions of human frailty, mortality, and finitude and in inculcating moral limits and constraints."[21]

Contrary to Poster's arguments, I suggest the conclusion that individual conscience is more securely formed in the child when deep, permanent relationships with parental figures are provided. And this points toward a defense of the nuclear family for the purpose of raising children. Our study suggests further that the normative model should be egalitarian and symmetrical, with concomitant changes in the images of mothering and fathering—themes that will be discussed in the chapters that follow.[22]

Before the bourgeois family can be given even a qualified affirmation, however, it must be subjected to a feminist critique. We now turn to an examination of family, ideology, and conscience from a feminist perspective.

6

THE FEMINIST CRITIQUE
OF WESTERN CHARACTER
FORMATION

THE NEW FEMINISM that emerged from the ferment of the 1960s took up once again the criticism of paternal dominance in Western society. At least one source of this renewed critique was a recognition on the part of women that even men in the ranks of the various reform movements—men who were calling for radical social reconstruction—were unwilling to relinquish their traditional male privileges. Thus the critique of patriarchy found in the literature of the Frankfurt School was a theme with immediate resonance for most feminists. Though some feminist thinkers on the left were attracted to the orthodox Marxian scheme, a larger contingent found that, in the light of women's experience, the thesis that all domination derives from the economic order was implausible. The contention of Wilhelm Reich that patriarchy is a nonderivative pattern of dominance, and that indeed it became the matrix out of which capitalist structures rose, commended itself to many feminists. The general thesis that patriarchal family structures, in alliance with patriarchal religion (and morality), have for millennia kept women in a subordinate position has had a deep impact on the feminist movement. This approach, however, puts little weight on historical changes that may have occurred, either in the family or in the ideological dimension. Horkheimer, Fromm, and Marcuse were valued for questioning why patriarchy endures in Western culture in spite of a lessening of patriarchal-authoritarian structures in the family and in spite of democratizing tendencies in general.

The issue that comes into focus for feminists is the need to explain the tenacity of patriarchy in the face of sociohistorical changes. This problem is comparable to the query that initiated the Frankfurt School in the 1930s: why were industrial workers submissive and conservative when the objective economic conditions were ripe for revolution? The initial question is similar for feminist study. Why do women as well as men acquiesce in patriarchal structures when objective conditions in the family as well as elsewhere would seem to allow for substantial changes? As in the thirties, it has proven necessary to turn to subjective factors, to the way in which psychology and ideology intersect in the context of the family. Why have ideological and characterological changes lagged behind other changes? Are the primary causes for the perseverance of patriarchy familial, psychological, or ideological? For many feminists these issues have served as a point of departure.

Thus having reached the point arrived at a generation earlier by critical theory, feminism needs a normative historical psychology that is attentive to familial and ideological factors as well as to biological and economic concerns. And just as Critical Theorists did in the thirties, some feminists have turned to Freud for assistance in developing the type of psychology needed. This "psychoanalytic feminism" begins with a close scrutiny of Freud's contention that father dominance and female subordination are inescapable due to "the centrality of the father to the struggle over the formation of the identity of both male and female child."[1] For Freud, sexual identity (gender) is not simply biological, it takes shape culturally in relation to paternal authority. But he saw no other path toward civilization than subordination of the female gender. Reich, seeking to escape the conclusion that the patriarchal family is unavoidable, urged that the nuclear family itself be jettisoned. Psychoanalytic feminism attempts to look behind the authority of the father to determine the reasons for the supposed necessity of the patriarchal pattern. In good Freudian fashion its attention is directed toward the pre-Oedipal period, the period before the ascendancy of the father. Nancy Chodorow summarizes this feminist project: "We continue to live in a male dominant society, even though the legal bases of male dominance are eroding. . . . [The] recognition of the tenacity of sexual asymmetry and inequality in the face of sweep-

ing historical changes has stimulated feminist attempts to articu-
late theoretically the systemic nature of the social organization of
gender, to move beyond descriptive generalizations about sexism,
patriarchy, or male supremacy to analysis of how sexual asymmetry and inequality are constituted, reproduced, and change."[2]

This inquiry into how gender inequality is constituted and reproduced and how it may be changed focuses attention upon the
gender structures of the psyche that are superimposed upon the
biological sexuality of the body, structures shaped by the complex
interactions of the individual child with his or her parents, both in
conflict and in identification. Freud analyzed these interactions in
careful detail, but did he "get it right" when he asserted paternal
supremacy as the inescapable result? The psychoanalytic feminists challenge Freud on this issue. Dorothy Dinnerstein and
Nancy Chodorow are often grouped together by virtue of the similarity of their analyses of Freud to the extent that their viewpoint
has been termed the Dinnerstein-Chodorow thesis. By examining
the way these two theorists construct a feminist explanation of
"the tenacity of sexual asymmetry," we can pursue the implications of their viewpoint for conscience theory.[3]

It is appropriate to view psychoanalytic feminism against the
background of critical theory because of inherent connections
between the two perspectives. Sondra Farganis suggests that feminist theory provides a kind of practicum for critical theory, and
Chodorow acknowledges an indebtedness to this tradition.[4] Fred
Alford contends that "the true successors to Horkheimer, Adorno,
and Marcuse are not critical theorists such as Habermas but the
so-called psychoanalytic feminists."[5] It is my contention that this
perspective points the way toward the continuation of the Frankfurt School's critique of conscience.

Dinnerstein and Chodorow agree in maintaining that Freud's
case for the centrality of the father "flies in the face of an im-
pressive array of evidence that establishes the centrality of the
mother."[6] According to the two analysts, infants of both sexes
develop love-hate feelings first toward the mother, the primary
caretaker. These ambivalent feelings include gratitude and affection for nurturance and need gratification but also fear of the
mother's power, aversion to one's dependency, and resentment of
regulation. For both sexes, then, the father emerges as a counterweight to the overwhelming power of the mother. As Balbus expresses it, "The Law of the Father is a welcome shelter from the
power of the mother."[7] The persistent inclination of men to pre-

serve the subordination of women has the same origin: the fear of the power of the mother.[8] According to this approach, the paternally oriented Oedipal superego and father identification take shape in reaction to the pre-Oedipal mother relation, and the character and intensity of the father relation are affected by the quality of the mother relation.

This emphasis on the primacy of the mother constitutes a correction of the priority given to the father in the Freudian schema. It does not as such represent a fundamental break with the Freudian framework. Freud himself referred to the early mother relation as unexplored territory, though he gave relatively little attention to it. Melanie Klein among others in the Freudian school had already begun this investigation. In pursuing the further implications of this shift of emphasis, however, our analysts diverge from Freud in different directions. It will serve our purposes here to summarize Dinnerstein's perspective and then to indicate how Chodorow develops and modifies it.

Dorothy Dinnerstein on Our "Gender Arrangements"

We have noted that Freud viewed the father-centered, patriarchal family as an institution essential to human civilization (that is, civilization requires a break from the incestuous tie to the mother). Reich saw the patriarchal family as prevailing up to the present; a new nonpatriarchal civilization will require the abolition of the nuclear family altogether. Dorothy Dinnerstein also sees the father-centered family prevailing into the present day. She begins to diverge from Freud's position as she pursues the reasons that this is the case. Her emphasis is not on the exclusively sexual or libidinal relation (as is the case with Freud) but on the social-human relation of infant to mother. Put in the broadest and simplest terms, in Dinnerstein's account the infant credits the mother for the pleasures of life and blames the mother for life's suffering and sorrow. Expecting to receive unlimited nurturance from the mother, the infant is inevitably disappointed and blames the mother for its disappointment. In awe of the mother's power, rebelling against the sense of dependency upon her, frustrated by her inability to satisfy its every desire, the infant turns to the father as to a safe haven from the mother. Ultimately the hostility of children of both sexes toward women-mothers is an expression of rebellion against the human condition—a rejection of human mortality. These feelings toward women, somewhat mitigated later in the case of female children, eventuate in the male in the desire to control and dominate women, perceived by men as those beings who possess the power to nurture or to withhold nurturance. Thus Dinnerstein's point is that the whole structure of our adult gender arrangements is based upon the fact that "the main adult presence in infancy and early childhood is female."[9] Patricentricity appears as a defense against matricentricity.

It is clear that for Dinnerstein patriarchy (or patricentricity, to use Erich Fromm's term) is a mode of relating to the human world, a psychological-ideological construct. Furthermore, it is not rooted in biology nor is it essential for the emergence of civilization; rather, it is response to a pathological gender arrangement, mother-monopolized child rearing. For if fathers were equally involved in the care and maintenance of infants, this entire attitudinal structure would be fundamentally altered. By inclusion of the father in infant nurturance and care, Dinnerstein contends that the credit for all the satisfactions and the blame for all the "ills that flesh is heir to" could both be laid at the doorstep of men as well as women. All of the wordless feelings of infancy—adoration, fear, rage—will no longer have as their single focus "the magically powerful goddess mother of infancy."[10]

In Dinnerstein as in Freud there is internalization of the father's authority. Against Freud she views the flight to the father not simply as an escape from a sexual relation with the mother; it is also an escape from the authority and power of the mother and from a sense of dependency upon her. For Dinnerstein the infant's relations to both mother and father are distinctively human, not strictly biological, and refer to human dilemmas, not strictly to biological needs. These dilemmas require an answer, but the typical human answer thus far has been pathological; we have not yet devised fully human answers to the problems of human existence. Our societal madness will not be replaced by sanity until we do.

In the views just summarized, Dinnerstein falls into the camp of the neo-Freudian revisionists, of which Fromm is our prime example. But in her accounts of the consequences of matricentricity and patricentricity, she diverges significantly from Fromm. He considers an initial matricentricity to be inescapable and healthy. The intrusion of the father at a later stage is equally essential. Superego formation, associated with the father, is different from nurturance but equally a stage on the path to maturity. At the patriarchal stage individualization is enhanced, as well as reasoning (through the use of abstract principles) and the capacity for obedience to rules. Fromm's final stage is a return (or partial return) to matricentric principles after the achievement of individuality, reason, and self-control.

Dinnerstein rejects the notion of a necessary progression from mother to father in favor of the egalitarian concept of shared parenting. This revision has important implications for moral formation; clearly the Freudian interpretation of conscience as superego must be revised to fit Dinnerstein's framework. The meaning of the father relation, and of the internalization of the father, is now no longer the breaking of the natural, incestuous mother relation and the accession to human culture. Rather, the father represents safety in the neurotic flight from the overwhelming mother. As a result, a controlling mentality vis-à-vis mother-nature-woman emerges from the father relation, a mentality that is valuable in certain respects but highly destructive in others. From this perspective the fact that conscience is patriarchal constitutes deformity, not maturity. The patricentric conscience constitutes one possible avenue of entrance into human culture, but not the only one, in Dinnerstein's view.

Alternatively, if the father is present from the beginning of infancy as nurturer and enabler as well as disciplinarian, the exclusiveness of the mother relation never develops, and neither the male nor the female child develops a fixation (as described above) toward the mother figure. From this perspective, superego formation seems to fade in moral significance (a point to be discussed in the next chapter). Gone are the sexual tensions that led to the Oedipus complex and its resolution. One senses that the Freudian perception of inevitable conflict between individual libidinal drives and the requirements of civilization is muted in Dinnerstein (as in Fromm). Nature-culture conflicts can be minimized if a fully egalitarian family is allowed to develop.

Also missing in Dinnerstein's revisionist model is the role played by the superego in individualization. In Dinnerstein's analysis, the process of individualization is perceived as occurring naturally in human development rather than through the mechanism of the guilty conscience. Fromm saw the superego as something to rebel against in order to affirm one's individuality. The need even for this negative function of the superego seems to have fallen away in Dinnerstein. What is needed is the early participation of men in the "initiation of infants into the human estate."[11] When this happens, it seems, there will be no need for the later decisive break with the mother, for there will be no exclusive tie with her in the first place. The concerns voiced by both Fromm and Horkheimer regarding the loss of individuality that may result from the absence of paternal authority are not raised in *The Mermaid and the Minotaur*.

Nancy Chodorow on Capitalism and the Bourgeois Family

Dinnerstein is like Wilhelm Reich in proposing as a future possibility a fundamental alteration of our "gender arrangements," while finding in past history only repetitions of a flawed pattern. Her analysis is therefore largely independent of the sociohistorical context. Nancy Chodorow on the other hand directs her attention to patterns of child rearing in the modern West, recognizing that culture-specific needs shape child-rearing practices. She summarizes her approach as follows: "Women's mothering in the isolated nuclear family of contemporary capitalist society creates specific personality characteristics in men that reproduce both an ideology and psychodynamic of male superiority and submission to the requirements of production."[12] Thus Chodorow follows the Frankfurt School in combining sociological and psychological dimensions in her critique of gender arrangements. Like them she links patriarchy with capitalism; like Fromm rather than Reich she connects patriarchy and capitalism with the nuclear family of modernity.

Chodorow takes note of the fact that gender roles are affected by familial and economic changes, such as the relative degree of presence or absence of the father in the domestic setting and the concomitant extent of mother dependency.[13] Yet it is Chodorow's contention that the gender system "stays the same in fundamental ways," namely, that women continue to mother.[14] The relative differences in mother domination found at different stages in the modern period are not truly fundamental, and therefore the controlling attitudes of men toward women (here Chodorow mirrors Dinnerstein) have remained to plague us throughout modernity. As a result, as Catherine Keller suggests, for Chodorow the nuclear family is "the villain of the piece."[15]

Like Dinnerstein, Chodorow holds that fundamental change is possible, but it requires a shift to shared parenting. "The elimination of the present organization of parenting in favor of a system of parenting in which both men and women are responsible would be a tremendous social advance. This outcome is historically possible, but far from inevitable."[16] The projected model is not inconsis-

tent with a revised form of the nuclear family in which fathers play
a far greater nurturant role. However, Chodorow's brief description
of alternative models focuses on more collective forms of child
rearing, and she questions the value of the exclusivity of the nuclear family.[17] Chodorow gives more attention than Dinnerstein to
the Oedipus complex and its resolution, though her interest is
more in gender identity than in moral development. She writes:
"For boys the major [Oedipal] goal is the achievement of personal
masculine identification with their father and sense of secure masculine self, achieved through superego formation and disparage-
ment of women."[18] Superego development for girls reaches a less
clear resolution: "They neither repress nor give up so absolutely
their preoedipal and oedipal attachment to their mother, nor their
oedipal attachment to their father."[19] The primary consequence of
the Oedipal period for the development of identity, then, has to do
with the male sense of separateness, the female sense of connection. "Boys come to define themselves as more separate and distinct, with a greater sense of rigid ego boundaries and differentia-
tion. The basic feminine sense of self is connected to the world, the
basic masculine sense of self is separate."[20] Chodorow does not
attempt to draw out the ethical implications of this formulaic
conclusion. Aspects of this project will concern us in the next
chapter.

In spite of her remarks about the personality characteristics
distinctive of capitalist society, and even her reference to stages in
the development of character types within that society to which
we will refer in the next chapter, Chodorow makes little attempt
to trace the historical development of our modern gender arrangements. Her descriptions of the nuclear family, like those of Dinnerstein, tend to be largely ahistorical; therefore changes in the
family and ideological changes that might have a bearing upon
character structure are largely unexamined.[21]

Isaac Balbus suggests ways of linking the Dinnerstein-Chodorow thesis to contemporary characterological debates. He notes
that the attack on the superego-dominated individual—engaged
in not only by Reich, Fromm, and the early Horkheimer but also
by many feminists—is to a considerable extent outmoded. This
type, says Balbus, "is increasingly being replaced by the 'narcissistic' individual with an underdeveloped superego and an over-
developed identification with his mother."[22] These individuals,
and indeed the families from which they derive, might well be
described as matricentric rather than patricentric. Such individ-

uals are less alienated from their feelings, less calculative and instrumental; indeed, they are more "feminine." Yet, Balbus argues, the unconscious fear of mother-identification on the part of men of this type leads them to a compensatory exaggerated assertion of their masculinity and to a need to deny dependence on the mother. These tendencies lead in turn to "an unconscious proclivity to dominate women."[23] Thus, even though the structure of the present-day family does not appear to be father dominated, destructive patriarchal attitudes are still generated.

Balbus therefore contends that the characterological trends of the present can be understood in terms of the theories of Dinnerstein and Chodorow. They provide a perspective that explains why men still seek to dominate women even after the marked decline of the father-dominated family. The patriarchal attitudes generated in our present culture derive from mother-monopolized child rearing.[24] Not fear of the father but fear of the mother is the ultimate cause of our social pathology. Cultures vary regarding the intensity of mother identification. It is likely, says Balbus, that the tendency toward "more indulgent, as well as father-absent, modes of child rearing . . . may well mean that mother-identification has increased and that compensatory masculine denigration of women . . . has likewise intensified."[25]

As Dinnerstein and Chodorow have recognized, then, the path toward a domination-free future, according to Balbus, lies in the direction of "authentic forms of shared parenting."[26] When fathers share fully in the nurturance of children, the psychological basis for male domination will disappear.[27] As Balbus interprets the psychoanalytic feminist position, the mode of child rearing is primary in determining character formation. Familial patterns interact with ideological factors, but the former predominate over the latter.[28]

The view that ideological factors are subordinate to familial patterns is an extrapolation from Dinnerstein and Chodorow, but it seems to be in accord with their perspectives. In fact they both deal only sparingly with ideological developments. Though both take for granted the feminist project of overcoming male domination, they leave aside moral and religious dialogues that might be provoked by their formulations. Both recognize a mythic-ideological dimension in gender relations, but neither initiates reflection as to how myth may be revised. There is, to be sure, an implicit ideology critique in Dinnerstein. She views the presently prevailing gender arrangements as a neurotic way of responding to the human predicament, even though they constitute a culturally induced neurosis that is defined as normal. Like Erich Fromm, the implied perspective for her critique of the prevailing ideology is from the standpoint of an ideal or essential human nature. But she largely ignores debates about and criticisms of this type of humanism. Chodorow's immediate purpose is descriptive, but more broadly, her intent also is to discover how the predominant mode of child rearing can be changed.[29] She grants that understanding how gender is constituted and how it may be changed in turn requires an understanding of our society's "ideology of gender."[30] Even so, Chodorow does not engage systematically in the critique of ideology. She clearly shares the Frankfurt School's criticism of capitalist ideology, but she does not explore how it may have contributed to the rise of mother-monopolized child rearing, nor does she clearly link new modes of child rearing to ideological change. One has to agree with Catherine Keller's assessment, "Chodorow underemphasizes the work of social and ideological structures beyond the family in requiring, exploiting, and institutionalizing that sexism to which the family structure already tends."[31]

As these discussions already suggest, the analysis of gender identity as found in Dinnerstein and Chodorow is closely connected with issues regarding conscience formation; "the process of becoming gendered subjects" (a phrase from Patricia Elliot)[32] is linked with the process of becoming conscientious subjects. The questions we want to ask, then, are as follows: What are the implications of the postulate that morality emerges from conflict-laden interactions with the mother as well as with the father? What will be the fate of conscience in the context of the altered gender arrangements advocated by Dinnerstein and Chodorow? If mother and father images are socially constructed, how can the mode of child rearing be changed without ideological change? Which ideological changes are required to effect the desired change in the mode of child rearing? Our next chapter explores possible answers to these questions.

7

PSYCHOANALYTIC
FEMINISTS
ON CONSCIENCE

IF THE PREVAILING IDEOLOGY of a society is reproduced in the character structure of individuals through the medium of the family, the mechanism of this reproduction is—if we follow the Freudian model—through internalization in the superego understood as a distillate of tradition within the psyche.[1] If patriarchy is perpetuated through superego formation, what position do psychoanalytic feminists take regarding this agency? Can it be eliminated or transformed? What is the shape of the feminist critique of the superego? This is an important issue for feminism and for our study of conscience and moral character. Though the psychoanalytic feminists deal with closely related matters, ambiguities remain on this crucial point. An examination of their possible answers to the following related questions will assist us in achieving some clarification: (1) Can and should the superego be dissolved into the ego? (2) Can distinctions be made within the superego between content derived from fathers and content derived from mothers? (3) Can distinctions be made between the superego and other components of the moral sense that have nonpaternal origins?

Dinnerstein and Chodorow on the Dissolution of Superego into Ego

The effort to dissolve the superego into the ego was undertaken by Freud in his quest for individual rational autonomy. Freud did not believe that many people could fully achieve this goal, but he regarded anything less as a form of immaturity. Submission to dictates of the superego is submission to an alien authority; the ego must become its own authority. This for Freud is the final stage of growing up; it means being scientific or rational rather than religious. Dinnerstein and Chodorow both speak as if they share with Freud the goal of achieving such autonomy.[2] Chodorow urges that the new gender arrangement (when both parents share in child rearing) will assist women in gaining the autonomy so often denied them, "which too much embeddedness in relationship has often taken from them."[3] If in fact the self cannot altogether escape the need for a "magic parent" (whether mother or father), it at least can learn, says Dinnerstein, to become parent for itself so that in some sense the ego becomes its own magic helper.[4]

Although both appear to share the Freudian goal of autonomy, Dinnerstein and Chodorow also share in the Frankfurt School's critique of character domination by the ego. As we have seen, Horkheimer, Adorno, and Marcuse (in contrast to Fromm) regarded the Western ego as itself patriarchal, as itself a form of internalized domination. (In this context they do not address the difference between male and female egos.) The approach of the Western ego to nature—both external and internal—is that of gaining control. Dinnerstein's account gives an explanation for this drive toward control: the masculine drive to control and dominate the mother, the nourishing woman. It is this urge to dominate the woman that lies behind what she calls our "compulsive, world-conquering spirit."[5] She expresses approval of Norman O. Brown's criticism of our "aggressive, dominating attitude toward reality."[6]

Dinnerstein expresses dismay at the fact that advances in science and technology have not weakened our "destructive infantilism." Indeed, what has been weakened is the ability to judge and to govern ourselves:

> As science and technology advance, formal theological belief in a parental deity has of course come to seem less plausible. But what has changed in the stance most people take toward nature-the-parent is not the destructive infantilism of this stance. What has weakened is a later-born feeling toward parental authority, a feeling which lies closer to the rational surface of awareness, and which is apt to be focused in good part on the father, who represents the more mature human world: that a parent can state valid moral impera-

tives, and impose predictable penalties if they are not met. The fading away of God the Father, the righteous judge, should in principle motivate his lopsidedly developed offspring to learn how to judge and govern themselves, but so far this has not happened. The loss of supernatural moral guidance in the light of scientific reason has not made people more grown-up; it has only unleashed the amoral greed of infancy.[7]

According to standard psychoanalytic perspectives, the dissolution of the paternal superego under the impact of scientific reason should make us more autonomous, should replace superego with ego. Dinnerstein grants that this has not happened. In effect, in her view we have freed ourselves from our fathers' tutelage, but not from the fear and awe of our mothers. Freed from the father but still under the sway of the mother, we lapse into greedy, infantile self-seeking.

It is not entirely clear what Dinnerstein favors at this point. If the father appears along with the mother as early nurturer, much of the magical power of the mother will be diffused, and the anxious desire for control on the part of males may be dissipated. But is an internalized parental superego still needed? Will fathers still represent the more mature human world? Or will superego-conscience formation be altered in the shared nurturance family she recommends? Or does society need to reform its valid moral imperatives before the family and conscience can be fundamentally altered? Dinnerstein stops short of debating these issues, and her position on the fate of the superego remains unclear.

Chodorow also gives an unclear picture of autonomy. In her view the present gender arrangements enable boys to gain separate identities by denying attachment to and identification with the mother.[8] At an earlier stage in Western history, this pattern was combined with a strong internalization of paternal authority, resulting in "inner moral direction and repression."[9] Contemporary social conditions have tended to lessen the intensity of internalization, with a consequent loss of inner autonomy.[10] Boys still establish their gender identity by denial of attachment, but moral autonomy seems to have been weakened. And Chodorow regards the establishment of "a sufficiently individuated and autonomous sense of self" as a recurring need and problem for women, that is, women have never been encouraged to achieve what men are now in danger of losing.[11] This analysis suggests that, for Chodorow, formation of a strong superego contributes to the process of gaining moral autonomy. The basic questions for Dinnerstein and Chodorow, then, are: Was it the case that formerly the superego, ripening into a mature conscience, assisted the individual in gaining a secure moral autonomy and a perspective from which to judge present existence, and that therefore the loss of this conscience is detrimental to moral selfhood? Or was it the case that this superego was largely the product of a patriarchal internalization and therefore socialization that minimizes internalization processes will lead to stronger ego development? Or was it the case that this superego was excessively patriarchal and therefore we need to cultivate an alternative superego? These questions remain unanswered by Dinnerstein and Chodorow. But themes in their work that give an affirmative answer to the third question will be explored in the next sections of this chapter.

Psychoanalytic Feminists on Melanie Klein and a
Motherly Content in the Superego

Chodorow's analysis of differential superego development in men and women is not entirely consistent with her account of historical changes in the formation of the masculine superego. She provides a vigorous critique of Freud's account of this difference, disputing Freud's claim that woman's superego—being different from man's—is therefore less culturally valuable. By discussing these differences, Chodorow raises the question whether there is motherly as well as fatherly content in the superego, thereby introducing the second topic we want to explore. Building upon Freud's analysis while rejecting his evaluations, Chodorow describes the difference between men and women as follows: "Denial of sense of connectedness and isolation of affect may be more characteristic of masculine development and may produce a more rigid and punitive superego, whereas feminine development, in which internal and external object-relations and affects connected to these are not so repressed, may lead to a superego more open to persuasion and the judgments of others, that is, not so independent of its emotional origins."[12]

This comparative, largely ahistorical, analysis of men and women stands in somewhat uneasy juxtaposition with her historical account of changes in masculine superego formation. She asserts that earlier in Western history men tended to form strong superegos. Today, however, when "individual goals have become

increasingly superseded by the goals of complex organizations,"
internalized standards are no longer crucial to the workplace, and
present-day families tend to produce individuals who are more
willing to accept external standards.[13] "Instead of internalizing
paternal authority, and developing a sense of self with autonomous inner principles, sons remain both fearful of and attracted to
external authority."[14]

Though Chodorow does not offer explicit evaluations of these
variant male character types, it seems apparent that she favors the
earlier inner-directed type. Yet the other-directed person (a term of
David Riesman, not used by Chodorow), lacking in inner autonomy, is surely closer to Chodorow's description of feminine development, as described in the previous chapter. This "organization man" is more relational, less separative, than older types, and
therefore appears to be more feminine. But is the weakened, less
rigid and punitive superego a step toward its dissolution into ego?
Does she accept the Freudian characterological model? Or is she
advocating a different sort of superego (especially for men), one
constructed more along the lines of the feminine type or combining elements from the masculine and the feminine types?

To address the question whether it would make sense to speak of
motherly as well as fatherly aspects of the superego and whether
this distinction will enable us to identify and separate regressive
and progressive aspects of the superego, we must explore other
dimensions of the Dinnerstein-Chodorow thesis. In discussing the
pre-Oedipal mother relation, both Dinnerstein and Chodorow
draw upon the work of psychoanalytic theorist Melanie Klein
(1882–1960). An introduction to certain of Klein's concepts will
help to clarify how the psychoanalytic feminists might develop a
distinction between motherly and fatherly components of the
superego.

Klein postulates an early and primitive superego fueled by the
infant's own aggressive tendencies and anxieties about these tendencies. This is to be distinguished from the "wise and mitigated
superego" of later development, as well as from a sense of gratitude
and a need to make reparation, all developing in connection with
both mother and father.[15] Klein contends, contrary to Freud, that
superego formation and even the Oedipus complex begin in infancy in relation to the mother, and especially in connection with
the infant's positive and negative reactions to the mother's breast
(or breast substitute).[16] Although, as Klein says, the "core of the
superego" is "the mother's breast, both good and bad," she imme-

diately brings the father into the picture: "The father too, who soon plays a role in the child's life, early on becomes a part of the infant's world."[17] The early superego consists largely of mother and father fantasies, constructed in response to anxieties growing out of feelings of aggression and rage, initially overwhelming the developing feelings of gratitude. This primitive superego tends to be "immeasurably harsher and more cruel than that of the older child or adult."[18] At every stage the superego is oriented toward both parents: "The various aspects of the superego derive from the way in which, throughout successive stages of development, the child conceives of his parents."[19] Given progressive development, the later superego plays a constructive role: "At this [later] stage the superego makes itself felt as conscience; it forbids murderous and destructive tendencies and links with the child's need for guidance and some restraint by his actual parents. The superego is the basis for the moral law which is ubiquitous in humanity."[20]

Thus in summary Klein argues for the beginning of superego formation in early infancy, views it as taking shape in interaction with both mother and father (but with a particular emphasis on the early mother relation), and makes a distinction between the harsh and punitive (hence partly destructive) early superego and the later constructive and benign superego (conscience). For Klein, therefore, the moral sense has its roots in the totality of parent-child relations, most fundamentally in the longing for reconciliation with the loved and hated parents. She concludes *Envy and Gratitude*:

> However far we feel removed from our original dependencies, however much satisfaction we derive from the fulfillment of our adult ethical demands, in the depths of our minds our first longings to preserve and save our loved parents, and to reconcile ourselves with them, persist. There are many ways of gaining ethical satisfaction; but whether this be through social and cooperative feelings and pursuits, or even through interests which are further removed from the external world—whenever we have the feeling of moral goodness, in our unconscious minds this primary longing for reconciliation with the original objects of our love and hatred is fulfilled.[21]

Both Dinnerstein and Chodorow pick up and carry forward Klein's emphasis on early infant-parent relations. However, they resist Klein's tendency to move the Oedipus complex to the earliest stage of life, and they focus their attention on the father-absent family of recent and contemporary modernity. Thus they effectively remove the father from the earlier stages of infancy and concentrate on the infant-mother relation. Therefore the morally important feeling of the need to compensate for greed, rapacity, and anger by making reparations (Dinnerstein speaks of "compunction" and "tender, healing solicitude" as well as "reparation")[22] is understood as being directed exclusively toward the mother. Since it is the mother toward whom the feelings of both the negative and positive sorts mentioned above are primarily directed, Chodorow concludes that these feelings develop differently in the cases of women and men. She writes: "The whole preoedipal relationship has been internalized and perpetuated in a more ongoing way for women than for men. Women take both parts in it. Women have capacities for primary identification with their child through regression to primary love and empathy. Through their mother identification, they have ego capacities and the sense of responsibility which go into caring for children. In addition women have an investment in mothering in order to make reparation to their own mother (or to get back at her)."[23]

Dinnerstein argues that men's reparative (we might say conciliatory) feelings toward women are different from those of women. For boys, the mother to whom reparation needs to be made is a gratifying or withholding "idol that has been flouted and must now be mollified lest she exact vengeance," while for girls she is this but also a fellow creature "who needs to be soothed and protected."[24] And Dinnerstein extends this difference to the attitude toward nature. Women are less prone to be "plunderers of [nature's] treasure" because of this "special compunction": identification with the first parent and thus with Mother Nature makes women less likely to exploit either in a rapacious way.[25]

Thus if the implication for Klein, Dinnerstein, and Chodorow is that the later superego is mitigated by reparative feelings toward parents (and hence reconciliatory feelings toward others), this becomes in Dinnerstein and Chodorow a point of difference between the superegos of men and of women: those of men remain more mixed with controlling, exploitative, fearful impulses, less mitigated by "tender, healing solicitude." The implicit assumption in Klein is drawn out in Dinnerstein and Chodorow: if the father were involved in early parental care, these reparative feelings would be directed toward men as well as women, and therefore the superegos of women and men would develop in a similar fashion.

The changes in the relationships within the family that are

favored by Dinnerstein and Chodorow have significant implications for superego theory. Their proposals regarding the family involve a modification of Freudian theory. They in effect project the inclusion within the superego of a new component: identification with and internalization of the nurturant parent (alongside of identification with and internalization of the disciplining parent). Recalling Freud's claim that the child internalizes the father's superego (rather than the father's actual behavior), the hypothesis may be offered in the present context that the mother's superego may also be internalized.

It must be granted that Freud did not develop the concept of a motherly superego. But it can be observed that not all women in fact display the kind of generous nurturance that in our culture is attributed ideally to mothers. This ideal might be called the mother's cultural superego, or perhaps the "Law of the Mother." To internalize a behavioral rule of empathy and concern for others is to develop a motherly superego. If, as Freud maintained, the parental superego influences the child more than the parent's actual behavior, the child can be affected in this way by both the father and the mother.

If there is a motherly superego, corresponding to it there is a culturally authenticated discipline and ideal. But this mother image in our culture is, at least in part, an ideology in the pejorative sense. It mystifies and distorts the actual process of mothering. By declaring that mothering is purely natural, this ideology places nurturance in the private, virtually precultural sphere. This ideological denigration of nurturance at the same time places a social premium on separative autonomy that excludes nurturance.

Implicit in the Dinnerstein-Chodorow thesis is the view that the inclusion of fathers in early nurturance will bring this ideology of mothering into question. (It may be supposed that the social resistance to nurturant fathers derives in part from the fact that this behavior challenges the ideology.) In an important discussion, however, Jessica Benjamin argues against the notion that the inclusion of fathers in nurturance will be sufficient to alter the cultural ideology favoring control and separation and denigrating nurturance.[26] On the one hand the ideology inhibits males from internalizing a nurturant model even if their fathers in fact display this behavior. More importantly from Benjamin's standpoint, the very rationality of the public sphere is affected by this ideology. Reason in bourgeois society represses in itself a dimension that it might otherwise possess; it is a "gendered" rationality.[27] Independence-seeking, controlling, instrumental reasoning is not value neutral; it presupposes a paternal model and excludes a maternal model.

Benjamin's primary interest is in alternative paths toward autonomy, rationality, and individualization, rather than alternative paths toward conscience formation. She contends that the masculine version of autonomy obscures the dependence of such individuals upon prior nurturance. "In this way," says Benjamin, "the political morality can preserve the fiction of the wholly independent individual."[28] Correlatively, as she suggests elsewhere, "since girls are denied identification with the father, who stands for difference and separation, they are unable to achieve the accepted form of autonomy."[29] Benjamin therefore criticizes the bourgeois ideology for its failure to recognize that mothers can "model autonomy."[30] By implication, if women-mothers were to provide a model of autonomy, they would offer an individuality less averse to connection and interdependency and less addicted to control.

Benjamin's position regarding alternative superegos is less clear. She contends that mothers are in fact just as active as fathers in fostering autonomy in children and in inculcating social and moral values, in spite of ideological views to the contrary.[31] But she combines this emphasis with an apparent reversal of position on internalization. In the earlier "Authority and the Family Revisited," she proposed that women can play an increasing role as cultural authorities: "The mother is clearly as capable as the father of bringing about a highly developed rationality in the child, of inducting [sic] internalization."[32] More recently, however, she has criticized internalization theory and denies that "internalization of authority is the only source of human reason and morality."[33] Instead of arguing that the superegos of mothers can be internalized, she seems to conclude that internalization only takes place with paternal authority.[34] Valid morality need not involve internalization; it can derive rather from our innate capacity for mutual recognition.[35]

Our analysis leads us to an alternative view: that mothers can induce internalization.[36] In this view, psychoanalytic feminism pushes toward a goal of never-as-yet accomplished symmetry. If fathers also nurture and mothers also represent cultural disciplines and ideals, the resulting superegos of children will be more maturely formed. Consciences informed by nurturant and disciplining fathers and mothers will contribute both to autonomy and to conciliation. Women of conscience will find it easier to gain autonomy, and men of conscience will find it easier to value connectedness and mutuality.

Our inquiry into the idea of a motherly dimension of the superego has led us into a discussion of two separable issues: can and do mothers represent cultural rules, restrictions, and disciplines? and are the rules, restrictions, and disciplines that mothers represent different from the ones fathers represent? Our responses are that mothers can and do represent cultural "laws," although the prevailing ideology of motherhood disguises and denies this fact; and the content of maternal "law" has heretofore been at least partly distinctive—the rule that one ought to be concerned for others, Benjamin's rule of mutual recognition, in short, the law of love. Our argument, as opposed to Benjamin's, is that a mature superego can be visualized, one that internalizes a motherly model as well as a fatherly model. If fathers nurture (and nurturance is no longer denigrated), and if mothers model an alternative autonomy, the resulting superegos would include both nurturance and autonomy, but the gender linkage of these qualities would be removed. In that case love would no longer be linked with mothers or autonomy with fathers.

This discussion of alternative superegos will remain incomplete until we take account of another approach to conscience suggested by the literature of psychoanalytic feminism. This approach builds upon a distinction suggested by Freud that has thus far been glossed over: the distinction between the superego and the ego ideal.

Chodorow and Benjamin on Chasseguet-Smirgel and the
Distinction between the Superego and the Ego Ideal

Our third area of inquiry relative to a feminist critique of conscience has to do with efforts to distinguish between the superego and other components of conscience that have a different, nonpaternal origin. The writings of the contemporary French psychoanalytic theorist Janine Chasseguet-Smirgel have been influential in this area. Dinnerstein does not show evidence of her influence, but Chodorow cites her extensively in *The Reproduction of Mothering* (1978).[37] However, Chodorow's interest is in Chasseguet-Smirgel's "reformulation of female development"[38] rather than in her approach to morality. Chodorow's important conclusion that "the basic feminine sense of self is connected to the world, the basic masculine sense of self is separate" shows Chasseguet-Smirgel's indirect influence.[39] Benjamin offers an explicit critique of Chasseguet-Smirgel's formulations. A brief introduction to some of Chasseguet-Smirgel's key themes will point us toward another possible development in a feminist theory of conscience.

Working from a relatively orthodox Freudian position, Chasseguet-Smirgel explores and develops further a distinction suggested but not maintained consistently by Freud, the distinction between the superego and the ego ideal. Like Freud, Chasseguet-Smirgel associates the superego with the father and views it as the "heir of the Oedipus complex."[40] She proposes, however, that the ego ideal should be more definitely distinguished from the superego than was done by Freud. As "heir to primary narcissism," the ego ideal derives from the mother relation.[41] The infant, identifying itself with the loved object, loves itself as one with the loved object (initially the mother). In Chasseguet-Smirgel's perspective the ego ideal and the incest fantasy "are closely linked."[42] Further, the incest wish is not simply sexual; it is motivated by "the search for our lost omnipotence."[43] These two impulses—the desire for fusion and the desire for omnipotence—characterize all ego ideal processes according to Chasseguet-Smirgel and those influenced by her.

Chasseguet-Smirgel summarizes the relation of superego and ego ideal: "There appears to be a fundamental difference between the ego ideal, and the superego. . . . The former is the product of an attempt to regain omnipotence, the latter of the castration complex, the former impelling the subject toward incestuous fusion, the latter separating the child from the mother by the incest barrier."[44] Clearly the ego ideal has regressive potential, and for Chasseguet-Smirgel the superego plays an essential role in prohibiting the incestuous return to the mother. But, according to her, the desire for our lost omnipotence, for our lost sense of unity and fusion, for our lost sense of completeness and happiness, is not forgotten; it can play a constructive role in life if the illusory possibility of an immediate reunification is given up and the much longer route of accepting finitude and learning to love and sublimate is taken.[45] Thus one important contribution of Chasseguet-Smirgel is to suggest that impulses toward reunion with a mother symbol are not necessarily regressive.

This analysis, then, takes themes from Freud and gives them a distinctive twist. While an ego ideal is generally thought of, following Freud's description, as a model to be emulated, Chasseguet-Smirgel argues that it is this only in a secondary sense. Models are chosen in consequence of the fundamental desire to regain the lost senses of omnipotence and fusion.[46] For her the key feature of holding an ego ideal is narcissistic identification with a loved object. Thus, if one identifies himself or herself with an ideal (which must be regarded as a mother symbol), he or she recovers (or is accorded by this ideal) something of the lost sense of plentitude and power possessed as an infant.

Perhaps this reading of the ego ideal and its relation to the superego may be clarified by setting it alongside a late formulation by Freud. In *Civilization and Its Discontents,* Freud spoke of the way civilizations justify renunciations by cultivating identifications. "Civilization has to use its utmost efforts in order to set limits to man's aggressive instincts, and to hold the manifestations of them in check by psychical reaction-formations. Hence, therefore, the use of methods intended to incite people into identifications and aim-inhibited relationships of love."[47] Nicolas Duruz explains Freud's perspective: "The ruse (stratagem) of civilization consists of imposing renunciations which appear to be sources of satisfaction; this is possible because these renunciations are narcissistically idealized."[48] Thus Freud portrays the linking of two distinguishable processes: internalization of a renunciatory rule (superego process) and identification with an admired ideal (ego ideal process). Chasseguet-Smirgel agrees in emphasizing the need for this linkage; she simply spells out how various properties that Freud at one time or another associated with primary narcissistic identification (feelings of omnipotence, of perfection, of completion, of fusion) might become progressive rather than regressive when linked with appropriate renunciations. It seems clear that for Chasseguet-Smirgel the remembered sense of omnipotence and unity that fuels the desire for identifications derives from the early mother relation.[49]

When Chodorow's schematism is combined with Chasseguet-Smirgel's analysis of the ego ideal and the superego, these two aspects of conscience seem clearly to be gender specific. When the distinction of superego and ego ideal is combined with Chodorow's formula—"the basic feminine sense of self is connected with the world, the basic masculine sense of self is separate"—it seems to follow that the masculine self tends to be governed by the superego, the feminine self by the ego ideal. And the superego derives principally from the father relation, the ego ideal from the mother relation.

Again, Benjamin objects to this formulation. She takes exception to the orthodox Freudian notion (affirmed by Chasseguet-Smirgel and left standing by Chodorow) that "the mother seems to play no active role in bringing the child to reality. In this polarized scheme, the mother exercises the magnetic pull of regression and the father guards against it; he alone is associated with the progression toward adulthood, separation, and self-control."[50]

Thus, even though Chasseguet-Smirgel affirms the possibility of a progressive ego ideal, Benjamin is not convinced that the mother's contribution to culture is protected. In Chasseguet-Smirgel's reading, the superego is unambiguously progressive as the representative of the reality principle; the ego ideal may contain progressive elements, but only in combination with a strong superego. If the ego ideal is exclusively of the mother, the motherly contribution to culture is somewhat precarious. However, if the schematism I have proposed is adopted, the superego will not be exclusively paternal. In this case Benjamin's objection would seem to be met.

The next step in this analysis would be the attempt to achieve a further reconciliation of our approach to the superego as presented above and the concept of ego ideal as proposed here. Since Christopher Lasch contributes to this topic of discussion, we shall postpone consideration of it until his concepts are reviewed in the next chapter. However, it is appropriate at this point to attempt a connection between the ego ideal concept and certain themes in the religious ethics of Paul Tillich.

In my view Tillich brings to the fore dimensions of the ego ideal concept not thematized by Chasseguet-Smirgel, Benjamin, or Lasch. I suggested earlier that Tillich's concept of the "trans-moral conscience" can be interpreted as a motherly conscience. We can now add that this dimension of conscience corresponds to the ego ideal. Characteristics that Tillich assigns to the trans-moral conscience may therefore illuminate ego ideal theory. I find two themes in Tillich's analysis that may be transposed into the theory of the ego ideal. First, Tillich reminds us of the difference between the experience of being nurtured and the experience of being required to follow a rule. Both have a passive aspect; but nurturance is a gift, while restriction is a demand. The primary fusion with mother and with the world is a state of being, independent of the will of the self. The recovery of this unity is a task to be achieved, but it also is and remains already in existence as presupposition and promise, something remembered and even present as well as something sought. By the same token, love (from parents to children) is given. It can also be required ("thou shalt love . . ."), but the requirement can be effective only on the basis of the prior gift. The specific point of overlap between superego and ego ideal, it would seem, is the motive of gratitude (we love because we first were loved). This leads us to a second relevant theme in Tillich. The presence of the transmoral conscience or the ego ideal has a formative influence on the superego. Rules are followed without resentment when they stand within the context of secure relationships and identifications. This insight has a bearing on the influence of the motherly element in culture. Superego restrictions become destructive (whether on the individual or on the social level) when they are separated from a nurturant context. Thus the motherly element in culture (and in religion as a part of culture) provides the context for fatherly superego demands.

In this chapter we have examined the questions of the dissolution of superego into ego, of motherly and fatherly content within the superego, and of the separability of superego and ego ideal, each issue viewed from the standpoint of psychoanalytic feminism. Many of the concepts discussed in this chapter have been explored in a series of writings by the cultural historian, Christopher Lasch. My next chapter is devoted to an examination of his perspective on these issues.

8

CHRISTOPHER LASCH
ON FEMINISM
AND CONSCIENCE

Lasch's Engagement with Feminism

ALTHOUGH THE FEMINIST GOAL of gender equality seems unambiguous and has come to enjoy the support of the majority of thoughtful persons in the Western world, the wider ramifications of the attack on patricentricity continue to generate debate both within feminism and beyond it. In particular the implications of the feminist critique in the realms of the family, character structure, morality, and ideology continue to be hotly debated. One of the major participants in these debates has been the cultural historian, Christopher Lasch. In a succession of books and articles, Lasch can be seen engaging directly and indirectly in a running dialogue with certain currents of feminist thought.[1] It is important to note at the outset that Lasch's criticism of feminists on specific issues must be placed within the context of his broader agreement with them on basic goals. Lasch acknowledges "the justice of women's demand for equality;"[2] his questions are about specific strategies and directions advocated within the movement. These queries raise important value considerations that deserve attention.

Lasch can be interpreted as focusing attention on the cultural consequences of the decline of the patriarchal family and of patriarchal culture more generally, developments that he sees as having a significant impact on the internalization of authority, that is, on the formation of the superego, and on authority structures in the family and the society at large. He has been accused of a "'nostalgia' for the patriarchal family"³—or even more broadly of a nostalgia for patriarchy generally.⁴ But what Lasch in fact calls for is a reassessment of the ambiguous legacy of the traditional family and of patriarchal culture, and a recognition of the threat to the social fabric as well as to individual maturation occasioned by its decline. At the deepest level the key issue for Lasch is the nature of cultural authority. He is interested in an analysis of the way individuals internalize socially legitimated authority and in a critique of "the devaluation of authority in modern society."⁵

Lasch's engagement with feminism began to take shape in his critical review of Juliet Mitchell's 1974 work, *Psychoanalysis and Feminism*. In her book Mitchell attempts to rehabilitate Sigmund Freud in the face of earlier feminist attacks. Following the rereading of Freud developed in French structuralism (especially in Claude Levi-Strauss), Mitchell finds in psychoanalysis a description of the laws upon which human culture has heretofore been established (the patriarchal laws of incest prohibition, exogamy, and what Levi-Strauss refers to as the "exchange" of women).⁶ Human culture is built upon the control and restraint of nature, and this law has in fact always been the law of the father. Mitchell claims that theorists such as Reich and Fromm, who postulate the existence of earlier matriarchal cultures and seek ways of returning to matriarchy, have projected a too easy victory over patriarchy. Freud's insight that heretofore paternal controls and proscriptions have been constitutive of culture must be respected.

What options then are open to feminists, according to Mitchell? Attempting to remain true to orthodox Freudian theory, but combining it with Wilhelm Reich's "sexual politics," she offers a new version of the Marx-Freud synthesis in the concluding sections of *Psychoanalysis and Feminism*. Patriarchy has heretofore been the ideology of human culture in its totality. The laws underlying culture, however, have become redundant and no longer essential. Furthermore, "the bourgeois family was so to speak created to give that law a last hearing."⁷ The present-day tensions and contradictions of the nuclear family represent the point of greatest weakness of patriarchal culture. Therefore Mitchell advocates supplementing the Marxist critique of capitalism with a Reichian-feminist critique of patriarchy and the nuclear family; only the

combination of the two critiques—and in consequence the overthrow of both capitalism and the nuclear family—will lead us
beyond our culture of domination.

To determine Lasch's reaction to Mitchell's proposals, we can
refer to his review of her book, which appeared in the *New York
Review of Books* in 1974.[8] There Lasch gives his approval to her
structuralist reading of Freud and to her assessment of the weakness of matriarchal theories. Regarding her attack on the bourgeois family, however, he strikes a note of dissent that I believe to
be crucial to his later work. He writes: "In bourgeois society the
family still serves not only as an agency that inculcates work
discipline and respect for authority but as a bulwark of privacy, in
which values opposed to those of the market-place retain some
vigor, however attenuated."[9] Contained in this brief comment are
overtones of another perspective that weighs strongly in the subsequent shaping of Lasch's work: the view of the family developed by
Max Horkheimer and his colleagues, especially regarding the liberating potential of the bourgeois family. Lasch's subsequent dialogue has been with the psychoanalytic feminists surveyed in the
preceding chapters.[10] It is possible to see in these debates a resur-
facing of the two sides of the Frankfurt School's evaluation of the
nuclear family: the feminists stressing its oppressive characteristics and Lasch emphasizing its positive functions.

In *The Minimal Self,* Lasch attempts to clarify his earlier positions and to sharpen his critique of feminism. Noting that his
viewpoint as stated in *The Culture of Narcissism* could be misin-
terpreted as an unqualified defense of tradition-oriented, patriarchal superego formation, he admits that the book "is not sufficiently critical of superego controls," in spite of its distinction
between archaic and Oedipal superegos.[11] Additionally Lasch
seeks to clarify his approach to narcissism, which has also been
misunderstood. He argues that the understanding of narcissism as
selfishness or egotism is inaccurate (though this mistake is commonly made). In Lasch's words: "Prevailing social conditions . . .
not only encourage a defensive contraction of the self but blur the
boundaries between the self and its surroundings. As the Greek
legend reminds us, it is this compression of self and the not-self—
not 'egoism'—that distinguishes the plight of Narcissus. The minimal or narcissistic self is, above all, a self uncertain of its own
outlines."[12]

Lasch's critique then is not directed primarily toward the "I've
got mine" self-centeredness often regarded as prevalent today, but

he asks about the self upon which one is centered and the causes for anxiety about this self. In his view narcissism is loss of selfhood, not self-assertion.

This discussion leads Lasch to a further encounter with feminism. Some feminists and their allies have sought to identify the Western sense of separate selfhood as masculine while identifying unitive and relational tendencies as feminine. Some of these writers have used the term *narcissism* to refer to this feminine desire for mutuality and relatedness. Lasch is then criticized either implicitly or explicitly for failing to see the need for a new relatedness and oneness with the world and with other persons, for failing to advocate an overcoming of the individualism with which patriarchal cultures are identified.

As I interpret Lasch's concluding chapters of *The Minimal Self*, he is warning feminists not to identify with the flight from self that is observable in present-day American culture, even in the interest of overcoming the "fortress self" or the domineering self that is also observable. Lasch sees these, rather, as two sides of the same narcissistic coin and asserts that both are forms of escape from authentic selfhood. He does not deny that we need a renewal of relatedness and mutuality, but this cannot be achieved through the denial of that in us which is uniquely human (and neither male nor female). Though feminists are correct in challenging the "arrogance of power" so often associated with male dominance, this should not be done in the Romanticist fashion by dissolving the tensions of selfhood or (to quote Lasch) "dreaming of a symbiotic reunion" with nature.[13] These points are of a piece with Lasch's qualified defense of the bourgeois family in *Haven in a Heartless World* and elsewhere. He agrees with the position of Horkheimer that the traditional family, through its privacy and intimacy and secure parental authority, provided both love and control and served as a kind of second womb for the growing child. In this context the internalization of values that gave shape to character and conscience and that fostered individualization could take place. On the basis of these considerations, Lasch rejects the call of some psychoanalytic feminists for the collectivization of child rearing.[14]

In a 1983 article, "A Society without Fathers: Cooperative Commonwealth or Harmonious Ant-Heap?," and in his introduction to Janine Chasseguet-Smirgel's *The Ego Ideal* (1985), Lasch elaborates further on his view that feminism errs in seizing upon the narcissistic character type as a viable alternative to the patricentric type.[15] In Chasseguet-Smirgel's perspective, as we have seen, the ego ideal is separable from the superego: while the superego is "heir to the oedipus complex," the ego ideal is "heir to the state of primary narcissism." Lasch considers the distinction between superego and ego ideal—consistent with Freud's early formulations but abandoned by Freud later—to be a useful clarification of psychoanalytic concepts. In his introduction to *The Ego Ideal* he observes, "Often misunderstood simply as a role model based on internalized images of parents and other authorities, the ego ideal, as explained by Chasseguet-Smirgel, originates in the earliest experiences and embodies the 'fundamental human desire to return to the maternal womb.' "[16] Lasch grants that the ego ideal "can become the basis for later identifications founded on a loving symbiosis with the world rather than on fear of punishment." At the same time, however, the regressive potential of this desire must be acknowledged, and Lasch thinks that present cultural conditions favor regression rather than progressive development.[17] As explained by Lasch, Chasseguet-Smirgel stresses that there are two solutions to the problem of separation from the mother—"the shortest route, the most regressive one, or the evolutionary one."[18] It is only in the abandonment of the original illusion of perfect fusion and the frustration of its easy recovery that the individual is pushed onto "the long and difficult road of motivation and development." On the latter path the sense of oneness is recaptured "not by denying the fact of separation but by overcoming it in the pursuit of an ideal—erotic, aesthetic, or religious—of devotion and self-sacrifice."[19]

Lasch finds in an article by Stephanie Engel the most balanced expression of the tendency in some psychoanalytic feminism to incorporate the drive toward reunion into its characterological model. He quotes the following passage from Engel, a passage that shows the clear influence of Chasseguet-Smirgel:

> The super-ego, heir to the oedipus complex, insists on reality and the separation of the child from the mother, whereas the ego-ideal, heir to the state of primary narcissism, restores the promise of the imagination, of desire, and the fantasy of refusion. The exclusive reign of the ego-ideal, the infantile fantasy of narcissistic triumph, forms the basis of illusion, of blind adherence to ideology and of the perpetual desire—characteristic of narcissists. Yet the desire to reconcile ego and ego-ideal, the drive to return to the undifferentiated infantile state of primary narcissism, helps to provide the content

and drive for imagination as well as for the emotions that are the heart of our creative life. Thus an alternative [to the Freudian model of emotional development, with its alleged overemphasis on the superego] is the insistence that neither agency of morality should overpower the other . . . this challenge to the moral hegemony of the super-ego would not destroy its power but would instead usher in a dual reign.[20]

Lasch finds this formulation—which is similar to Fromm's call for a combination of patricentric and matricentric characteristics— persuasive so long as it is emphatically recognized that the narcissistic dream of reunion may be pursued along regressive as well as progressive paths (and that the regressive path is a distinct hazard in our period). Engel attempts to forestall the regressive solution to narcissistic longing by combining ego ideal and super-ego, holding that the latter "insists on reality and the separation of the child from the mother." Lasch does not oppose this effort at combination.[21] But he objects to the implicit assignment of gender to the qualities associated with ego ideal and superego, "so that feminine 'mutuality' and 'relatedness' can be played off against the 'radically autonomous' masculine sense of self."[22]

To provide a fuller explication of Lasch's position on this issue, it is necessary to clarify his view of certain pathologies of narcissism. Following Chasseguet-Smirgel, he maintains that the longing for omnipotence expresses itself in two regressive forms: solipsism and self-obliteration.[23] That is, the self may seek to assert its own "narcissistic omnipotence" (its own self-sufficiency), or, failing this, to assert the omnipotence of some ideal object with which the self identifies in a self-obliterative fashion.[24] Narcissistic desire may also have a more progressive outcome, as Chasseguet-Smirgel and Engel suggest, but the power of these regressive impulses must be acknowledged.

Lasch argues that all persons experience the pain of separation and the frustration of the craving for omnipotence and long for the restoration of a lost unity; both men and women experience these feelings and are faced with the alternative paths mentioned above. Lasch seems willing to grant, however, that the path toward self-obliteration is more likely to be taken by women, the path to solipsism by men;[25] the mature path is perhaps equally difficult for each. Likewise he is willing to term mutuality and union with others as feminine virtues and a strong sense of moral autonomy as a masculine virtue, if the above warnings are noted. He admits that his pejorative description of present-day culture as a "culture of narcissism" "may obscure the positive contributions which primary narcissism may make to emotional development."[26]

Lasch on Conscience, Family, and Ideology

We are now in a position to pull together from these debates the various strands of Lasch's theory of conscience. First he advocates acknowledgment of the distinction between superego and ego ideal. What this means from our perspective is that a mature conscience will have these two aspects. Following Klein, he further distinguishes between the archaic, punitive superego and the more mature, "loving and beloved" superego.[27] Thus superego demands may assist the self in achieving autonomy, but in immature forms they may contribute to authoritarian dependency. Distinction must also be made between regressive and progressive ego ideals. The regressive ego ideal may encourage regressive fusion with mother or mother substitutes, or it may result in illusions of solipsistic omnipotence. Progressive ego ideals on the other hand contribute to the developmental overcoming of separation through constructive identifications.

A mature conscience in a Laschian perspective, then, will consist of a developed superego and a progressive ego ideal. Both men and women are tempted to adopt more infantile, regressive patterns; maturity is equally difficult for both. Women are more inclined toward self-obliterative regression, men toward the illusion of total self-sufficiency. By the same token men are more likely to achieve superego-assisted individualization while they tend to lack that mutuality toward which ego ideal contributes; for women the opposite is the case.

Taken in toto and along with his recent concessions, Lasch's views on character structure and conscience are not as distant from a position acceptable to psychoanalytic feminists as might be supposed. Differences remain, however, regarding at least two issues. First, Lasch—though he is inconsistent on this—tends toward the view that the formation of the superego is associated exclusively with the father. As we saw earlier, Melanie Klein's theory permits the interpretation of superego development as a process of continual interaction with both parents beginning in earliest infancy. Lasch in fact comes close to this view in passages such as this one: "We might speculate further that the Oedipal superego—'the loving and beloved superego,' as Roy Schafer calls it—rests as much on the wish to make amends as on the fear of reprisals, though even here it is apparent that feelings of grati-tude—the most important emotional basis of what is called con-science—first arise in connection with the mother."[28]

Running counter to this tendency toward drawing the mother into superego formation is Lasch's support for the view that fa-thers "protect us from our mothers." Here he emphasizes the discontinuity between the primitive superego, which arises from attraction to and fear of the mother, and the mature Oedipal superego, which brings in a "more impersonal principle of author-ity associated with the father."[29]

The claim that the superego must derive from the father relation leads back to the Freudian position (held also by Chasseguet-Smirgel) that only men can represent the disciplines and controls of culture. This is an implicit rejection of the idea suggested earlier that gratitude and reparation can be a cultural discipline repre-sented by mothers. To the extent that Lasch subscribes to this claim, he fails to acknowledge that the typical superego derives from a culture that puts a premium on masculine separative au-tonomy and relegates mutuality to the private sphere where it has been disvalued. (This idealization of the masculine model is not inconsistent with idealization of the mother in a different sense. Mothers can be put on a pedestal and denigrated at the same time.) Lasch then, fails to acknowledge the possibility of an alternative superego.

By combining insights from Klein, Chasseguet-Smirgel, and Benjamin, a broader symmetry can be suggested than that favored by Lasch. On the one hand both mothers and fathers can represent cultural discipline, and their models can be internalized by the young. In the case of mothers, this symmetry will no doubt occur more extensively the more the privatization of women is over-come. On the other hand both fathers and mothers can be the source of ego-ideal formation. In the case of fathers this will no doubt occur more extensively the more they participate in the early nurturance of children. Revisions in the cultural ideology of mothers and fathers are also required for these steps to occur.

It remains unclear whether Dinnerstein, Chodorow, Benjamin, and Lasch are heading in the direction of this kind of symmetry. We have seen that all four seem to shy away from the idea of mater-nal involvement in superego formation and paternal involvement in ego-ideal formation; they do not indicate whether they would see these patterns developing in the family in which nurturance is shared, the goal they all project as desirable. It does seem probable that feminism will tend in this direction, however, if only against Freudian resistance.

Differences between Lasch and the feminists also appear in attitudes toward the bourgeois family. Lasch refuses to enter into a blanket condemnation of the patriarchal family, contending that at its best this family was able to combine superego and ego ideal in ways that were conducive to maturity for its offspring. In consequence he speaks favorably of trends that call for renewal, rather than further dissolution, of family ties. He attacks those feminists, such as Juliet Mitchell and possibly Chodorow, who favor abolishing the nuclear family. He faults feminists for not joining other radicals who have "rediscovered the importance of family ties."[30] Women should seek liberation not from the family but from the dehumanizing organization of work that requires women to sacrifice their families to it.[31] His charge against feminism is that in its present form it is contributing to the emergence of an individualistic culture with regressive ego ideals. The attack on patriarchy as presently constituted tends to augment bourgeois individualism. Thus while Lasch acknowledges the "justice of the central feminist demands," he maintains that the movement has tended to mirror the destructive trends of bourgeois culture rather than offering a constructive alternative to them.

Lasch's position is again subject to Jessica Benjamin's counter-argument: the defense of the privatized nuclear family with traditional gender roles leaves in place the Freudian assumption that the father plays the civilizing role in the family, as the representative of the outside world. As she suggests, "The idea that the father *intervenes* in the mother-child dyad" makes the implicit assumption "that the father is the only possible liberator and way into the world."[32] Benjamin grants that "there is much valuable thinking in [Lasch's *The Minimal Self*]." But, she asserts, "there appears to be a dreamlike blind spot in his presentation of mothers and fathers."[33] What may be at stake here is Lasch's failure to discuss the need to change the cultural images of mothering and fathering and in particular to overcome the denigration of nurturance.

Lasch's analyses of patricentricity and his dialogues with feminists have thus far been focused mainly upon issues relating to character structure (*The Culture of Narcissism*) and the family (*Haven in a Heartless World*). His recently published large work, *The True and Only Heaven: Progress and Its Critics*, can be regarded as ideology critique—a commentary on our spiritual disrepair and a quest for a viable moral tradition beyond ideological liberalism and conservatism.[34] This work is only indirectly related to the present study; we will conclude this chapter with brief reflections on how *The True and Only Heaven* correlates with his studies of character and family. But first we might explore Lasch's comments on Puritan religion in a recent essay.

In several essays during the 1980s, Lasch discussed religious and ideological issues.[35] In the 1983 essay, "A Society without Fathers," he calls for a reconsideration of the Puritan heritage. Here he reviews new research that suggests that "Puritan patriarchy in effect sought to promote a union of superego and ego ideal."[36] According to Lasch's treatment, the Puritan emphasis upon individuals recognizing their dependency had the effect of preventing regressive infantile feelings of omnipotence. The goal of Puritan spiritual development—its ego ideal—was reunion (with God and God's world), which could occur only after an acknowledged separation and the painful process of spiritual growth. Thus Lasch agrees with Chasseguet-Smirgel's assessment that religion—at least Puritan religion—unlike mysticism or some of the new cults, represents the longer, more arduous path toward the ego ideal. The father God, the god of the superego, stands in opposition to the easy fusion with the primary object, the "equivalent of the mother-prior-to-the-loss-of-fusion." The moral discipline, remorse, and repentance associated with superego religion represent hurdles to be overcome on the path toward reunion. If religious symbolism collapses, says Lasch, more insidious symbols may appear, even the magic of science itself, which appears to offer an easy omnipotence to the believer. Lasch concludes that Puritan imagery and doctrine in important respects "anticipated recent developments in psychoanalysis itself."[37]

By implication, then, the Puritan conscience in Lasch's view contributed to maturity rather than preserving authoritarian dependency. If the final developmental goal is the linking together of superego and ego ideal, this becomes a kind of linking of separation and union, of father-symbol and mother-symbol. Conscience in the Puritan tradition was not simply Oedipal (identification with an authority figure). It was also gratitude for, and remorse for wronging, those we love; it was the "awareness of the gulf between human aspirations and human limitations."[38] Protestantism at its best was a progressive response to individualization, a way of preserving moral autonomy while at the same time transcending it in a recovered unity. Lasch's view entails that moral-spiritual development requires both separative and unitive tendencies. Since each of these tendencies can have regressive as well as progressive effects, it is not satisfactory to associate either to the exclusion of the other with progressive development. Superego development may lead to regression and is not therefore always constructive; ego ideal development may be progressive or regressive. So even though it may be correct to associate mothers with unitive tendencies and fathers with separative tendencies, neither sex has an exclusive association with morality or cultural discipline, nor is either associated with progressive reunion to the exclusion of the other.

In *The True and Only Heaven,* Lasch resumes his pursuit of Puritan themes in such thinkers as Carlyle, Emerson, William James, and Reinhold Niebuhr in quest of an alternative to the ideology of unlimited progress. Lasch's basic assumption is that in "the impending age of limits"[39] we will need to draw upon those ideological traditions that acknowledge limits to human freedom.[40] We must learn again that dependency and submission do not necessarily involve weakness or passivity.[41] And Lasch draws the contrast between the unbridled greed of ambitious young careerists and the "sense of having been called to a given task."[42] I would argue that Lasch's discussion of limits is an exploration of the ideological side of the conscience question as I have posed it here.

Running through the book is a discernable effort to recover something of the moral realism of our ancestors.[43] The book is not explicitly religious, but it repeatedly engages the moral and religious traditions of American society. The dialogue with feminism is muted in these pages, but one might anticipate that Lasch will once again generate a creative exchange with feminists, this time perhaps with feminist theologians. I allude to this dialogue in my concluding chapter.

Lasch is important for the discussion in this book because he gives attention to all three dimensions of the critique of conscience that our study has emphasized: the characterological, the familial, and the ideological. I have contended that with regard to the first two dimensions Lasch and the psychoanalytic feminists represent somewhat divergent strands of the Frankfurt School heritage. On matters of ideological critique and reconstruction Lasch engages issues first broached by Tillich. In the concluding chapter, I attempt to draw from these discussions a constructive view of conscience that may be viable for our time.

9

CAN CONSCIENCE
BE RECOVERED?

HAS THE EXPERIENCE of conscientiousness become too problematical to be defended at the end of the twentieth century? Have we psychoanalyzed ourselves—individually and collectively—to the point at which the internalization of authority becomes an anachronistic pathology? Has feminism completed the process begun by Freud: the exposure of conscience as "internalized domination"? Or alternatively are we—individually and collectively—frightened into reaction by the specter of consciencelessness? Are we turning to reaffirmations of old ideologies and the traditional family in order to restore conscience to its accustomed place? Are we shoring up old authorities in order to avoid a downward slide into individual and collective self-indulgence?

Our study has sought a third alternative: the recovery of what is valuable in conscience through critique. We have drawn upon psychological, sociological, and historical perspectives in order to develop more nuanced judgments about conscientiousness and have employed the framework of critical theory in order to develop an evaluative critique of the basic theory in this area, the Freudian concept of the superego.

Interestingly we found the first-generation Critical Theorists to be decidedly ambivalent regarding the contribution of a developed superego to human maturity. Fromm, Horkheimer, Adorno, and

Marcuse all gave a mixed assessment, as did Tillich from a more theological perspective. Later Horkheimer and Adorno adopted a more unqualified affirmation of superego processes. This turn was viewed as reactionary in some circles, as the legatees of critical theory tended to polarize into two opposing factions on this question. Such thinkers as Poster in family studies and Benjamin in psychoanalysis have spoken strongly against internalization, while Lasch among others has defended it. Feminists—drawing upon Reich and Fromm—have criticized Lasch for his position on the superego, and Habermas's effort to find a more intermediate perspective has also met feminist opposition.

The topic deserves to be pursued further. I attempt to carry the discussion forward, but certain cautions are appropriate as I pursue that end. First, one should be reminded again that such terms as *superego* and *internalization* are metaphorical in nature. They do not refer to organs or physical spaces; they are attempts to describe what goes into the structural constitution of the human psyche as distinguished from what passes through it as momentary experience. The basic question is whether moral structuration requires the psychic incorporation of cultural-familial norms. Second, a concern might be raised that in emphasizing the origin of conscience we are guilty of the genetic fallacy in failing to distinguish between the origin of something and what it becomes through development. Certainly conscience, like intellect, develops in the individual. However, the studies reviewed here suggest that the early structure given to conscience affects its later outcome. Furthermore, if our analysis is correct, conscience in its origins and development differs in different societies. There is a typical conscience or social character in a given society. If so, this fact has a specific bearing on morality. Persons with strict consciences are observable as a particular social type, apart from the content of the norms in question, and the rise and subsequent decline of this type have been observed in modern Western society. Which psychosocial type is more desirable? is a question that is inescapable, unless one adopts a purely value-neutral standpoint. This question arises apart from any and all specific moral judgments. In answering it, we are drawn into issues regarding the genesis of conscience as well as its mature fulfillment. Moral philosophers as well as psychologists, sociologists, and historians have a role to play in this debate.[1]

Within psychoanalytic theory, discussions about moral structuration have tended to center upon the fate of the superego in the mature character. While some theorists agree with Franz Alexander that the superego is "an anachronism of the mind [which] has to be eliminated and the ego put in its place,"[2] others find a continuing need on the part of the mature psyche for a benign superego.[3] Two contemporary theorists, Hans Loewald and Eli Sagan, provide further insights pointing toward the construction of a model of beneficent conscience.

Several essays of Hans Loewald capture positive aspects of superego formation in ways that would seem compatible with the late view of Horkheimer and Adorno.[4] Two themes from Loewald deserve mention here. First, a stable superego structure represents the self-transcendence of the psyche toward the future.

> The superego watches, commands, threatens, punishes, forewarns, admonishes, and rewards the ego, it loves and hates the ego. All of this we can do with ourselves only insofar as we are ahead of ourselves looking back at ourselves from a point of reference that is provided by the potentialities we envisage for ourselves or of which we despair. . . . Conscience, the mouthpiece of the superego, speaks to us, one might say, in the name of the inner future that envisages us as capable or incapable, as willing or unwilling to move toward it and encompass it, just as parents envisaged us in our potentialities and readiness for growth and development.[5]

In other words, for Loewald, the structural arrangement of the psyche, as far as the superego is concerned, is temporal rather than spatial.[6] The future that the superego represents, however, is not, in Loewald's view, disconnected from the past. "Considering psychic past and psychic future from a different angle, we can say that the future state of perfection, which is the viewpoint of the superego by which we measure, love and hate, judge ourselves and deal with ourselves, recaptures the past state of perfection that we are said to remember dimly or carry in us as our heritage and of which we see signs and traces in the child's innocence when he is at one with himself and his environment."[7] Loewald's articulation of the temporal character of the superego is, I believe, a valuable contribution to discussions of mature conscience, and one that accords with the approach being taken here.

A second valuable emphasis of Loewald is upon a clarification of superego internalization as a distinctive process. Internalization in his sense is different from repression in that anything repressed is split off from the ego. By contrast, says Loewald, "what is internalized . . . is not split off from the coherent ego but becomes or has become an integral part of a coherent ego."[8] Indeed that which is internalized as superego in his view "enter[s] into the formation of higher psychic structure, leading in turn to the development of object relations of a higher order of organization."[9]

Loewald contends further that internalization is not a matter of preserving identifications with the parents. "In internalization it is a matter of transforming these relations into an internal, intrapsychic, depersonified relationship, thus increasing and enriching psychic structure: The identity with the object is renounced."[10] The internalization of the parent (as distinguished from that identification with the parent which preserves archaic libidinal and aggressive ties) frees the individual for nonincestuous object relations. "Internalization as a completed process implies an emancipation from the object [the parent] . . . the individual is enriched by the relationship he has had with the beloved object, not burdened by identification and fantasy relations with the object."[11] In this emphasis Loewald extends and amplifies the Frankfurt School perspective on internalization. However, he loses some of the ambivalence Horkheimer and Adorno displayed regarding the superego. By minimizing the role of coercion in superego formation, Loewald is able to imagine the realization of a fully healthy conscience, something Adorno felt was not possible apart from social critique (healthy conscience, Adorno thought, cannot be realized in an unfree society). Even when addressing social changes, Loewald reaffirms the centrality of the Oedipus complex, ignores the difference between male and female superegos, and fails to take account of the feminist critique of patriarchy.[12] We must look elsewhere for the necessary social-ideological critique.

A different psychoanalytically informed approach to the healthy conscience is offered by Eli Sagan in *Freud, Women, and Morality.* Influenced by the argument of psychoanalytic feminists and others that the early mother relation is more important than Freud granted, Sagan proceeds to find the origins of genuine morality in early nurturance. The superego, understood in Freud's sense (though Freud, Sagan states, was not completely consistent here), originates in conflict and in fear (of castration). In Sagan's view, Freud is to be faulted for finding the origin of all morality in the resolution of Oedipal conflicts.[13] Alternatively, an idea that Freud occasionally hinted at but never developed was closer to the truth, says Sagan: "Conscience (morality, the moral function) has its genesis in the original nurturing situation between the child and its primary caretaker(s). Love and morality cannot be sundered. All morality is a sublimated and transformed manifestation of the Eros of nurturing."[14]

Sagan's viewpoint can be interpreted as associating morality exclusively with the ego ideal (a theme that we have found elaborated upon by Janine Chasseguet-Smirgel, Stephanie Engel, and Christopher Lasch), or with Tillich's transmoral conscience. Sagan's view minimizes the constructive role of the superego as a separate component of morality and tends to absolutize the moral structuration deriving from the infant-mother relation, viewing it as independent of society to a significant degree. Here once again an infallible source of moral insight is found. Sagan writes: "It is the argument of this book that *conscience* [in our terms, the ego ideal based upon relations with the nurturant mother] . . . unlike the superego, knows clearly which actions are moral and which immoral . . . [and] is incapable of corruption and pathology."[15]

In critique of Sagan I would assert that while there is something universally human in the structure of the ego ideal, this component of conscience is an insufficient ground for morality. The universal component of the relation of nurturance is the memory of, and the longing for, a blissful unity with a source of nurturance. But this longing can eventuate in either regressive or progressive desires, depending upon the quality of nurturance experienced by the infant and upon the development of a stable and benign superego. Unlike Sagan I would argue that mothering-nurturance is in large measure culturally relative (like fathering-discipline), even though it may have a rudimentary instinctual basis and even though the memory and anticipation just referred to point toward a potential universality. The fact is that we do not know what the ideal community "looks like"; we are faced with problematic choices between models that may be progressive or regressive.

Furthermore, morality cannot be solely a matter of desire for, or promise of, the good. Self-discipline is required, and it is a function of a developed superego. As Fred Alford has commented in another connection: "Ideals are too weak to constrain unintegrated desire, the self too likely to transform ideals into the image of desire. Ideals cannot take the place of self-control, nor can they perform the function of self-control."[16] As one might say in Tillich's terms, love and grace must be integrated with justice and law. In the end, however, I would suggest with Loewald and Sagan—and in accord with the Frankfurt School—that the "future state of perfection" is the viewpoint—even though we do not know it fully—from which the mature conscience (both superego and ego ideal) judges the self and offers a meaningful task for striving.

These psychoanalytic critiques of conscience must be supplemented by sociological and ideological critiques. Conscience is being transformed by changes in society and in ideology; these changes must be evaluated, and to the extent possible, guided in desirable directions.

Issues that have arisen between Juergen Habermas and certain feminist critics are instructive and provide a starting point for a social-ideological critique. Habermas describes traditional conscience formation as the creation of a naturelike internalization in the psyche; conscience in traditional societies came to seem a part of the natural organism. But enlightened analysis shows this to be a deception; the internalized norms are really culturally and familially relative. After this disenchantment, the only basis for moral norms, says Habermas, is conscious argumentation. As we saw earlier, Habermas makes one exception; we must internalize language, and it has a moral presupposition: the need for uncoerced discourse.

The claim that this disenchantment of morality is occurring irreversibly in our society is crucial to Habermas's case. A feminist objection raised at just this point is that internalization of normative tradition is not being eliminated in contemporary character structure. As Nancy Fraser argues, Habermas overlooks the fact that gender identity is "normatively secured" (that is, based on internalized tradition) rather than "communicatively achieved."[17] She contends, contra Habermas, that "feminine and masculine gender identity run like pink and blue threads" through most regions of the society.[18] It is clear that in this feminist view normative structures continue to be internalized; becoming naturelike, they are incorporated into the character structure of individuals. These patriarchal structures persist, according to the argument offered by Isaac Balbus and others, even with the absence of a dominant, Oedipal father in the current family structure. Patriarchy is preserved in the dominant ideology and is internalized even without the classic Oedipal relationships because of mother-monopolized child rearing. Habermas's optimism that the "diminishing significance of the oedipal problematic" alone—without substantial changes in child-rearing practices and in the ideologies of fathering and mothering—will lead to egalitarian attitudes is questioned by these analyses.

Our further argument here is that the patriarchal family and ideology has generated a kind of conscience that has the capacity for self-criticism. Feminism speaks for and to this conscience; it is the Western moral tradition that "contains the presuppositions for its own critique." There are no strong reasons for believing that the erosion of this conscience is leading or will lead to egalitarian attitudes. The proposal here is that rather than eliminating conscience we should proceed to the self-critique of the pathologies of conscience, with an eye toward the rescue of a more mature conscientiousness. But, as we have seen, critique of conscience extends to critique of the pathologies of family and of ideology.

This project was suggested but was not in fact accomplished by the original members of the Frankfurt School. As we have noted, Adorno envisioned a critique of conscience that would rescue its potential. Erich Fromm carried reflections of this sort a bit further by proposing a distinction between authoritarian and humanistic conscience, and he recognized correlatively the need to distinguish authoritarian and humanistic ideologies (religion). We found one version of Fromm's distinctions leading to a kind of precritical naturalism, where conscience becomes simply a natural "voice of oneself." Jessica Benjamin and possibly Dorothy Dinnerstein lean toward a similar view. But we found more provocative the suggestion that the fully mature, humanistic conscience and culture must recover a repressed motherly content, that patricentricity in character and culture ought to be qualified by matricentricity. Fromm's effort to delineate what might constitute a nonauthoritarian conscience, while instructive, was not sufficiently historical. Though he gave attention to developments in the realms of ideology and of conscience formation, he did not integrate these with consideration of the history of the family.

Aspects of the thought of the psychoanalytic feminists (here I have in mind principally Dinnerstein, Chodorow, and Benjamin) can be interpreted as carrying forward the project initiated by Fromm and others by means of a critique of the family. Viewed from this vantage point, these theorists belong in the cultural and interpersonal school of psychoanalysis, sharing Fromm's interest in psychosocial pathologies. They give specific attention to the bourgeois family and how it might be changed in order to overcome relationships of domination. They return to the theme of recovery of a repressed motherly content in conscience and culture, and they provide insights into various pathologies of conscience. However, even though they clearly share certain ideological value commitments among themselves, they have been reluctant to spell out these implications of their positions, and they have had relatively little to say directly about the characteristics of the mature conscience. Indeed they do not make it explicitly clear whether they favor the dissolution of conscience into ego or the achievement of mature conscience.

My effort, then, is to glean elements for a critical and constructive view of conscience from these feminist discussions. Scrutinizing the debates about gender identities (including the exchanges between the psychoanalytic feminists and Christopher Lasch), I find two analyses that bear implications for a description of conscience, for critique of its pathologies, and for an indication of ways these pathologies might be corrected.

The first analysis is a discussion of how the superegos of men and women develop differently. Dinnerstein and Chodorow suggest that women in their development tend to combine fear of the mother and desire to control her with a "tender, healing solicitude" toward her. The latter tendency is less likely in men, since they cannot identify with the source of nurturance. The presence of this tendency in women renders their superegos more reparative and reconciling than those of men. We have extended this line of thought to the hypothesis that if fathers participate more fully in primary nurturance, the conciliatory attitude toward the nurturing parent will be found in male superegos as well. This change in family pattern then can be seen as a means for overcoming the excessive drive toward separation and the aggressively controlling tendencies found in the superegos of many men.

This hypothesis, taken by itself, would seem to suggest that the process of superego formation found in women in the bourgeois family should be taken as a model for both men and women. In this view only the male superego is damaged by mother-monopolized child rearing. Following Jessica Benjamin's discussion, however, I have suggested that the superegos of women are damaged by the obverse of that situation. Fathers have been understood in bourgeois culture to stand over against nurturant mothers as representatives of cultural restriction and aspiration and as models of autonomy. Mothering has consequently been privatized and devalued by being placed in a quasi-natural sphere within the privatized family. To the extent that young women cannot identify with their fathers, they find cultural models and ideals less compelling. The devaluation of nurturance and the societal preference for separation over connection both tend to put a social premium on the traditional male superego over the female superego.

Only when women along with men are acknowledged as representatives of cultural ideal and restriction and as models of autonomy will young women be able fully to identify with these ideals, restrictions, and models. When this happens, mothers will share equally with fathers in the formation of the child's superego, and the cultural value of men's and women's superegos will be the same. This change will represent a major departure from Freud's view that cultural discipline is built upon the father's prohibition of a regressive return to the mother. It is, however, more in accord with the psychoanalytic feminists' revisionist viewpoint. In their approach bourgeois superego formation derives from fear of the mother rather than from a need to counteract erotic attraction to the mother. Freud viewed civilization as inevitably patriarchal because patriarchy constitutes the only path away from the inevitable incestuous tie to the mother. Dinnerstein and Chodorow, on the other hand, view the patriarchal structure of culture as a reaction to a particular type of early nurturance that can be changed. If fathers nurture, the whole dynamic will be altered (and, according to the hypothesis, altered for the better). But by the same token, if mothers model autonomy and cultural ideal the dynamic will also be altered for the better.

My proposal then is that the superego can become more constructive with a movement toward a double symmetry (or a movement away from Freud's asymmetry): mothers and fathers both fully participant in early nurturance, and fathers and mothers both acknowledged as representatives of cultural ideal and restriction. This new pattern will help to overcome pathologies in the superegos of both men and women. For men, it suggests that the aggressive, controlling mentality and the excessive tendency toward moral isolation may be overcome. For women, the lack of self-confidence and autonomy in moral judgment may be overcome and individualization may be heightened. It should be noted, however, that these changes involve not only a change in familial pattern but also an ideological change—a change in the images of mothers and fathers. We will return to this point later.

A second structural analysis gleaned from the literature of psychoanalytic feminism that assists us in identifying and correcting pathologies of conscience has to do with the distinction between the superego and the ego ideal that was suggested by Freud and developed further by Janine Chasseguet-Smirgel. While in the previous discussion we have treated internalization of restriction and identification with model or ideal as parts of the same process,

Freudian theorists such as Chasseguet-Smirgel find that the superego and the ego ideal have different points of origin. In this development of Freudian theory, the superego is associated with the
father, who "lays down the law," while in the case of the ego ideal
the child's identifications with ideal figures and values has its
roots in the original symbiosis with the mother and the longing
to recover this lost unity and wholeness. The superego and the
ego ideal can be viewed as separable (because they have different
points of origin) and still be considered interlocking aspects of
conscience.

Following Chasseguet-Smirgel, Stephanie Engel, and Lasch, we
have proceeded to identify pathologies of the ego ideal. Regressive
narcissism leads to self-obliteration, the abdication of autonomy
(as has been suggested, a pathology more typical of women, having
affinities with the pathologies of the feminine superego mentioned earlier). Avoidance of this pathology, according to Chasseguet-Smirgel, requires connection with a mature superego, which
serves the function of preventing regressive reunification. Additionally, following Lasch's interpretation of the ego ideal, a second
pathology can be found in its development: solipsistic grandiosity.
This pathology is more typical of men and has affinities with the
pathologies of the masculine superego mentioned earlier.

If now we accept a broadened concept of conscience that combines superego and ego ideal, we begin to see the outlines of an
approach that would identify pathologies of conscience and point
the way toward maturity. Conscience combines renunciations
connected with internalization and narcissistic gratification based
upon identifications. When the nurturant and the superego-mold-
ing functions of parenting are polarized as the functions of mother
and father, respectively, male moral structuration tends to be deficient in conciliation and female in autonomy. When these functions are shared by both parents, however, the resulting superegos
can be both conciliatory and autonomy inducing. For females
formation of the ego ideal can avoid self-obliteration if superego
formation contains an autonomy-inducing component deriving
from an autonomy-modeling mother. For males formation of an
ego ideal can avoid solipsism if superego formation contains a
component of conciliation deriving from a nurturant father.

These are the lineaments of an internalization-identification
that break the grip of the patriarchal-authoritarian structure predominating in Western culture. It remains an internalization of
parental-cultural authority and of cultural-personal ideal; hence,

it serves to avoid the conscienceless culture of narcissism. Yet it allows a fluidity and openness that permits the emergence of a more communicative ethic as well. It points the way to a new social character that preserves autonomy while providing for a greater intersubjectivity.

As suggested earlier, movement toward a mature conscience and the removal of pathologies will require not only familial change but also ideological change. Ideology can lend legitimation to infantile or pathological as well as to mature behavior. In the context of our study, this means that the Western ideologies of motherhood and fatherhood must be scrutinized. As we have argued, in modern bourgeois societies mothering has been interpreted in terms of natural categories. Women have been viewed as naturally inclined toward all those functions that are required for the "care and feeding" of children and husbands. All of these nurturing functions require generous, self-disregarding behavior. In fact women have been taught a renunciatory ideal that is internalized as the conscience of women. As one writer expresses the point, women "are psychologically prepared for enormous personal sacrifices as a moral duty."[19]

This ethic of self-abnegation has been cloaked by the ideology of naturalness—that women naturally mother in all of the approved ways. This ideological pattern was accentuated in the early modern period by the privatization of the family. One could say that a Protestant ethic for women emerged in this period along with the bourgeois family: a female form of this-worldly asceticism with its locus in the familial cloister. This ethic legitimated the subordination of women just as it authorized the denigration of nurturance. By relegating the activity of mothering to nature, the mothering or nurturing aspect of culture was minimized. At the same time masculine aggressiveness and isolation were given a social premium, as the self-sacrificial ethic for women was paralleled by a solipsistic ethic for men.

This ethic of mothering cannot be dismissed as a simple exploitation of women, just as the masculine individualistic ethic cannot be regarded in a purely negative light. There was a perfectionist, utopian aspect to this moral demand and vocation prescribed for women, an aspect that contributed to human liberation. Many women found meaningful vocation in creating a context of generous care for the forming of autonomous, conscientious individuals. In so doing they provided a foretaste of an ideal loving community and a perspective from which the exaggerated individualism of the larger society could be criticized. As Horkheimer suggests, in these mothers something "essential to authentic humanism became concretized." Undeniably, the personal cost to women was very high; the ideology of mothering provided meaning but not justice. The separation of the ethic of selfless generosity into the private, familial sphere—the privatization of love—meant in effect that men were to a considerable extent absolved of this duty, while women were coerced into it. And the ethic was viewed as inapplicable in the public world of affairs.

Thus it should be recognized that motherly behavior is just as culturally conditioned as fatherly behavior. Although mothers may have an initial motherly instinct vis-à-vis their infants, it is short-lived and socially malleable. Everyone recognizes a difference between immature and mature mothering, which suggests that mature mothering is a cultural construct (not something women simply possess by instinct). Women are not naturally more virtuous than men (although they may be prone to different virtues and defects). Women who try to be personally successful in a public realm that denigrates nurturance will not necessarily remain more nurturant themselves.

The ethic of nurturance appears to be natural to women in bourgeois culture, but this appearance is a part of the bourgeois ideology. Nurturance has been culturally relegated to the natural sphere because it is inconsistent with bourgeois individualism but essential to the reproduction of bourgeois individuals. Like the family and Protestant religion, mothering is a nonbourgeois presupposition for bourgeois culture. This placing of nurturance into an unsullied private sphere leads to a male-female dualism: each gender represents something denied in the other. Males are expected to develop their individuality while denying dependence and interconnectedness; females are expected to cultivate nurturance at the expense of autonomy. Their consciences develop in different directions, although neither is more or less morally rigorous than the other.

The ideological change required for the maturing of conscience, then, is first and foremost a movement toward overcoming the privatization and denigration of nurturance. To an extent the participation of fathers in nurturance along with the ensuing alterations in the bourgeois family structure will facilitate this change. But the ideologies of fathering and mothering are not simply a reflection of the familial structure; they have a certain degree of independence as well—hence the need for critique of ideology.

In modern Western culture mother and father images have been closely interconnected with the Western religions. Therefore critique of ideology leads into critique of religion. One of the difficulties with the latter is finding an appropriate standpoint. One such standpoint is that of maturity of conscience, itself a religiously informed ideal. One way of posing the question is whether religion as it has been observed and practiced in the modern West has been predominantly or exclusively a pathology of conscience or whether in some of its forms it has had the capacity to induce maturity. What has been the effect upon conscience of the mother and father images fostered by modern Western religion?

Many thinkers in the psychoanalytic tradition have held that religion has been a pathology of conscience. In a recent essay on Horkheimer and Adorno, Joel Whitebook has restated the case against religion. He expresses the view that religion "represents a sublimation of the search for the certainty of absolute parental authority." If human beings can relinquish the quest for this absolute authority, they will mature by giving up "the heteronomous appeal to dogmatic tradition."[20] Maturity in this view means giving up the longing for absolute authority. This critique derives from a standpoint based upon a self-concept of separative autonomy, rationality, and denial of dependency.[21] Dorothy Dinnerstein, while sympathetic with Whitebook's position, nevertheless enunciates the problematic of Whitebook's Enlightenment perspective in a passage quoted earlier: "The fading away of God the Father . . . should in principle motivate his . . . offspring to learn how to judge and govern themselves, but so far this has not happened . . . it has only unleashed the amoral greed of infancy." Dinnerstein here poses the question: if heteronomous authority causes a pathology of conscience, does not the collapse of authority also cause pathology? The further question therefore arises: Can there be a nonheteronomous religious authority that could foster a nonauthoritarian conscience? Both Erich Fromm and Paul Tillich spent their careers pondering this question.

In Fromm's account, as we grow up we should become for ourselves our own fathers, our own authority; likewise we should provide mothering, or nurturance, for ourselves. Thus for Fromm the development of a healthy, humanistic conscience entails our becoming for ourselves our own (good) mothers and our own (good) fathers. This thesis, however, involves an implausible transmutation. Fromm's claim is that the motherly and fatherly voices are transmuted into a kind of natural "voice of oneself." But Fromm cannot explain how this second nature is transformed from culture into nature. Mothering and fathering are given to us, not supplied by ourselves to ourselves. The images of mother and father that we internalize are derived from the culture and its ideology as well as from our experience of actual parents and our internalization of their superegos. It is a romantic illusion to suppose that "the child is father to the man." Maturity must first be embodied in ideology and in the institution of the family and then internalized by children. The contrary effort—to free children from internalization in order to allow them to develop naturally—is doomed to failure. Culture improves upon nature. Mature conscience is given to us, even though it dictates what is required of us.

Fromm's approach to god-concepts is in harmony with his ideas about conscience and suffers a similar limitation. His approach is reductive: the projected qualities of divinity must be recovered for ourselves. By implication we must become god for ourselves. External authorities and ideals are restrictive and repressive. All norms that would prevent us from becoming fully human (thus fully ourselves) must be regarded as authoritarian. True religion for Fromm is critique of idols ("idology"); the only proper outcome of religious tradition is a negative theology.[22] Only human nature has a legitimate positive authority over individuals. In the end for Fromm, nature, not culture, constitutes authority. The consequence of this view, however, is the dissolution of moral demand into subjective, natural desire.

Tillich agrees with Fromm that there has been an element of authoritarianism in Western religion. He seeks to accommodate this insight by distinguishing between regressive and progressive religious authority. Religion becomes progressive, he thinks, when the demand of father religion is radicalized and made unconditional. Tillich clearly has in mind here the moral imperative that, becoming unconditional, judges not only individual desires and impulses but also all finite authorities from the standpoint of an absolute justice. The Calvinist conscience, itself a sublimation of the paternal superego, is the forerunner of the Kantian categorical imperative. For this prophetic religion, the various pathologies of conscience are different ways human beings attempt to become God—regressive fusion, solipsism, identification with a powerful authority. All can be criticized as forms of idolatry. Thus far Tillich agrees with the Frankfurt School's negative theology.

For Tillich, however, the negative theology, the voice of the

critical superego, taken by itself, is deficient and even pathological. The universalized demand can be harsh and destructive. Conscience becomes repressive and control oriented. Beyond it, Tillich postulates the appearance of a transmoral conscience, which
itself provides a perspective for criticizing the moral conscience.
Interpreting Tillich, I have suggested that he finds in certain modern religious trends (derived primarily from Luther) the reintro-
duction of the motherly element in religion and conscience. Seen
in this light Tillich's position is in considerable accord with that of
Fromm, but Tillich finds in the motherly conscience a positivity
that Fromm omits. Likewise a parallel can easily be drawn between Tillich's moral and transmoral consciences and the superego and ego ideal as developed by Chasseguet-Smirgel, Engel, and
Lasch, but there is in Tillich an emphasis not thematized in these
other theorists. The motherly component of conscience (the ego
ideal) is seen by Tillich as gift and promise rather than simply as
ideal, the goal of desire. This gives the ego ideal an active, rather
than a merely passive, aspect. What we are required to do (superego demands) is derived from what we are given (goals of the ego
ideal, hence meaning and vocation). This theme of promise (of
happiness, redemption, reunion) as the basis for hope and motivation finds resonance in some passages of the Frankfurt School
literature, but only fleetingly; the predominant tone, in Horkheimer and Adorno at least, is stoic resignation. Because of this
emphasis on gift, Tillich is able to include as an important motive
for moral action the impulse of gratitude. His formulation accords
well with the perspective of Melanie Klein, and, although it strikes
a note that seems lacking in most of the Frankfurt School texts, it
is in keeping with Lasch's perspective.

Lasch finds in Puritanism a paradigm case of an ideology that
strikes a creative balance of the fatherly and motherly elements.
(Fromm interestingly saw this being achieved in certain socialist
movements; Tillich would have agreed, at least partially.) Lasch
points out that the Puritans both cultivated the guilty conscience
and sought reconciliation beyond this conscience. Lasch goes beyond Fromm and Tillich in at least noting a correlative feature of
the Puritan family (Fromm was disappointingly brief on family
history and Tillich gave little attention to it). The Puritan father,
according to Lasch, "concerned himself with every phase of his
children's intellectual and emotional development."[23] This suggests Lasch's acknowledgment of the need for paternal participation in nurturance, a development not considered by Fromm or

Tillich. What all three overlook is that Protestant-Puritan religion and family may have provided nurturance and a push toward autonomy for men, but they failed to encourage autonomy for women. The Protestant ideology and the cultural ideology of mothering minimized the mother's role in modeling autonomy and hence contributed to the cultural denigration and privatization of mothering-nurturance.

Recent trends in Western culture have further altered the religion-family-conscience dynamic that prevailed in the Protestant era. Religion has itself become more and more privatized, along with the family. Correlatively the nurturant aspect of religion—emphasized by Fromm, Tillich, and Lasch—has come more and more to the forefront. But this feminization of religion tends to become a regressive influence, so long as the patriarchal ideology prevails in the public sphere. If religion, like the family, is confined to the private sphere, men are pulled away from it toward autonomy along solipsistic lines; when women are drawn into religion, the self-obliterative pattern tends to be preserved. Change will occur only when masculine as well as feminine models of achievement and competence (autonomy) include the characteristic of nurturance. This will involve both drawing men into nurturance and encouraging women to model autonomy. In the end it is "public patriarchy" that needs to be broken, whether by means of the deprivatization of religion (without denying religious pluralization), or by means of moral reform. Efforts to construct a political theology can be seen as contributing to this project by attempting to bring an element of nurturance back into the public arena.[24]

In this connection the question might be raised whether a god concept is implicit in these discussions. The language of our entire study suggests acknowledgment of the provisional usefulness of a reductive approach; by implication god concepts have been viewed as absolutizations of familial relationships. We must recognize the parent in god concepts; that recognition is a necessary "disillusion." But after disillusionment the question of appropriate symbolization arises. Here the picture may be more complex than some feminist theology has been inclined to acknowledge. For example Catherine Keller asserts that the father-god of Western religion represents "separative transcendence," and this representation is the mirror image of the bourgeois father's dominating relation to the world.[25] This is an important critical insight; but it ignores the counterbalancing claim that biblical patriarchal religion may also have involved a significant feminization of the father. Noting that in a broad historic frame fatherly nurturance of the young could not be taken for granted, John W. Miller suggests that "[the Bible's] firm belief in God as effectively caring father undergirds and encourages human fathers in the taking on of caretaking roles."[26] In this same vein, however, it would be appropriate to question whether Western patriarchal religion has been successful in encouraging individualization and moral autonomy on the part of women. Further discussion of these questions is beyond the scope of this book. Feminist theology rightly continues the search for a more appropriate symbolization of transcendence that will include fatherly and motherly components. Suffice it to say that the absolutizing tendency inherent in the narcissistic wishes for perfection, omnipotence, and fusion is both the source of the ennobling human desire for a relation to transcendence and the origin of numerous pathologies—in inextricable mixture. To paraphrase Calvin, religion and conscience are "factories of idols." But they both foster criticism of idols as well.

What seems more clearly inherent in conscientious experience is the intimation of an ideal self in an ideal community. God is not a personification of existing society (an idea associated with the French sociologist, Emile Durkheim), but, for conscience at least, God is closely associated with the kingdom of God—the ideal community. The idea of Habermas that an ideal speech community is presupposed by language can be extended beyond the verbal, hence purely mental, sphere.[27] As he suggests, we as human beings are individuated through socialization. It is in community that we become individuals. But this socialization is intergenerational, fostered in the first instance by families, not by peer groups. The ideals and disciplines of culture are not created ab ovo by the rising generation but are passed on from parents to offspring. It is the family that liberates individuals from bondage to the merely natural and enables the emergence of autonomous selves. It is true that the desire to recover a lost unity—hence the impulse toward connectedness—can properly be regarded as natural, but nature cannot distinguish between immature and mature unity. The existence of moral selves who seek mature unity presupposes the reality of a nurturant and disciplining community of adults. As Alford suggests, the original Frankfurt theorists rightly perceived that the family, not simply an amorphous language community, plays the crucial role in the creation of moral selves.[28] It is my contention that conscience is the voice of the ideal self in the ideal community, a community that is presupposed and sought. Certain communities, preeminently the familial ones, give us a foretaste of a longed-for future. Approval by conscience means approval by that person who I want to be (or want to emulate). In the internalization of conscience I become parent to myself. The pathologies of conscience are rooted in the pathologies of community. A conscience cured of pathologies is the voice of the past, the voice of our communal origin; but it is also, and preeminently, the voice of a longed-for future, the voice of the perfected self in perfected community. It is this conscience that our age must seek to recover.

NOTES
BIBLIOGRAPHY
INDEX

NOTES

Introduction

1. The following are representative works dealing with conscience: John Donnelly and Leonard Lyons, eds., *Conscience* (Staten Island, N.Y.: Alba House, 1973), esp. David J. Jones, "Freud's Theory of Moral Conscience," pp. 85–114; C. Ellis Nelson, ed., *Conscience: Theological and Psychological Perspectives* (New York: Newman Press, 1973); Eric D'Arcy, *Conscience and Its Right to Freedom* (London: Sheed and Ward, 1961); John C. Staten, *Conscience and the Reality of God: An Essay on the Experimental Foundations of Religious Knowledge* (New York: Mouton de Gruyter, 1988); Eli Sagan, *Freud, Women, and Morality* (New York: Basic Books, 1988); Thomas E. Wren, *Caring about Morality: Philosophical Perspectives in Moral Psychology* (Cambridge: MIT Press, 1991); Donald E. Miller, *The Wing-Footed Wanderer: Conscience and Transcendence* (Nashville: Abingdon Press, 1977); Sidney Callahan, *In Good Conscience: Reason and Emotion in Moral Decision Making* (San Francisco: Harper, 1991). For an example of a sermonic use of conscience, see Reinhold Niebuhr, *Justice and Mercy,* ed. Ursula M. Niebuhr (Louisville: Westminster/John Knox Press, 1974), pp. 38–45, 105–11; see also "Conscience" in *The Encyclopedia of Religion,* ed. Mircea Eliade, 16 vols. (New York: Macmillan, 1987); and James F. Childress, "Appeals to Conscience," *Ethics* 89, no. 4 (July 1979): 315–35.
2. *Webster's New Collegiate Dictionary* (Springfield, Mass.: G. and C. Merriam, 1981).
3. D'Arcy, *Conscience and Its Right to Freedom,* pp. 4–5.
4. For an excellent example of this approach see Callahan, *In Good Conscience,* esp. pp. 14–32; 38–41; 190–95; 212–14; for a major reconsideration of the import of psychoanalysis for ethics and the argument that Freud's view leads in the direction of rational ethics, see Ernest Wallwork, *Psychoanalysis and Ethics* (New Haven: Yale Univ. Press, 1991), esp. pp. 221–43; 288–91. For a

range of perspectives on these questions see Thomas E. Wren, ed., *The Moral Domain: Essays in the Ongoing Discussion between Philosophy and the Social Sciences* (Cambridge: MIT Press, 1990).

5. The approach taken here has much in common with the discussion of "the contribution that parental upbringing makes to a good moral character" in Laurence Thomas, *Living Morally: A Psychology of Moral Character* (Philadelphia: Temple Univ. Press, 1989), pp. 75–96.

6. Heinz Hartmann, *Psychoanalysis and Moral Values* (New York: International Universities Press, 1960), pp. 38–39, quoted in Sagan, *Freud, Women, and Morality*, p. 91. The issue of rationality is reopened when the question of rational authority is posed. The question here is whether rationality (and even liberation) can be embodied in social institutions (such as the family) and in ideologies (such as those of fatherhood and motherhood). My analysis tends toward a positive answer to this question.

7. One widely read work on this topic is Robert Bellah, et al., *Habits of the Heart* (Berkeley: Univ. of California Press, 1985); for reconsiderations of individualism and community see Leroy S. Rouner, ed., *On Community* (Notre Dame, Ind.: Univ. of Notre Dame Press, 1991); Juergen Habermas, to be discussed later in this essay, argues for a concept of selves "individuated through socialization" in *Moral Consciousness and Communicative Action* (Cambridge: MIT Press, 1990), p. 199. See also Gil G. Noam, "Beyond Freud and Piaget: Biographical Worlds—Interpersonal Self," in *The Moral Domain*, ed. Thomas E. Wren, esp. pp. 381–85.

8. The term *patriarchy* will be used throughout this study. Its root meaning is "rule by fathers." A distinction should be preserved between fatherly rule and male rule, though they are sometimes equated. Although some earlier approaches—including ones referred to here—found patriarchy to be a repetitive pattern remaining essentially the same throughout history, current theory has historicized this concept. Paternal dominance has taken different forms, and its meaning has varied in different historical epochs. The term remains useful in the context of studies about conscience, however, and some of its alternative senses will be discussed here. See Sagan, *Freud, Women, and Morality*, p. 57, where he criticizes the generalized use of the term, and argues for "differentiating the crucially distinct forms of patriarchy." Richard Sennett discusses patriarchy, paternalism, and authority in *Authority* (New York: Vintage Books, 1981), esp. pp. 50–83. See also Philip Greven, *Four Generations: Population, Land and Family in Colonial Andover, Massachusetts* (Ithaca: Cornell Univ. Press, 1970), pp. 72–79.

9. See the brief "history" of psychoanalytic feminism in Nancy Chodorow, *Feminism and Psychoanalytic Theory* (New Haven: Yale Univ. Press, 1989), pp. 15–16. In a footnote (p. 243 n. 8) Chodorow sketches out the strand of "critical psychoanalytic social theory" that I am investigating.

10. See Roy Schafer's discussion of the use of this term in *A New Language for Psychoanalysis* (New Haven: Yale Univ. Press, 1976), pp. 155–78; and Hans Loewald's discussion, *Papers in Psychoanalysis* (New Haven: Yale Univ. Press, 1980), esp. pp. 69–86, 257–76.

11. This formulation differs from, but has been influenced by, that of Juergen Habermas in *Moral Consciousness and Communicative Action*, esp. pp. 164–65.

12. Hans Loewald, "Superego and Time," *Papers on Psychoanalysis*, p. 46; see also Johannes Metz's use of the concept of a "conscience for the future," *Theology of the World* (New York: Seabury Press, 1969), pp. 100, 150–56.

13. This term was chosen by Horkheimer to identify the emerging perspective of the Frankfurt School as a group. Aspects of the perspective to which it points will be examined as we proceed. Here it can simply be noted that their use of "critical" derives in perhaps equal measure from the philosophies of Immanuel

Kant and Karl Marx. See Max Horkheimer, "Traditional and Critical Theory," in *Critical Theory: Selected Essays* (New York: Seabury Press, 1972), pp. 188–243, esp. pp. 206–10.

1. Origins of the Critical Perspective on Conscience

1. For a discussion of Hegel's influence on the Frankfurt School, see e.g. David Ingram, *Critical Theory and Philosophy* (New York: Paragon House, 1990), pp. 10–18. Two basic texts of Hegel relevant to topics discussed here are *The Phenomenology of Mind* (New York: Harper and Row, 1967) and T. M. Knox, trans. and ed., *Hegel's Philosophy of Right* (London: Oxford Univ. Press, 1952). Hegel's approach to the family is discussed in Joan B. Landes, "Hegel's Conception of the Family," in *The Family in Political Thought*, ed. Jean Bethke Elshtain (Amherst: Univ. of Massachusetts Press, 1982), pp. 125–44, and in Rudolf J. Siebert, *Hegel's Concept of Marriage and Family: The Subjective Origin of Freedom* (Washington, D.C.: Univ. Press of America, 1979).

2. The word *ideology* is useful but ambiguous. Its modern usage derives from the Marxian context, where the term takes on the pejorative implication of moral-philosophical-religious ideas that rationalize and justify oppression. When internalized, ideology shapes and motivates behavior and becomes embedded in character structure. In this essay the focus is upon ideologies of "mother" and "father." These images play an important role in shaping our value systems and have considerable religious import. Therefore at times here the term *ideology* becomes a near equivalent for religious ideas. These various connotations should be clear from the context.

   The connection of ideology with character type and the pathologies thereof may be one of the original contributions of Wilhelm Reich and the Frankfurt School. See Martin Jay, *The Dialectical Imagination: A History of the Frankfurt School and the Institute of Social Research, 1923–1950* (Boston: Little, Brown, and Co., 1973), p. 94. The standpoint of ideology critique, as interpreted here, is that a kernel of truth can be rescued from the ideology by criticism of the elements of "false consciousness" contained within it. To term the bourgeois ideals of motherhood and fatherhood and the religious image of the "heavenly father" ideologies is not to identify them simply as false ideas. Their utopian "truth" can be rescued by critique. Consequently the word *ideology* has a neutral usage, referring to ideas that may or may not be used falsely. Adorno once observed, "It is not ideology in itself which is untrue but rather its pretension to correspond to reality": Theodor Adorno, *Prisms* (Cambridge: MIT Press, 1967), p. 32. For examples of this kind of usage see Dorothee Soelle, *Political Theology* (Philadelphia: Fortress Press, 1974), esp. pp. 23–27; Dorothee Soelle, *Beyond Mere Obedience* (New York: Pilgrim Press, 1982), esp. pp. 67–71; Dorothee Soelle, *The Strength of the Weak: Toward a Christian Feminist Identity* (Philadelphia: Westminster Press, 1984), esp. pp. 106–17. Also see J. A. Colombo's discussion of the functions of ideology, *An Essay on Theology and History: Studies in Pannenberg, Metz, and the Frankfurt School* (Atlanta: Scholars Press, 1990), pp. 79–81.

3. Max Weber, *The Protestant Ethic and the Spirit of Capitalism*, trans. by Talcott Parsons (1920; reprint, New York: Charles Scribner's Sons, 1958). For contemporary discussion of the Weber thesis see Richard van Duelmen, "Protestantism and Capitalism: Weber's Thesis in the Light of Recent Social History," *Telos* 78 (Winter 1988–1989):71–80.

4. David Little, *Religion, Order, and Law: A Study in Pre-Revolutionary England* (Chicago: Univ. of Chicago Press, 1969), p. 1.

5. Gianfranco Poggi, *Calvinism and the Capitalist Spirit: Max Weber's Protestant Ethic* (Amherst, Mass.: Univ. of Massachusetts Press, 1983), p. 52.

6. See Weber, *The Protestant Ethic*, pp. 62–63. For a discussion of "vocation" in Weber, see Harvey Goldman, *Max Weber and Thomas Mann: Calling and the Shaping of the Self* (Berkeley: Univ. of California Press, 1988).

7. Weber, *The Protestant Ethic*, pp. 118–21, 149.

8. Ibid., pp. 109, 117–20.

9. Bellah, *Habits of the Heart*, pp. 32–33.

10. See Arthur Mitzman's discussions of Weber on asceticism in *The Iron Cage: An Historical Interpretation of Max Weber* (New York: Alfred A. Knopf, 1970), esp. pp. 194–201, 242–54. The term *Protestant* is used broadly here to refer to a character (and culture) type that can be found elsewhere in human society. Credence can be given to Weber's thesis without attributing historic uniqueness to Protestantism. It may well represent a recurrent tendency in ethics, repeatable in other historical circumstances and other religious traditions.

11. Weber, *The Protestant Ethic*, p. 182.

12. The phrase was applied to Weber's analysis by Benjamin Nelson. See Otto Stammer, ed., *Max Weber and Sociology Today*, (New York: Harper and Row, 1971), pp. 167, 169.

13. Weber, *The Protestant Ethic*, p. 90.

14. See H. Stuart Hughes, "Weber's Search for Rationality in Western Society," in *Protestantism, Capitalism, and Social Science: The Weber Thesis Controversy*, ed. Robert Green (Lexington, Mass.: D. C. Heath and Co., 1973), pp. 159, 168. For comments on the intersections of Weber and Freud see Lawrence A. Scaff, *Fleeing the Iron Cage: Culture, Politics and Modernity in the Thought of Max Weber* (Berkeley: Univ. of California Press, 1989).

15. Sigmund Freud, *The Ego and the Id*, in John Rickman, ed., *A General Selection from the Works of Sigmund Freud* (Garden City, N.Y.: Doubleday Anchor, 1957), p. 227; also found in *The Complete Psychological Works of Sigmund Freud*, vol. 19 (London: Hogarth Press, 1961), p. 48. The term *superego* is useful but also subject to misuse. Eli Sagan appropriately reminds us of the pitfalls. He notes that the parts of the psyche as described by Freud do not "exist in the way we conceive of the liver or the heart existing." Rather, they are metaphors and "are extremely useful in our attempt to understand psychic conflict, and their continued use is theoretically legitimate, provided we do not forget that we are describing things metaphorically, not actually." When we employ ego, superego, and id, "we are in the world of drama and myth, not of 'science.' There are nonetheless many truths to be discovered in these realms, and therefore there is no reason to repress the metaphorical mode of talking about the psyche, provided we continually bear in mind what mode of discourse we are actually using" (*Freud, Women, and Morality*, p. 184). See a similar warning and a similar defense of the use of these concepts in Christopher Lasch, *The Minimal Self: Psychic Survival in Troubled Times* (New York: W. W. Norton and Co., 1984), p. 176.

16. Freud, *The Ego and the Id*, in *The Complete Psychological Works of Sigmund Freud*, p. 31.

17. Ibid., p. 36.

18. Ibid., p. 37.

19. Ibid., p. 37.

20. Ibid., p. 37.

21. This is the implication of Freud's discussion of the primal father in *Civilization and Its Discontents* (New York: W. W. Norton and Co., 1961), pp. 46–48.

22. Melanie Klein, "The Early Development of Conscience in the Child," (originally published in 1933) in Melanie Klein, *Contributions to Psychoanalysis 1921–1945* (London: Hogarth Press, 1968), p. 267.

23. Sigmund Freud, *New Introductory Lectures* (New York: W. W. Norton and Co., 1964), p. 69. For discussion of contemporary superego theory see, for example,

Phyllis Tyson and Robert Tyson, *Psychoanalytic Theories of Development* (New Haven: Yale Univ. Press, 1990), pp. 195–245. With the emphasis on the origin of conscience in interpersonal relations, we diverge from another strand of conscience interpretation. Some theorists link it more closely with cognitive development. Speaking historically we align ourselves more with the tradition of Paul, Augustine and Luther than with Aquinas (see Tyson and Tyson, *Psychoanalytic Theories of Development*, p. 202n).

24. See Freud, *Civilization and Its Discontents*, pp. 89–91.
25. See Judith Van Herik, *Freud on Femininity and Faith* (Berkeley: Univ. of California Press), 1982.
26. Freud, *Civilization and Its Discontents*, p. 89.
27. Ibid., p. 90.
28. An observation made recently by Peter and Brigitte Berger in *The War over the Family: Capturing the Middle Ground* (New York: Doubleday Anchor Press, 1983), p. 98.
29. Friedrich Engels, *The Origin of the Family, Private Property, and the State*, in *Marx-Engels Reader*, ed. Robert Tucker (New York: W. W. Norton and Co., 1972), p. 739.
30. Ibid., p. 736. For a summary of Engels's views on the family, see Mark Poster, *Critical Theory of the Family* (New York: Seabury Press, 1978), pp. 42–46.
31. See Isaac Balbus, *Marxism and Domination* (Princeton, N.J.: Princeton Univ. Press, 1982), pp. 61–83.
32. See, for example, Karl Marx, *The German Ideology*, excerpted in *Marx and Engels: Basic Writings on Politics and Philosophy*, ed. Lewis Feuer (Garden City, N.Y.: Doubleday Anchor Book, 1959), pp. 246–61.
33. See Erich Fromm, *The Sane Society* (New York: Rinehart and Company, 1955), pp. 262–65.
34. See Andrew Arato and Paul Breines, *The Young Lukács and the Origins of Western Marxism* (New York: Seabury Press, 1979). In his 1922 work, *History and Class Consciousness* (Cambridge: MIT Press, 1971), Lukács provided a vigorous critique of what was called "vulgar Marxism," that is, that version of Marxism that sought to be "scientific" by reducing mental or ideological causation to causal factors emanating from the "material base." By reemphasizing "the relative autonomy of ideology" (Arato and Breines, *The Young Lukács*, p. 202), Lukács authenticated Marxian interest in ideology critique, making possible a Marxian dialogue with Max Weber (as well as reviving Marxian interest in the idealism of Hegel). Lukács provides a basis for combining the Marxian and the Weberian attacks on bourgeois-capitalist culture, but he does not attempt a historical psychology—a theory about how the bourgeois ethic is mediated to individuals; therefore he did not contribute substantially to the debates about character types. As a result, although he contributed to the Marx-Weber synthesis, Lukács is less central to the specific currents of thought being traced here. (For a discussion of Lukács's Marx-Weber synthesis, see Andrew Arato and Eike Gebhardt, eds., *The Essential Frankfurt School Reader* (New York: Urizen Books, 1978), pp. 191–97.
35. Wilhelm Reich, *The Invasion of Compulsory Sex-Morality* (New York: Farrar, Strauss, and Giroux, 1970), pp. 145–50. As I suggested earlier, the term *patriarchy*, as used in the present essay, entails "rule or control by the father." In the Freudian perspective patriarchy takes on the character of inevitability, but Reich gives the term a pejorative connotation (including the suggestion of "domination by the father"). Frankfurt School usage reflects a degree of ambivalence, but the Reichian view tends to prevail. *Matriarchy* for Reich means mother centeredness, with favorable connotations. Fromm picks up Reich's usage and adopts the term *matricentricity*.
36. Wilhelm Reich, *The Mass Psychology of Fascism* (New York: Farrar, Strauss, and Giroux, 1970), pp. 30–31, 60.

37. Ibid., pp. 86–87; see Christopher Lasch, *Haven in a Heartless World: The Family Besieged* (New York: Basic Books, 1979), p. 94.
38. Reich, *The Invasion of Compulsory Sex-Morality*, pp. 145–46; see Russell Jacoby, *Social Amnesia: A Critique of Contemporary Psychology from Adler to Laing* (Boston: Beacon Press, 1975), pp. 90–91.
39. Reich, *Mass Psychology*, p. 163.
40. Ibid., pp. 151, 163.
41. Reich, *Mass Psychology*, 3d ed. (1942), p. xv.
42. Juliet Mitchell's phrase, in *Psychoanalysis and Feminism: Freud, Reich, Laing and Women* (New York: Pantheon Books, 1974), p. 149; see also p. 186.
43. Ibid., p. 413.
44. Reich, *Mass Psychology*, 3d ed., pp. xxvi–xxvii.
45. Balbus, *Marxism and Domination*, pp. 215–17.

2. Frankfurt School Perspectives on Conscience

1. See Rainer Funk, *Erich Fromm: The Courage to be Human* (New York: Continuum Publishing Company, 1989), esp. pp. 296–97, n. 11; Martin Jay, *The Dialectical Imagination*, esp. pp. 88–106; Gerhard Knapp, *The Art of Living: Erich Fromm's Life and Works* (New York: Peter Lang, 1989); and Guyton B. Hammond, *Man in Estrangement: A Comparison of the Thought of Paul Tillich and Erich Fromm* (Nashville: Vanderbilt Univ. Press, 1965). Regarding Fromm's influence Douglas Kellner writes: "Fromm's important role during the earlier stages of the development of Critical Theory has been underestimated by most interpreters. His contributions deserve to be studied in much more detail than has previously been the case": *Critical Theory, Marxism, and Modernity* (Baltimore: Johns Hopkins Univ. Press, 1989), p. 240 n 20.
2. Rainer Funk, *Erich Fromm: The Courage to be Human*, p. 103; see Funk's summary of the essay, pp. 101–4.
3. Erich Fromm, *The Dogma of Christ and Other Essays on Religion, Psychology, and Culture* (New York: Holt, Rinehart, and Winston, 1955), pp. 67–68; Freud was to arrive at a not wholly dissimilar view of Christianity in his 1939 work, *Moses and Monotheism* (New York: Random House, 1939).
4. Ibid., p. 91.
5. Ibid., p. 91.
6. Erich Fromm, *The Crisis of Psychoanalysis: Essays on Freud, Marx, and Social Psychology* (New York: Holt, Rinehart and Winston, 1970), pp. 116–17.
7. Ibid., p. 117; see also Fromm's review of Reich's *The Invasion of Compulsory Sex-Morality* (1933) in Erich Fromm, *Gesamtausgabe*, band 8 (Stuttgart: Deutsche Verlags-Anstalt, 1981), pp. 93–96.
8. Fromm, *The Crisis of Psychoanalysis*, pp. 136–47; he draws on Freud's essay, "Character and Anal Eroticism" (1908).
9. Ibid., p. 148.
10. Ibid., pp. 153, 155. Fromm and the other members of the Frankfurt School use the term *bourgeois* to refer to that which pertains to middle-class and commercial interests. Their usage carries Marxist and Weberian connotations, so for them the term has a critical edge. Later in our study we will find a more favorable usage in Peter Berger's work.
11. Ibid., pp. 97, 104. The shift in terminology from *patriarchy* and *matriarchy* to *patricentricity* and *matricentricity* suggests a shift of interest from political (-archy = rule) to psychological and cultural factors (-centricity = focus, line of influence). Mothers may play a more or less decisive role in character formation without being in a position of "rule" politically speaking.
12. Ibid., p. 104. In a later supplement to this essay Fromm gave a somewhat more favorable account of patricentricity, associating it with "conditional love, hier-

archical structure, abstract thought, man-made law, the state and justice,"
p. 83.

13. Ibid., p. 104.

14. Fromm, *The Crisis of Psychoanalysis*, p. 105; see also Erich Fromm, *Escape from Freedom* (New York: Avon Books, 1969), p. 118.

15. Fromm, *Escape from Freedom*, p. 60.

16. Douglas Kellner, *Herbert Marcuse and the Crisis of Marxism* (Berkeley: Univ. of California Press, 1984), p. 165.

17. Fromm, *Escape from Freedom*, p. 325.

18. Fromm develops this thesis in chapters 2 and 3 of *Escape from Freedom*.

19. Fromm does not generally use the terms *patricentricity* and *matricentricity* in *Escape from Freedom*, but his descriptions of character types there are identical to the earlier ones.

20. See Max Weber, *Economy and Society* (Berkeley: Univ. of California Press, 1978), pp. 225–41.

21. Robert Moore in *Max Weber and Modern Sociology*, ed. Arun Sahay (London: Routledge and Kegan Paul, 1971), p. 88.

22. Weber, *Economy and Society*, pp. 372, 375.

23. Arun Sahay, ed., *Max Weber and Modern Sociology*, p. 94.

24. Weber, *Economy and Society*, pp. 605–6.

25. Peter and Brigitte Berger, *The War over the Family*, p. 98.

26. See Fromm's use of this word in Erich Fromm, *The Sane Society*, p. 82. He does give a generalized account of familial relations in *The Heart of Man* (New York: Harper and Row, 1964), chapter 5. But there he reverts to the Freudian universalization of the bourgeois family and refers only in a footnote to different family structures.

27. See Reich, *Invasion of Compulsory Sex-Morality*, p. 157; *Mass Psychology*, pp. 86–87.

28. See Erich Fromm, *The Art of Loving* (New York: Bantam Books, 1956), p. 35.

29. Fromm, *The Crisis of Psychoanalysis*, pp. 82–83, 103.

30. See Jay, *The Dialectical Imagination*, esp. pp. 6–7; 24–27; Stephen E. Bronner and Douglas M. Kellner, eds., *Critical Theory and Society* (New York: Routledge and Kegan Paul, 1989), pp. 1–21; Max Horkheimer, *Dawn and Decline: Notes 1926–1931 and 1950–1969* (New York: Seabury Press, 1978), Afterword by Eike Gebhardt, pp. 241–52.

31. Bronner and Kellner, eds., *Critical Theory and Society*, p. 33.

32. Max Horkheimer ed., *Autoritaet und Familie: Studien aus dem Institut fuer Sozialforschung* (Paris: Librairie Felix Alcan, 1936).

33. Max Horkheimer, *Critical Theory: Selected Essays*, p. 100. Horkheimer's 1936 essay, "Authority and the Family," appears in this collection.

34. Frankfurt Institute for Social Research, ed., *Aspects of Sociology* (Boston: Beacon Press, 1972), pp. 134–36.

35. Horkheimer, *Critical Theory*, pp. 105–6, 111.

36. Ibid., p. 114.

37. Ibid., pp. 100–101. Ernst Troelsch is cited in this passage.

38. Ibid., p. 108. Here Horkheimer uses the term *rational* in an ideal, positive sense rather than in the Weberian sense of "rationalization." See also Max Horkheimer and Theodor Adorno, *Dialectic of Enlightenment* (New York: Seabury Press, 1972), pp. 203–4, for a description of the rise and fall of the character type analyzed by psychoanalysis. For a discussion of the emergence of "psychoanalytic man" see J. H. Colombo, *An Essay on Theology and History*, 112–29.

39. Ibid., pp. 98, 124.

40. Ibid., pp. 114–21.

41. Ibid., pp. 118–19.

42. See Frankfurt Institute for Social Research, ed., *Aspects of Sociology*, pp. 141–

42. For a stronger, late expression of this view, see Max Horkheimer, *Critique of Instrumental Reason* (New York: Seabury Press, 1971), pp. 11–12.
43. The phrase is Marcuse's in Herbert Marcuse, *Studies in Critical Philosophy* (Boston: Beacon Press, 1973), p. 74.
44. *Telos 69* (Fall 1986):89.
45. Ibid., p. 98.
46. Ibid., pp. 95–96.
47. Ibid., pp. 106–8.
48. Ibid., pp. 113–14.

3. *Paul Tillich's Critical Theology and Its Implications for Conscience*

1. For discussion of Tillich and the Frankfurt School see my articles, "Patriarchy and the Protestant Conscience: A Critique," in *The Journal of Religious Ethics* 9, no. 1 (Spring 1981), pp. 84–102; "The Conscience-less Society and Beyond: Perspectives from Erich Fromm and Paul Tillich," in *Neue Zeitschrift fuer Systematische Theologie und Religions-Philosophie* 25, no. 1 (1983):20–32; "Tillich and the Frankfurt School on Protestantism and the Bourgeois Spirit," in *Religion et Culture: Actes du Colloque International du Centenaire Paul Tillich*, ed. Jean Richard (Quebec: Les Presses de l'Université Laval, 1987), pp. 327–37; and "Tillich, Adorno, and the Debate about Existentialism," in *Laval théologique et philosophique* 47, no. 3 (October 1991):343–55. See also John R. Stumme, *Socialism in Theological Perspective: A Study of Paul Tillich, 1918– 1933* (Atlanta: Scholars Press, 1978), esp. pp. 44–51; and Max Horkheimer et al., eds., *Werk und Wirken Paul Tillichs: Ein Gedenkbuch* (Stuttgart: Evangelisches Verlagswerk, 1967).
2. Paul Tillich, *The Religious Situation*, trans. by H. Richard Niebuhr (New York: Meridian Books, 1956).
3. Ronald H. Stone, *Paul Tillich's Radical Social Thought* (Atlanta: John Knox Press, 1980), p. 155.
4. Tillich, *The Religious Situation*, pp. 181–219.
5. Ibid., pp. 113–14, 139.
6. Ibid., p. 138.
7. Ibid., pp. 62, 135–40.
8. Paul Tillich, *The Socialist Decision*, trans. by Franklin Sherman (New York: Harper and Row, 1977).
9. Ibid., p. 15.
10. Ibid., p. 16.
11. Ibid., p. 20.
12. Ibid., p. 23.
13. See Stumme's discussion of the breaking of the myth of origin, *Socialism in Theological Perspective*, pp. 92–104.
14. Tillich, *The Socialist Decision*, p. 47.
15. Paul Tillich, "Protestantismus und Politische Romantik" (1932), in *Fuer und Wider den Sozialismus* (Muenchen: Siebenstern Taschenbuch Verlag, 1969), p. 86 (my translation).
16. Ibid., my translation.
17. Weber, *The Protestant Ethic*, esp. pp. 79–92. For a discussion of the importance of the theme of vocation in Weber, see Goldman, *Max Weber and Thomas Mann*, esp. pp. 18–51.
18. Weber, *The Protestant Ethic*, p. 166.
19. See, for example, Paul Tillich, *The Protestant Era* (London: Nisbet and Company, 1951), pp. 50–53.
20. Paul Tillich, *Political Expectation* (New York: Harper and Row, 1971), p. 61.
21. See esp. Tillich, *The Socialist Decision*, pp. 20–23.

22. See Tillich's reference to a "summons," ibid., p. xxxi.
23. Ibid., p. 4.
24. Ibid., pp. 3–8. Langdon Gilkey emphasizes the importance of this triad in *The Socialist Decision*. See Langdon Gilkey, *Gilkey on Tillich* (New York: Crossroad, 1990), pp. 4–6.
25. Tillich, *The Socialist Decision*, p. 15.
26. See e.g. Tillich's use of this term, ibid., p. 5; his discussion of Marxism, pp. 117–25; and his reference to the "recent" discovery of Marx's early manuscripts, p. 175 n. 12.
27. Ibid., p. 134.
28. See e.g. Paul Tillich, *The Protestant Era*, pp. 50–53.
29. Paul Tillich, *The Socialist Decision*, pp. 167–68 n. 12.
30. Paul Tillich, "Die Bleibende Bedeutung der Katholischen Kirche fuer den Protestantismus," in Paul Tillich, *Der Protestantismus als Kritik und Gestaltung* (Muenchen: Siebenstern Taschenbuch Verlag, 1966), pp. 137–38, my translation.
31. Paul Tillich, *Systematic Theology*, vol. 3 (Chicago: Univ. of Chicago Press, 1963), p. 274.
32. Paul Tillich, "The Impact of Pastoral Psychology on Theological Thought," in Paul Tillich, *The Meaning of Health*, ed. by Perry LeFevre (Chicago: Exploration Press, 1984), p. 146.
33. Tillich, *The Religious Situation*, pp. 191–92.
34. Tillich, *Political Expectation*, p. 31.
35. Ibid., p. 38.
36. Ibid.
37. Tillich, "The Transmoral Conscience," in *The Protestant Era*, pp. 152–66; see also Tillich's briefer treatment of conscience: "Ethical Principles of Moral Action," in *Being and Doing: Paul Tillich as Ethicist*, ed. John J. Carey (Macon, Ga.: Mercer Univ. Press, 1987), pp. 205–17; and Benjamin Nelson's discussion of the transmoral conscience in *On the Roads to Modernity: Conscience, Science, and Civilizations* (Totowa, N.J.: Roman and Littlefield, 1981), esp. pp. 49–54, 74–77.
38. Tillich, *The Protestant Era*, p. 163.
39. Ibid.
40. Ibid., p.165.
41. For "New Being," see e.g. Tillich, *Systematic Theology*, pp. 140–61.
42. Tillich, *The Protestant Era*, p. 154. See also Tillich, *Systematic Theology*, pp. 38–41.
43. See R. H. Tawney's argument to this effect in his Foreword to Weber, *The Protestant Ethic*, pp. 9–10.
44. See Paul Connerton, *The Tragedy of Enlightenment: An Essay on the Frankfurt School* (Cambridge: Cambridge Univ. Press, 1980).
45. For other efforts to relate theology to the perspective of the Frankfurt School, see Charles Davis, *Theology and Political Society* (Cambridge: Cambridge Univ. Press, 1980); Helmut Peukert, *Science, Action, and Fundamental Theology: Toward a Theology of Communicative Action* (Cambridge: MIT Press, 1984); Matthew Lamb, *Solidarity with Victims: Toward a Theology of Social Transformation* (New York: Crossroad, 1982); and Guyton B. Hammond, *Man in Estrangement.*

4. Later Developments in Critical Theory

1. Reich, *Mass Psychology*, pp. 7–8.
2. Fromm, *Escape from Freedom*, pp. 185–86.
3. See ibid., pp. 84, 97, 102.

4. Ibid., p. 189.
5. Fromm, *Man for Himself* (New York: Rinehart and Co., 1947), pp. 157–58.
6. Fromm, *Escape from Freedom*, p. 240.
7. Ibid.
8. See ibid., pp. 117–18; Christopher Lasch makes this point about Fromm in *Haven in a Heartless World*, pp. 89–90.
9. Fromm, *Escape from Freedom*, p. 279; see also Fromm, *The Sane Society*, pp. 152–55.
10. Fromm, *Escape from Freedom*, p. 282.
11. Fromm, *The Sane Society*, p. 158.
12. Ibid., p. 153.
13. Frankfurt Institute for Social Research, ed., *Aspects of Sociology*, p. 143.
14. Ibid., p. 143. This approach can be linked with Fromm's discussion of "anonymous" authority.
15. Ibid., pp. 142–43.
16. Max Horkheimer, "The Lessons of Fascism," in *Tensions That Cause Wars*, ed. Hadley Contril (Urbana: Univ. of Illinois Press, 1950), pp. 209–42.
17. Ibid., pp. 213–14.
18. Ibid., p. 214.
19. Ibid., p. 217.
20. Theodor Adorno, "Freudian Theory and the Pattern of Fascist Propaganda," in *The Essential Frankfurt School Reader*, ed. Arato and Gebhardt, p. 137.
21. Ibid., p. 120.
22. Theodor Adorno et al., *The Authoritarian Personality* (New York: W. W. Norton and Company, 1950), esp. pp. 230–34, 316–17, 454–56, 744–83.
23. Ibid., p. 234.
24. Ibid., pp. 759–74.
25. Ibid., pp. 231–34.
26. Frankfurt Institute for Social Research, ed., *Aspects of Sociology*, p. 142.
27. For Fromm's discussion of Judaism, see Erich Fromm, *You Shall Be as Gods: A Radical Interpretation of the Old Testament and Its Tradition* (New York: Holt, Rinehart, and Winston, 1966), esp. pp. 46–55, 72–76. For Protestantism's positive contribution, see esp. Fromm, *Escape from Freedom*, pp. 92–93.
28. See Fromm, *Escape from Freedom*, pp. 123–56; Fromm, *Man for Himself*, pp. 82–88; Fromm, *The Sane Society*, pp. 25–36.
29. Fromm, *Man for Himself*, p. 158.
30. Ibid., p. 172.
31. Fromm, *The Sane Society*, p. 47.
32. See, for example, ibid., p. 95, where the patriarchal character of capitalist man is discussed.
33. Fromm, *The Crisis of Psychoanalysis*, p. 82. This passage is from a 1970 essay.
34. Fromm, *The Sane Society*, p. 57; see Fromm, *The Crisis of Psychoanalysis*, p. 83.
35. Fromm, *The Sane Society*, pp. 47–48.
36. Ibid., p. 47.
37. Erich Fromm, *To Have or To Be?* (New York: Harper and Row, 1976), pp. 55, 59.
38. Ibid., p. 201.
39. Douglas Kellner suggests that Fromm anticipates "recent feminist theories of mothering" by showing "how the activity of mothering produces certain nurturing maternal character traits associated with women." Kellner, *Critical Theory, Marxism, and Modernity*, p. 39, see p. 240 n. 25.
40. Jay, *The Dialectical Imagination*, pp. 107–12; see Herbert Marcuse, *Eros and Civilization* (Boston: Beacon Press, 1955), Epilogue; see also Erich Fromm, "The Human Implications of Instinctive Radicalism," in *Dissent* 2, no. 4 (Autumn 1955):342–49; Herbert Marcuse, "A Reply to Erich Fromm," *Dissent* 3, no. 1 (Winter 1956):79–81; Erich Fromm, "A Counter-Rebuttal," *Dissent* 3,

no. 1 (Winter 1956):81–83. Chodorow also notes their actual convergence in *Feminism and Psychoanalytic Theory*, pp. 133, 248 n. 94.

41. Marcuse, *Eros and Civilization*, p. 16.

42. Ibid., p. 129.

43. See Sigmund Freud, "Formulations Concerning Two Principles in Mental Functioning," in *Collected Papers* (London: Hogarth and Company, 1950), 4:14ff; see Douglas Kellner's discussion of these themes in *Herbert Marcuse and the Crisis of Marxism*, pp. 158–74.

44. Kellner, *Herbert Marcuse and the Crisis of Marxism*, p. 158; see Marcuse, *Eros and Civilization*, pp. 14–15.

45. Kellner, *Herbert Marcuse*, pp. 172–73; see Marcuse, *Eros and Civilization*, p. 129.

46. Herbert Marcuse, *Five Lectures* (Boston: Beacon Press, 1970), pp. 46, 50.

47. Marcuse, *Eros and Civilization*, pp. 96–97.

48. See Kellner, *Herbert Marcuse*, pp. 116–17.

49. Marcuse, *Five Lectures*, pp. 14–15; 46–47; 50–51.

50. Marcuse, *Eros and Civilization*, p. 97.

51. Ibid., p. 129.

52. Ibid., p. 167.

53. Ibid., p. 198.

54. Marcuse, *Five Lectures*, p. 24.

55. Ibid., pp. 229–30.

56. Chodorow, *Feminism and Psychoanalytic Theory*, pp. 139, 144, 145.

57. Herbert Marcuse, *Counterrevolution and Revolt* (Boston: Beacon Press, 1972), p. 75.

58. Fromm, "The Human Implications of Instinctivistic Radicalism," pp. 344–45.

59. Theodor Adorno, *Negative Dialectics* (New York: Seabury Press, 1973), pp. 211–99.

60. Ibid., p. 261.

61. See Fromm, *Escape from Freedom*, p. 189, where he includes Kant in his analysis of coercive conscience.

62. Adorno, *Negative Dialectics*, p. 273.

63. See Max Horkheimer, *Eclipse of Reason* (New York: Seabury Press, 1974), p. 109.

64. Adorno, *Negative Dialectics*, p. 273 n. 11.

65. Ibid., p. 282; see p. 273.

66. Ibid., p. 275.

67. See this idea in Jessica Benjamin, *The Bonds of Love: Psychoanalysis, Feminism, and the Problem of Domination* (New York: Pantheon Books, 1988), p. 293 n. 56.

68. See Sagan, *Freud, Women, and Morality*, p. 210.

69. For a helpful discussion of this topic, see C. Fred Alford, *Melanie Klein and Critical Social Theory* (New Haven: Yale Univ. Press, 1989), pp. 142–45; for the psychodynamics of internalization, see Hans Loewald, *Papers on Psychoanalysis*, "On Internalization," 69–86.

70. Frankfurt Institute for Social Research, ed., *Aspects of Sociology*, p. 138.

71. Ibid., p. 145.

72. Ibid., p. 139.

73. Juergen Habermas, *The Theory of Communicative Action*, vol. 1 (Boston: Beacon Press, 1984), p. 391.

74. Phrase used by Joel Whitebook in "Reason and Happiness: Some Psychoanalytic Themes in Critical Theory," in *Habermas and Modernity*, ed. Richard J. Bernstein (Cambridge: MIT Press, 1985), p. 153. My analysis of Habermas has been aided by Whitebook's article.

75. Ibid., pp. 148–49.

76. Juergen Habermas, *Legitimation Crisis* (Boston: Beacon Press, 1975), p. 72.

77. Whitebook, "Reason and Happiness," p. 149; see Habermas, *Legitimation Crisis*, pp. 89–92.
78. Habermas, *The Theory of Communicative Action*, 2:387.
79. Ibid., p. 388.
80. Ibid., 1:398.
81. Ibid., p. 391.
82. Habermas, *Moral Consciousness and Communicative Action*, p. 183. See Peter Dews, ed., *Habermas: Autonomy and Solidarity* (London: Verso, 1986), pp. 19–21.
83. Habermas, *Legitimation Crisis*, p. 87.
84. Habermas, *Moral Consciousness*, p. 199. Habermas continues his reflections on individuation through socialization and on the role of conscience in individuation in a recently published essay, "Individuation through Socialization: On George Herbert Mead's Theory of Subjectivity," in Juergen Habermas, *Postmetaphysical Thinking: Philosophical Essays*, trans. by William Hohengarten (Cambridge: MIT Press, 1992), pp. 149–204.
85. Ibid., p. 207.
86. See ibid., p. 178.
87. For a discussion of Habermas's turn away from the concreteness of family and full selfhood see C. Fred Alford, *Narcissism: Socrates, the Frankfurt School, and Psychoanalytic Theory* (New Haven: Yale Univ. Press, 1988), esp. pp. 164–65. I have confined my attention here to Habermas's use of psychoanalytic thought. In his later work Habermas turns his attention to developmental theories of morality deriving from Piaget and Kohlberg. Consideration of how Habermas attempts to combine Freud and Kohlberg would require lengthy treatment, and I have not attempted it here. See Juergen Habermas, *Communication and the Evolution of Society* (Boston: Beacon Press, 1979), pp. 69–129; and the biographical references in Dews, *Habermas: Autonomy and Solidarity*, pp. 151, 160. The extensive debates in the Kohlbergian tradition generated by Carol Gilligan's work are germane to the present essay, but I have had to set them aside. See Carol Gilligan, *In a Different Voice* (Cambridge: Harvard Univ. Press, 1982).

5. Family Studies on Conscience

1. On the development of studies in the history of the family since Philippe Ariès's seminal work, *Centuries of Childhood: A Social History of Family Life* (London: Cape, 1962), see Tamara K. Hareven's bibliographic essay, "The History of the Family and the Complexity of Social Change," in *The American Historical Review* 96, no. 1 (February 1991):96–124. For one example of a work focusing on recent and contemporary developments, see Arlene Skolnick, *Embattled Paradise: The American Family in an Age of Uncertainty* (Basic Books, 1991).
2. Mark Poster, *Critical Theory of the Family*. Page references in this section of Chapter 5 are to this work. In a recent essay Poster reports on his continuing research on the family. His approach there is largely empirical and descriptive; his conclusions do not seem inconsistent with the work surveyed here: see Mark Poster, *Critical Theory and Poststructuralism: In Search of a Context* (Ithaca: Cornell Univ. Press, 1989), pp. 143–69.
3. Page references in this section of Chapter 5 are to the Bergers' work, *The War over the Family*.
4. I suggested difficulties with this formulation in Chapter 2.
5. Weber, *The Protestant Ethic*, pp. 181, 182.
6. Poster, *Critical Theory of the Family*, pp. 152, 204–5; Berger and Berger, *The War over the Family*, pp. 157–58.

7. See esp. Poster, *Critical Theory of the Family*, p. 152.
8. Ibid., p. 204; Berger and Berger, *The War over the Family*, p. 158.
9. Poster, *Critical Theory of the Family*, p. 205.
10. This same debate is replicated in feminist literature. Nancy Chodorow, in *The Reproduction of Mothering: Psychoanalysis and the Sociology of Gender* (Berkeley: Univ. of California Press, 1978) (a work we will discuss in the next chapter), speaks favorably of children reared in the kibbutz (p. 217). This view provoked a spirited rebuttal by Jean Bethke Elshtain in *Public Man, Private Woman: Women in Social and Political Thought* (Princeton: Princeton Univ. Press, 1981), pp. 293–96. Elshtain cites Bettelheim's analysis in her critique of Chodorow.
11. Bruno Bettelheim, *The Children of the Dream* (London: Macmillan Co., 1969), pp. 125–31.
12. Ibid., p. 127.
13. Ibid., p. 128.
14. Ibid.
15. Ibid., p. 130.
16. Poster, *Critical Theory of the Family*, pp. 58–63.
17. Berger and Berger, *The War over the Family*, p. 161.
18. Ibid., p. 117.
19. See Benjamin's critique of the Bergers' work, *The Bonds of Love*, pp. 199–203.
20. Callahan, *In Good Conscience*, p. 205.
21. Jean Bethke Elshtain, *Power Trips and Other Journeys: Essays in Feminism as Civic Discourse* (Madison: Univ. of Wisconsin Press, 1990), p. 60. See also essays by Elshtain and others collected in Elshtain, ed., *The Family in Political Thought*. Elshtain's essays on the family are valuable contributions to these debates.
22. See discussion of the "symmetrical" family in Arlene Skolnick, *Embattled Paradise*, esp. pp. 193, 204.

6. The Feminist Critique of Western Character Formation

1. Isaac Balbus, *Marxism and Domination*, p. 304; for a recent analysis of psychoanalytic feminism see Patricia Elliot, *From Mastery to Analysis: Theories of Gender in Psychoanalytic Feminism* (Ithaca: Cornell Univ. Press, 1991). Elliot studies a number of these thinkers, and provides a more extended list; see p. 10.
2. Nancy Chodorow, *The Reproduction of Mothering: Psychoanalysis and the Sociology of Gender*, pp. 6–7.
3. My account of Dinnerstein and Chodorow has drawn upon the detailed study of the Dinnerstein-Chodorow thesis found in Isaac Balbus, *Marxism and Domination*, pp. 304–97. See also Sondra Farganis, *Social Reconstruction of the Feminine Character* (Totowa, N.J.: Roman and Littlefield, 1986), p. 104; Alford, *Narcissism*, esp. pp. 182, 201–3; and Alford, *Melanie Klein*, esp. pp. 185–97. For criticism of Dinnerstein and Chodorow, see Elliot, *From Mastery to Analysis*, pp. 99–146.
4. Farganis, *Social Reconstruction of the Feminine Character*, p. 96; Chodorow, *The Reproduction of Mothering*, pp. 13, 36–37, 187–89.
5. Alford, *Melanie Klein*, p. 185.
6. Balbus, *Marxism and Domination*, p. 305. See Chodorow's comments on her relation to Dinnerstein, *Feminism and Psychoanalytic Theory*, pp. 81–82; 238 n. 14; 184–85.
7. Balbus, *Marxism and Domination*, p. 309.
8. Ibid., p. 311.
9. Dorothy Dinnerstein, *The Mermaid and the Minotaur: Sexual Arrangements and Human Malaise* (New York: Harper and Row, 1976), p. xii.

10. Ibid., p. 85.
11. Ibid., p. 94.
12. Chodorow, *The Reproduction of Mothering*, pp. 180–81. In *Feminism and Psychoanalytic Theory*, Chodorow qualifies this claim by recognizing that mothering is one of the factors in the construction of patriarchy. I confine my attention here to Chodorow's indebtedness to Melanie Klein and Janine Chasseguet-Smirgel. For her connection with object-relations theorists, see e.g. Elliot, *From Mastery to Analysis*, pp. 137–38.
13. Ibid., pp. 174–77, 187–88.
14. Ibid., p. 215.
15. Catherine Keller, *From a Broken Web: Separation, Sexism, and Self* (Boston: Beacon Press, 1986), p. 125.
16. Chodorow, *The Reproduction of Mothering*, p. 219.
17. Ibid., pp. 217–18.
18. Ibid., p. 165.
19. Ibid., p. 168.
20. Ibid., p. 169.
21. Chodorow offers an interesting critique (and defense) of the tendency toward universalization and absolutization of the mother-relation in her essay (with Susan Contratto), "The Fantasy of the Perfect Mother" (1982) found in *Feminism and Psychoanalytic Theory*. There the authors contend that the view that "what happens in the earliest mother-infant relationship determines the whole of history, society, and culture" (89) is a cultural ideology that came to be dominant in the nineteenth century. This ideological "belief in the all-powerful mother" (p. 90) is found in feminist as well as antifeminist writings. In one of its variations it appears in Chodorow's *The Reproduction of Mothering* as well (p. 238 n. 14). But the ideology in turn derives to a significant degree from the fact that we were all "mothered exclusively by one woman" (p. 90). Thus Chodorow and Contratto find a vicious circle: "Psyche and culture merge here and reflexively create one another" (p. 90). This analysis, while insightful regarding culture's repetitions, leaves unexplained how the nineteenth century could differ from earlier periods in this respect.
22. Balbus, *Marxism and Domination*, p. 391.
23. Ibid., p. 394.
24. See, for example, ibid., pp. 311, 342 n. 96.
25. Ibid., p. 322.
26. Ibid., p. 397.
27. Ibid., pp. 311–12.
28. See ibid., pp. 345–47, 388.
29. Chodorow, *The Reproduction of Mothering*, pp. 3, 211, 214–15.
30. Ibid., p. 218; see also pp. 178–90.
31. Keller, *From a Broken Web*, p. 131.
32. Elliot, *From Mastery to Analysis*, p. 239.

7. Psychoanalytic Feminists on Conscience

1. See, for example, Freud, *New Introductory Lectures in Psychoanalysis*, p. 67, a passage cited in chapter 1.
2. For Dinnerstein, see *The Mermaid and the Minotaur*, pp. 112–13, 187; for Chodorow, see *The Reproduction of Mothering*, pp. 211, 212, 218.
3. Chodorow, *The Reproduction of Mothering*, p. 218.
4. Dinnerstein, *The Mermaid and the Minotaur*, pp. 113–14.
5. Dinnerstein, "Afterword: Toward the Mobilization of Eros, " in *Face to Face: Fathers, Mothers, Masters—Essays for a Nonsexist Future*, ed. Meg McGavran Murray (Westport, Conn.: Greenwood Press, 1983), p. 302.

6. Dinnerstein, *The Mermaid and the Minotaur*, p. 136.
7. Ibid., p. 109.
8. Chodorow, *The Reproduction of Mothering*, p. 181.
9. Ibid., p. 188.
10. Ibid., p. 190.
11. Ibid., p. 212.
12. Ibid., p. 169.
13. Ibid., p. 188. Chodorow's discussion here appears to have been influenced by David Riesman's distinction between "inner direction" and "other direction" in *The Lonely Crowd: A Study of the Changing American Character* (Garden City, N.Y.: Doubleday Anchor Books, 1953).
14. Ibid., p. 189.
15. Melanie Klein, *Envy and Gratitude and Other Works, 1946–1963* (Delacorte Press/Seymour Lawrence, 1975), p. 297; see also Melanie Klein, "The Early Development of Conscience in the Child" in *Contributions to Psychoanalysis, 1921–1945*, pp. 267–77.
16. Klein, *Envy and Gratitude*, pp. 32–50. Dinnerstein interprets Klein's references to the breast not simply in a literal sense but symbolically as a metaphor for "source of good" (*The Mermaid and the Minotaur*), p. 96.
17. Klein, *Envy and Gratitude*, p. 321.
18. Melanie Klein, *Love, Guilt, and Reparation and Other Works, 1921–1945* (Delacorte Press/Seymour Lawrence, 1975), p. 248.
19. Klein, *Envy and Gratitude*, p. 321.
20. Ibid., p. 279.
21. Ibid., p. 323.
22. Dinnerstein, *The Mermaid and the Minotaur*, pp. 100, 102.
23. Chodorow, *The Reproduction of Mothering*, p. 204. She cites Klein in this connection.
24. Dinnerstein, *The Mermaid and the Minotaur*, p. 103.
25. Ibid., p. 103.
26. Benjamin, *The Bonds of Love*, pp. 185–87. For another argument that the "restructuring of parenting roles" will not be enough to change the social order, see Elliot, *From Mastery to Analysis*, esp. pp. 88, 141–43.
27. Benjamin, *Bonds of Love*, p. 187.
28. Ibid.
29. Jessica Benjamin, "The Oedipal Riddle: Authority, Autonomy, and the New Narcissism," in *The Problem of Authority in America*, ed. John P. Diggins and Mark E. Kamm (Philadelphia: Temple Univ. Press, 1981), p. 210.
30. Ibid., p. 211.
31. Benjamin, *Bonds of Love*, p. 152.
32. *New German Critique* 13 (Winter 1978):53, 54.
33. Benjamin, "Oedipal Riddle," in *Problem of Authority*, ed. Diggins and Kamm, p. 218; see Benjamin, *Bonds of Love*, p. 46.
34. Benjamin, "Oedipal Riddle," in *Problem of Authority*, ed. Diggins and Kamm, pp. 218, 219.
35. Ibid., p. 218.
36. See C. Fred Alford's criticism of Benjamin on this point in *Melanie Klein*, pp. 190–93.
37. Janine Chasseguet-Smirgel's major work, *The Ego Ideal*, was published in France in 1975; it is available in an English translation by Paul Barrows, Introduction by Christopher Lasch (New York: W. W. Norton and Co., 1985); *The Mermaid and the Minotaur* was published in 1976.
38. Chodorow, *The Reproduction of Mothering*, p. 121.
39. Ibid., p. 169. Another psychoanalytic feminist, Stephanie Engel, who suggests a feminist ethic built upon the concepts of Chasseguet-Smirgel, will be mentioned in the next chapter.

40. See, for example, Janine Chasseguet-Smirgel, *The Ego Ideal*, p. 182.
41. Ibid., p. 182. The concept of narcissism is complex, and current usages are "far from convergent": Nicholas Duruz, in *Psychoanalysis and Contemporary Thought*, ed. Leo Goldberger (New York: International Universities Press, 1981), 4:3. Here I follow the approach taken by Chasseguet-Smirgel. In the next chapter I review Christopher Lasch's approach, which is influenced by Chasseguet-Smirgel. For our purposes the concept of narcissism is ancillary to the analysis of the ego ideal. Review of the extensive literature on narcissism lies beyond the scope of this essay.
42. Chasseguet-Smirgel, *The Ego Ideal*, p. 183.
43. Ibid., p. 184.
44. Ibid., p. 184. She is aware (see p. 217) of the correlation of this description of the ego ideal with Freud's comments about the "oceanic feeling" in *Civilization and Its Discontents*.
45. Ibid., pp. 182, 187, 217–19.
46. Ibid., pp. 6–7.
47. Freud, *Civilization and Its Discontents*, p. 59.
48. Duruz, *Psychoanalysis and Contemporary Thought*, ed. Goldberger, p. 30. Duruz notes that "Freud offered five differing definitions of narcissism in a seven year period" (p. 8).
49. Chasseguet-Smirgel appears to confuse things somewhat by including the father in ego-ideal processes. Her point seems to be that fatherly objects can be idealized; but the basic desire to be reunited derives from the lost mother relation. Her analysis leaves open the question whether, if fathers were to participate in early nurturance, this desire would derive from the loss of the early father-relation as well.
50. Benjamin, *Bonds of Love*, p. 151. Benjamin does not intend to deny that the mother contributes to the "narcissistic ideal of rapprochement" (p. 153).

8. Christopher Lasch on Feminism and Conscience

1. See esp. the following works by Christopher Lasch: *The Culture of Narcissism: American Life in an Age of Diminishing Expectations* (New York: W. W. Norton and Co., 1980); *Haven in a Heartless World; The Minimal Self; The True and Only Heaven: Progress and Its Critics* (New York: W. W. Norton and Company, 1991). See also my article, "Christopher Lasch and a Renewed Theory of the Family," *Perspectives in Religious Studies* 10, no. 1 (Spring 1983):15–32.
2. Lasch, *Haven in a Heartless World*, p. xvi.
3. Ibid., p. xiii.
4. See Marjorie Bell Chambers, "A Political Diary of an Assertive Woman," in *Face to Face*, ed. Murray, pp. 233–35.
5. Lasch, *Haven in a Heartless World*, p. 183.
6. See e.g. Juliet Mitchell, *Psychoanalysis and Feminism*, pp. xiv–xv. Chodorow calls this work "the first major argument for psychoanalytic feminism" (*Feminism and Psychoanalytic Theory*, p. 16).
7. Mitchell, *Psychoanalysis and Feminism*, pp. 412–13.
8. Christopher Lasch, "Freud and Women," in *New York Review of Books* 21 (October 3, 1974):12–18.
9. Ibid., p. 17.
10. Lasch's approval of Mitchell's perspective was further qualified later when he criticized Mitchell for her doctrinaire Marxism. See Lasch, *The Minimal Self*, p. 295. *The Culture of Narcissism* is unquestionably Lasch's most widely read book. I concentrate here on his later works, some of which take account of criticism that *The Culture of Narcissism* received. For a greater focus on his

earlier work, see my article "Christopher Lasch and a Renewed Theory of the Family."

11. Lasch, *The Minimal Self*, pp. 286–87.
12. Ibid., p. 19.
13. Ibid., p. 256.
14. Ibid., p. 243.
15. Christopher Lasch, "A Society without Fathers: Cooperative Commonwealth or Harmonious Ant-Heap?" in *Face to Face*, ed. Murray, pp. 3–19.
16. Lasch, Introduction, in Chasseguet-Smirgel, *The Ego Ideal*, p. x.
17. Lasch, "A Society without Fathers," in *Face to Face*, ed. Murray, p. 4.
18. Chasseguet-Smirgel as quoted in ibid.
19. Lasch, Introduction to Chasseguet-Smirgel, *The Ego Ideal*, p. xii.
20. Stephanie Engel, "Femininity as Tragedy: Reexamining the 'New Narcissism,'" *Socialist Review* 53 (September-October 1980):101, quoted in Lasch, *The Minimal Self*, p. 245 (Lasch's omissions and brackets).
21. See Lasch, *The Minimal Self*, p. 245; Lasch, "A Society without Fathers," in *Face to Face*, ed. Murray, pp. 4–6; 15, n. 5; 17, n. 11.
22. Lasch, *The Minimal Self*, p. 245. See Benjamin's discussion of Lasch on Engel in *The Bonds of Love*, pp. 156–59. I suggest a qualification of Lasch's view in the next section.
23. Lasch, *The Minimal Self*, p. 246.
24. See Chasseguet-Smirgel, *The Ego Ideal*, pp. 6–7; as we saw above, the ego ideal for her is not so much a model to be emulated as an object that promises some fragment of the lost sense of omnipotence and fusion.
25. Lasch, *The Minimal Self*, p. 246.
26. Lasch, "A Society without Fathers," in *Face to Face*, ed. Murray, p. 6. Chodorow seems to have acknowledged the legitimacy of this critique. See her warning against a too-ready approval of "visions of pre-oedipal relatedness" (*Feminism and Psychoanalytic Theory*, p. 250 n. 127); see also Lasch, *The Minimal Self*, p. 185; his alternative suggestion—a culture of "the uninhibited ego ideal"— seems still unclear; perhaps "regressive ego ideal" would serve better.
27. See Lasch, *The Culture of Narcissism*, p. 41; Lasch, *The Minimal Self*, pp. 176–77. The phrase is Roy Schafer's.
28. Lasch, *The Minimal Self*, p. 177; see the corresponding reference in Lasch, "A Society without Fathers," in *Face to Face*, ed. Murray, p. 7.
29. Ibid., pp. 7–9.
30. Lasch, *Haven in a Heartless World*, New Preface, p. xv.
31. Ibid., p. xvii.
32. Benjamin, *The Bonds of Love*, p. 140.
33. Ibid., p. 291 n. 39. See similar criticisms of Lasch made by Poster in *Critical Theory and Poststructuralism*, pp. 143–69.
34. Lasch, *The True and Only Heaven*, p. 22.
35. Lasch holds that feminism, among other influences, has "exposed the shallowness" of the Marxist view that "a revolution in property relations would automatically revolutionize the relations between men and women": *The Culture of Narcissism*, p. 347. Changes are required in consciousness (subjectivity) as well as in the economic base of society, and this means that value systems, attitudes, and ideologies must be examined and criticized. This recognition has led Lasch to reflections on the continuing need for progressive spiritual vision and moral discipline. His assessment of Western religion seems ambivalent. In his Foreword to the 1980 edition of *The Culture of Narcissism* (New York: W. W. Norton Warner Books, 1980) he writes: "Neither humanism nor religion . . . any longer has much to teach us about the modern world. . . . The best of the classical tradition, the best of Christianity and Judaism, have been incorporated into the work of Marx, Freud, Darwin, Einstein, and other pioneers of modernism, while the humanist and religious rejection of that work

makes humanism and religion increasingly irrelevant to an understanding of our social life" (pp. xvii–xviii). Elsewhere, in partial contradiction to this view, he calls for moral and spiritual renewal. He speaks of "the need for community, stability and authoritative moral leadership—the need to submit to a vigorous and demanding spiritual discipline, and to give oneself to a cause higher than the self": Christopher Lasch, "The Cultural Civil War and the Crisis of Faith," in *Katallagete* 8, no. 1 (Summer 1982):16. See also Lasch, "1984: Are We There?" in *Salmagundi* 65 (Fall 1984):62, and the concluding pages of *The Minimal Self* for other reflections on vision and moral discipline.

36. Lasch, "A Society without Fathers," in *Face to Face*, ed. Murray, p. 17.
37. Ibid., p. 7.
38. Lasch, *The Minimal Self*, p. 258.
39. Lasch, *The True and Only Heaven*, p. 39.
40. Ibid., pp. 239–40.
41. Ibid., p. 264.
42. Ibid., pp. 33, 235.
43. Ibid., p. 265.

9. Can Conscience Be Recovered?

1. See the following statement from Thomas E. Wren regarding "the way moral psychologies treat motivation": "[We] can speak of [moral agents] as having consciences that are weak, strict, tender, and so on, all without regard to the contents or deliverances of those consciences. It is even possible, though often difficult, for us to esteem and commend people for being faithful to consciences that are radically different from our own": *Caring about Morality*, p. 21. It is conscience that motivates us to take moral questions seriously. Wren terms it *moral motivation*. Conscience provides an answer to the question, why be moral?
2. Quoted in Seymour C. Post, ed., *Moral Values and the Superego Concept in Psychoanalysis* (New York: International Universities Press, 1972), p. 25.
3. For alternative approaches to the "benign" superego and discussions of implications for conscience see the collection of articles in Post, ed., *Moral Values and the Superego Concept*. Two essays that have been influential in this debate are Roy Schafer, "The Loving and Beloved Superego in Freud's Structural Theory," *Psychoanalytic Study of the Child* 15 (1960):163–88; and Henry Lowenfeld and Yela Lowenfeld, "Our Permissive Society and the Superego," *Psychoanalytic Quarterly* 39 (1970):590–607 (reprinted in Post, ed., *Moral Values and the Superego Concept*).
4. See esp. Hans Loewald, "Superego and Time," and "On Internalization," in *Papers in Psychoanalysis*, pp. 43–52, 69–86, respectively. For a very favorable assessment of Loewald's work see Chodorow, *Feminism and Psychoanalytic Theory*, pp. 10–14.
5. Loewald, *Papers on Psychoanalysis*, p. 46.
6. Ibid., p. 43.
7. Ibid., p. 50.
8. Ibid., p. 78.
9. Ibid., p. 76.
10. Ibid., p. 83. In another essay Loewald distinguishes between "primary" and "secondary or superego" identification. It is the early Oedipal-incestuous identifications that are renounced (ibid., p. 398).
11. Ibid., p. 83.
12. See ibid., pp. 400–404.
13. Sagan, *Freud, Women, and Morality*, pp. 7–8.
14. Ibid., p. 21, see also p. 14.

15. Ibid., p. 14; see pp. 22–23; see Callahan's critique of this viewpoint, *In Good Conscience*, pp. 194–95.

16. C. Fred Alford, *The Self in Social Theory* (New Haven: Yale Univ. Press, 1991), p. 173.

17. Nancy Fraser, "What's Critical about Critical Theory?: The Case of Habermas and Gender," in *Feminism as Critique*, ed. Seyla Benhabib and Drucilla Cornell (Minneapolis: Univ. of Minnesota Press, 1987), pp. 38, 49.

18. Ibid., p. 45. For discussions of Fraser's criticism of Habermas, see Peter Uwe Hohendahl, *Reappraisals: Shifting Alignments in Postwar Critical Theory* (Ithaca: Cornell Univ. Press, 1991), pp. 221–28; and Francis S. Fiorenza, "The Church as a Community of Interpretation," in *Habermas, Modernity, and Public Theology*, ed. Don S. Browning and Francis S. Fiorenza (New York: Crossroad, 1992), pp. 77–78.

19. Bonnelle L. Strickling, "Self-Abnegation," in *Feminist Perspectives*, ed. Lorraine Code, et al. (Toronto: Univ. of Toronto Press, 1988), p. 199.

20. Joel Whitebook, "The Politics of Redemption," *Telos* 63 (Spring 1985):167.

21. For reflections on how Freudians may construct an absolutistic idol of rationality and how nonauthoritarian religion may assist in mediating between the psyche and external reality, see James DiCenso, "Religion as Illusion: Reversing the Freudian Hermeneutic," *Journal of Religion* 71, no. 2. (April 1991):167–79.

22. Erich Fromm, *You Shall Be as Gods*, pp. 46–47.

23. Lasch, "A Society without Fathers," in *Face to Face*, ed. Murray, p. 8.

24. See Dorothee Soelle's discussion of "politicizing the conscience of men and women," *Political Theology*, Foreword, p. xx. It is significant that one of the key terms that has surfaced in the context of liberation theology (broadly conceived as encompassing black theology, feminist theology, and Third World liberation theology) is *conscientization*. As Letty Russell explains, this concept includes but goes beyond "consciousness-raising," for it includes criticism of culture as well as reflection: Letty Russell, *Human Liberation in a Feminist Perspective: A Theology* (Philadelphia: Westminster Press, 1974), p. 115; see her discussion of conscientization and references to other literature, pp. 105–21. In our terms conscientization is a change in one's conscience, not just in one's consciousness (or understanding). If culture is oppressive to women because of the self-images the dominant culture imposes, this is just as much a function of the superego as of the ego (see Russell, p. 118). The new conscience has a utopian aspect (Russell, p. 117). For a discussion of conscientization in Gustavo Gutiérrez, see Curt Cadorette, *From the Heart of the People: The Theology of Gustavo Gutiérrez* (Oak Park, Ill.: Meyer-Stone Books, 1988), pp. 48–56.

25. Catherine Keller, *From a Broken Web*, p. 39. This feminist approach to God-concepts is anticipated by Tillich's concept of the "God beyond the God of theism."

26. John W. Miller, *Biblical Faith and Fathering: Why We Call God Father* (Mahwah, N.J.: Paulist Press, 1989), p. 52. See also David Bakan, *And They Took Themselves Wives: The Emergence of Patriarchy in Western Civilization* (San Francisco: Harper and Row, 1979). For a discussion of fatherly and motherly symbols for God see Dorothee Soelle, *The Strength of the Weak*, pp. 106–17.

27. See Seyla Benhabib's effort to recover the utopian dimension in communicative ethics, i.e., "those images and anticipations of a fulfilled life-history and of a collective life-form" that are implicit in critical theory: "The Utopian Dimension in Communicative Ethics," in *Critical Theory: The Essential Readings*, ed. David Ingram and Julia Simon-Ingram (New York: Paragon House, 1991), pp. 388–99.

28. Alford, *Narcissism*, p. 182.

BIBLIOGRAPHY

Abel, Elizabeth, and Emily K. Abel, eds. *The Signs Reader: Women, Gender, and Scholarship.* Chicago: Univ. of Chicago Press, 1983.

Adams, James Luther, Wilhelm Pauck, and Roger Lincoln Shinn, eds. *The Thought of Paul Tillich.* San Francisco: Harper and Row, 1985.

Adorno, Theodor. *Kierkegaard: Construction of the Aesthetic.* Translated and edited by Robert Hullot-Kentor. Minneapolis: Univ. of Minnesota Press, 1989.

———. *Minima Moralia.* London: NLB, 1974.

———. *Negative Dialectics.* New York: The Seabury Press, 1973.

———. *Prisms.* Cambridge: MIT Press, 1967.

Adorno, Theodor, et al. *The Authoritarian Personality.* New York: W. W. Norton and Co., 1950.

Alford, C. Fred. *Melanie Klein and Critical Social Theory.* New Haven: Yale Univ. Press, 1989.

———. *Narcissism: Socrates, the Frankfurt School, and Psychoanalytic Theory.* New Haven: Yale Univ. Press, 1988.

———. *The Self in Social Theory.* New Haven: Yale Univ. Press, 1991.

Andolsen, Barbara, Christine E. Gudorf, and Mary D. Pellauer, eds. *Women's Consciousness, Women's Conscience: A Reader in Feminist Ethics.* San Francisco: Harper and Row, 1985.

Arato, Andrew, and Paul Breines. *The Young Lukács and the Origins of Western Marxism.* New York: Seabury Press, 1979.

Arato, Andrew, and Eike Gebhardt, eds. *The Essential Frankfurt School Reader.* New York: Urizen Books, 1978.

Ariès, Philippe. *Centuries of Childhood: A Social History of Family Life.* London: Cape, 1962.

Balbus, Isaac. *Marxism and Domination.* Princeton, N.J.: Princeton Univ. Press, 1982.

Baum, Gregory, ed. *Sociology and Human Destiny.* New York: Crossroad/ Seabury Press, 1980.

Bellah, Robert, et al. *Habits of the Heart.* Berkeley: Univ. of California Press, 1985.

Benhabib, Seyla, and Drucilla Cornell, eds. *Feminism as Critique.* Minneapolis: Univ. of Minnesota Press, 1987.

Benjamin, Jessica. *The Bonds of Love: Psychoanalysis, Feminism, and the Problem of Domination.* New York: Pantheon Books, 1988.

Berger, Peter, and Brigitte Berger. *The War over the Family: Capturing the Middle Ground.* Garden City, N.Y.: Anchor Press, 1983.

Bernstein, Richard J., ed. *Habermas and Modernity.* Cambridge: MIT Press, 1985.

Bettelheim, Bruno. *The Children of the Dream.* London: Macmillan Co., 1969.

Boyers, Robert, ed. *Psychological Man.* New York: Harper and Row, 1975.

Bronner, Stephen E., and Douglas M. Kellner, eds. *Critical Theory and Society.* New York: Routledge and Kegan Paul, 1989.

Brown, Bruce. *Marx, Freud, and the Critique of Everyday Life: Toward a Permanent Cultural Revolution.* New York: Monthly Review Press, 1973.

Browning, Don S. *Religious Thought and the Modern Psychologies.* Philadelphia: Fortress Press, 1987.

Browning, Don S., and Francis S. Fiorenza, eds. *Habermas, Modernity, and Public Theology.* New York: Crossroad, 1992.

Buck-Mors, Susan. *The Origin of Negative Dialectics: Theodor Adorno, Walter Benjamin, and the Frankfurt Institute.* New York: Free Press, 1977.

Bulman, Raymond F. *A Blueprint for Humanity: Paul Tillich's Theology of Culture.* Lewisburg: Bucknell Univ. Press, 1981.

Cadorette, Curt. *From the Heart of the People: The Theology of Gustavo Gutiérrez.* Oak Park, Ill.: Meyer-Stone Books, 1988.

Callahan, Sidney. *In Good Conscience: Reason and Emotion in Moral Decision Making.* San Francisco: Harper, 1991.

Carey, John J., ed. *Being and Doing: Paul Tillich as Ethicist.* Macon, Ga.: Mercer Univ. Press, 1987.

———. *Theonomy and Autonomy: Studies in Paul Tillich's Engagement with Modern Culture.* Macon, Ga.: Mercer Univ. Press, 1984.

Chasseguet-Smirgel, Janine. *The Ego Ideal.* Translated by Paul Barrows. Introduction by Christopher Lasch. New York: W. W. Norton and Co., 1985.

Chodorow, Nancy. *Feminism and Psychoanalytic Theory.* New Haven: Yale Univ. Press, 1989.

———. *The Reproduction of Mothering: Psychoanalysis and the Sociology of Gender.* Berkeley: Univ. of California Press, 1978.

Code, Lorraine, et al., eds. *Feminist Perspectives: Philosophical Essays on Method and Morals.* Toronto: Univ. of Toronto Press, 1988.

Colombo, J. H. *An Essay on Theology and History: Studies in Pannenberg, Metz, and the Frankfurt School.* Atlanta: Scholars Press, 1990.

Connerton, Paul. *The Tragedy of Enlightenment: An Essay on the Frankfurt School.* Cambridge: Cambridge Univ. Press, 1980.

Contril, Hadley, ed. *Tensions That Cause Wars.* Urbana: Univ. of Illinois Press, 1950.

Cupitt, Don. *Crisis of Moral Authority.* Philadelphia: Westminster Press, 1972.

Daly, Mary. *Beyond God the Father: Toward a Philosophy of Women's Liberation.* Boston: Beacon Press, 1973.

D'Arcy, Eric. *Conscience and Its Right to Freedom.* London: Sheed and Ward, 1961.

Davis, Charles. *Theology and Political Society.* Cambridge: Cambridge Univ. Press, 1980.

Dews, Peter, ed. *Autonomy and Solidarity: Interviews with Juergen Habermas.* London: Verso, 1986.

Diggins, John P., and Mark E. Kamm, eds. *The Problem of Authority in America.* Philadelphia: Temple Univ. Press, 1981.

Dinnerstein, Dorothy. *The Mermaid and the Minotaur: Sexual Arrangements and Human Malaise.* New York: Harper and Row, 1976.

Donnelly, John, and Leonard Lyons, eds. *Conscience.* Staten Island, N.Y.: Alba House, 1973.

Douglas, Ann. *The Feminization of America.* New York: Alfred A. Knopf, 1977.

Dourley, John P. *C. G. Jung and Paul Tillich: The Psyche as Sacrament.* Toronto: Inner City Books, 1981.

Dunfee, Susan Nelson. *Beyond Servanthood: Christianity and the Liberation of Women.* Lanham, Md.: Univ. Press of America, 1989.

Eisenstadt, S. N., ed. *Max Weber: On Charisma and Institution Building—Selected Papers.* Chicago: Univ. of Chicago Press, 1968.

Elliot, Patricia. *From Mastery to Analysis: Theories of Gender in Psychoanalytic Feminism.* Ithaca: Cornell Univ. Press, 1991.

Elshtain, Jean Bethke. *Power Trips and Other Journeys: Essays in Feminism as Civic Discourse.* Madison: Univ. of Wisconsin Press, 1990.

———. *Public Man, Private Woman: Women in Social and Political Thought.* Princeton, N.J.: Princeton University Press, 1981.

Elshtain, Jean Bethke, ed. *The Family in Political Thought.* Amherst: Univ. of Massachusetts Press, 1982.

Epstein, Barbara L. *The Politics of Domesticity: Women, Evangelism, and Temperance in Nineteenth-Century America.* Middletown, Ct.: Wesleyan Univ. Press, 1981.

Farganis, Sondra. *Social Reconstruction of the Feminine Character.* Totowa, N.J.: Roman and Littlefield, 1986.

Feuer, Lewis, ed. *Marx and Engels: Basic Writings on Politics and Philosophy.* Garden City, N.Y.: Doubleday Anchor, 1959.

Fishburn, Janet Forsythe. *The Fatherhood of God and the Victorian Family: The Social Gospel in America.* Philadelphia: Fortress Press, 1981.

Floyd, Wayne Whitson, Jr. *Theology and the Dialectics of Otherness: On Reading Bonhoeffer and Adorno.* Lanham, Md.: Univ. Press of America, 1988.

Freud, Sigmund. *Civilization and Its Discontents.* New York: W. W. Norton and Co., 1961.

——. *Collected Papers.* London: Hogarth and Co., 1950.

——. *The Complete Psychological Works.* Vol. 19. London: Hogarth Press, 1961.

——. *The Future of an Illusion.* Garden City, N.Y.: Doubleday Anchor, 1944.

——. *Moses and Monotheism.* New York: Random House, 1939.

——. *New Introductory Lectures.* New York: W. W. Norton and Co., 1964.

Frankfurt Institute for Social Research, ed. *Aspects of Sociology.* Boston: Beacon Press, 1972.

Fromm, Erich. *The Anatomy of Destructiveness.* Greenwich, Ct.: Fawcett Books, 1973.

——. *The Art of Loving.* New York: Bantam Books, 1956.

——. *The Crisis of Psychoanalysis: Essays on Freud, Marx, and Social Psychology.* New York: Holt, Rinehart and Winston, 1970.

——. *Escape from Freedom.* New York: Avon Books, 1969.

——. *The Dogma of Christ and Other Essays on Religion, Psychology, and Culture.* New York: Holt, Rinehart, and Winston, 1955.

——. *For the Love of Life.* Edited by Hans Juergen Schultz. New York: Free Press, 1986.

——. *Gesamtausgabe.* Band 8. Stuttgart: Deutsche Verlags-Anstalt, 1981.

——. *Greatness and Limitations of Freud's Thought.* New York: New American Library, 1980.

——. *To Have or To Be?* New York: Harper and Row, 1976.

——. *The Heart of Man.* New York: Harper and Row, 1964.

——. *Man for Himself.* New York: Rinehart and Co., 1947.

——. *The Sane Society.* New York: Rinehart and Co., 1955.

——. *You Shall Be as Gods: A Radical Interpretation of the Old Testament and Its Tradition.* New York: Holt, Rinehart and Winston, 1966.

Funk, Rainer. *Erich Fromm: The Courage to Be Human.* New York: Continuum Publishing Co., 1989.

Gilkey, Langdon. *Gilkey on Tillich.* New York: Crossroad, 1990.

Gilligan, Carol. *In a Different Voice.* Cambridge: Harvard University Press, 1982.

Goldberger, Leo, ed. *Psychoanalysis and Contemporary Thought.* New York: International Universities Press, 1981.

Goldman, Harvey. *Max Weber and Thomas Mann: Calling and the Shaping of the Self.* Berkeley: Univ. of California Press, 1988.

Gould, Carol C., ed. *Beyond Domination: New Perspectives on Women and Philosophy.* Totowa, N.J.: Rowman and Allanheld, 1984.

Greeley, Andrew, ed. *The Family in Crisis or in Transition: A Sociological and Theological Perspective.* New York: Seabury Press, 1979.

Green, Robert W. *Protestantism, Capitalism, and Social Science: The Weber Thesis Controversy.* 2d ed. Lexington, Mass.: D.C. Heath and Co., 1973.

Greer, Germaine. *Sex and Destiny: The Politics of Human Fertility.* New York: Harper and Row, 1984.

Greven, Philip J. *Four Generations: Population, Land, and Family in Colonial Andover, Massachusetts.* Ithaca: Cornell Univ. Press, 1970.

———. *The Protestant Temperament: Patterns of Child-Rearing, Religious Experience, and the Self in Early America.* New York: Knopf, 1977.

Grimshaw, Jean. *Philosophy and Feminist Thinking.* Minneapolis: Univ. of Minnesota Press, 1986.

Habermas, Juergen. *Communication and the Evolution of Society.* Boston: Beacon Press, 1979.

———. *Legitimation Crisis.* Boston: Beacon Press, 1975.

———. *Moral Consciousness and Communicative Action.* Cambridge: MIT Press, 1990.

———. *Postmetaphysical Thinking: Philosophical Essays.* Translated by William Hohengarten. Cambridge: MIT Press, 1992.

———. *The Theory of Communicative Action.* Vols. 1 and 2. Boston: Beacon Press, 1984, 1987.

Hamerton-Kelly, Robert. *God the Father: Theology and Patriarchy in the Teachings of Jesus.* Philadelphia: Fortress Press, 1979.

Hammond, Guyton B. *Man in Estrangement: A Comparison of the Thought of Paul Tillich and Erich Fromm.* Nashville: Vanderbilt Univ. Press, 1965.

Harrison, Beverly Wildung. *Making the Connections: Essays in Feminist Social Ethics.* Edited by Carol S. Robb. Boston: Beacon Press, 1985.

Hartman, Heinz. *Psychoanalysis and Moral Values.* New York: International Universities Press, 1960.

Hauerwas, Stanley. *A Community of Character: Toward a Constructive Christian Social Ethic.* Notre Dame: Univ. of Notre Dame Press, 1981.

Hegel, G. F. W. *On Christianity: Early Theological Writings.* Translated T. M. Knox. Introduction by Richard Kroner. New York: Harper and Brothers, 1961.

————. *The Phenomenology of Mind.* New York: Harper and Row, 1967.

————. *Werke in Zwanzig Banden.* Vol. 1, *Fruehe Schriften.* Frankfurt: Suhrkamp Verlag, 1971.

Hohendahl, Peter Uwe. *Reappraisals: Shifting Alignments in Postwar Critical Theory.* Ithaca: Cornell Univ. Press, 1991.

Horkheimer, Max. *Critical Theory: Selected Essays.* New York: Seabury Press, 1972.

————. *Critique of Instrumental Reason.* New York: Seabury Press, 1971.

————. *Dawn and Decline: Notes 1926–1931 and 1950–1969.* New York: Seabury Press, 1978.

————. *Eclipse of Reason.* New York: Seabury Press, 1974.

————. *Die Gesellschaftliche Funktion der Philosophie.* Frankfurt: Suhrkamp Verlag, 1979.

————. *Gesellschaft im Uebergang: Aufsaetze, Reden, und Vortraege, 1942–1970.* Frankfurt: Fischer Taschenbuch Verlag, 1972.

————. *Die Sehnsucht nach dem ganz Anderen: Ein Interview mit Kommentar von Helmut Gumnior.* Hamburg: Furche Verlag, 1970.

Horkheimer, Max, ed. *Autoritaet und Familie: Studien aus dem Institut fuer Sozialforschung.* Paris: Librairie Felix Alcan, 1936.

Horkheimer, Max, and Theodor Adorno. *Dialectic of Enlightenment.* New York: Seabury Press, 1972.

Ingram, David. *Critical Theory and Philosophy.* New York: Paragon House, 1990.

Ingram, David, and Julia Simon-Ingram, eds. *Critical Theory: The Essential Readings.* New York: Paragon House, 1991.

Izenberg, Gerald N. *The Existentialist Critique of Freud: The Crisis of Autonomy.* Princeton, N.J.: Princeton Univ. Press, 1976.

Jacoby, Russell. *Social Amnesia: A Critique of Contemporary Psychology from Adler to Laing.* Boston: Beacon Press, 1975.

Jay, Martin. *Adorno.* Cambridge: Harvard Univ. Press, 1984.

————. *The Dialectical Imagination: A History of the Frankfurt School and the Institute of Social Research, 1923–1950.* Boston: Little, Brown, and Co., 1973.

Jones, James W. *Contemporary Psychoanalysis and Religion: Transference and Transcendence.* New Haven: Yale Univ. Press, 1991.

Keller, Catherine. *From a Broken Web: Separation, Sexism, and Self.* Boston: Beacon Press, 1986.

Kellner, Douglas. *Critical Theory, Marxism, and Modernity.* Baltimore: Johns Hopkins Univ. Press, 1988.

————. *Herbert Marcuse and the Crisis of Marxism.* Berkeley: Univ. of California Press, 1984.

Klein, Melanie. *Contributions to Psychoanalysis, 1921–1945.* London: Hogarth Press, 1968.

————. *Envy and Gratitude and Other Works, 1946–1963.* N.p.: Delacorte Press/Seymour Lawrence, 1975.

———. *Love, Guilt, and Reparation and Other Works, 1921–1945.* N.p.: Delacorte Press/Seymour Lawrence, 1975.

Knapp, Gerhard. *The Art of Living: Erich Fromm's Life and Works.* New York: Peter Lang, 1989.

Knox, T. M., trans. and ed. *Hegel's Philosophy of Right.* London: Oxford Univ. Press, 1952.

Kueng, Hans. *Freud and the Problem of God.* Enlarged edition. New Haven: Yale Univ. Press, 1990.

Lamb, Matthew. *Solidarity with Victims: Toward a Theology of Social Transformation.* New York: Crossroad, 1982.

Lasch, Christopher. *The Culture of Narcissism: American Life in an Age of Diminishing Expectations.* New York: W. W. Norton and Co., 1980.

———. *Haven in a Heartless World: The Family Besieged.* New York: Basic Books, 1979.

———. *The Minimal Self: Psychic Survival in Troubled Times.* New York: W. W. Norton and Co., 1984.

———. *The True and Only Heaven: Progress and Its Critics.* New York: W. W. Norton and Co., 1991.

———. *The World of Nations: Reflections on American History, Politics, and Culture.* New York: Alfred A. Knopf, 1973.

Leese, Kurt. *Die Religion des Protestantischen Menschen.* Berlin: Junker und Duennhaupt Verlag, 1938.

Leibrecht, Walter, ed. *Religion and Culture: Essays in Honor of Paul Tillich.* New York: Harper and Brothers, 1959.

Leiss, William. *The Domination of Nature.* Boston: Beacon Press, 1974.

Leites, Edmund. *The Puritan Conscience and Modern Sexuality.* New Haven: Yale Univ. Press, 1986.

Leverenz, David. *The Language of Puritan Feeling.* New Brunswick: Rutgers Univ. Press, 1980.

Lipton, Robert Jay. *Boundaries: Psychological Man in Revolution.* New York: Simon and Schuster, 1967.

Little, David. *Religion, Order, and Law: A Study in Pre-Revolutionary England.* Chicago: Univ. of Chicago Press, 1969.

Loewald, Hans. *Papers in Psychoanalysis.* New Haven: Yale Univ. Press, 1980.

Marcuse, Herbert. *Counterrevolution and Revolt.* Boston: Beacon Press, 1972.

———. *Eros and Civilization.* Boston: Beacon Press, 1955.

———. *Five Lectures.* Boston: Beacon Press, 1970.

———. *Hegel's Ontology and the Theory of Historicity.* Translated by Seyla Benhabib. Cambridge: MIT Press, 1987.

———. *One-Dimensional Man.* Boston: Beacon Press, 1964.

———. *Studies in Critical Philosophy.* Boston: Beacon Press, 1973.

Metz, Johannes. *Theology of the World.* New York: Seabury Press, 1969.

Milgate, Murray, and Cheryl B. Welch, eds. *Critical Issues in Social Thought.* New York: Harcourt, Brace, Jovanovich, 1989.

Mills, Patricia Jagentowicz. *Woman, Nature, and Psyche.* New Haven: Yale Univ. Press, 1987.

Mitchell, Juliet. *Psychoanalysis and Feminism: Freud, Reich, Laing and Women.* New York: Pantheon Books, 1974.

Mitchell, Basil. *Morality: Religious and Secular.* Oxford: Clarendon Press, 1980.

Mitscherlich, Alexander. *Society without the Father: A Contribution to Social Psychology.* New York: Schocken Books, 1970.

Mitscherlich, Alexander, and Margarete Mitscherlich. *The Inability to Mourn: Principles of Collective Behavior.* New York: Grove Press, Inc., 1975.

Mitterauer, Michael, and Reinhard Sieder. *The European Family: Patriarchy to Partnership from the Middle Ages to the Present.* Chicago: Univ. of Chicago Press, 1982.

Mitzman, Arthur. *The Iron Cage: An Historical Interpretation of Max Weber.* New York: Alfred A. Knopf, 1970.

Mount, Eric, Jr. *Conscience and Responsibility.* Richmond, Va.: John Knox Press, 1969.

Murray, Meg McGavran, ed. *Face to Face: Fathers, Mothers, Masters— Essays for a Nonsexist Future.* Westport, Conn.: Greenwood Press, 1983.

Nelson, C. Ellis, ed. *Conscience: Theological and Psychological Perspectives.* New York: Newman Press, 1973.

Nelson, Benjamin. *On the Roads to Modernity: Conscience, Science, and Civilizations.* Totowa, N.J.: Roman and Littlefield, 1981.

Nicholson, Linda J. *Gender and History: The Limits of Social Theory in the Age of the Family.* New York: Columbia Univ. Press, 1986.

Niebuhr, Reinhold. *Justice and Mercy.* Edited by Ursula M. Niebuhr. Louisville: Westminster/John Knox Press, 1974.

Ochs, Carol. *Behind the Sex of God: Toward a New Consciousness— Transcending Matriarchy and Patriarchy.* Boston: Beacon Press, 1977.

Ogilvy, James. *Many Dimensional Man: Decentralizing Self, Society, and the Sacred.* New York: Oxford Univ. Press, 1977.

Ozment, Steven. *When Fathers Ruled: Family Life in Reformation Europe.* Cambridge: Harvard Univ. Press, 1983.

Pauck, Wilhelm, and Marion Pauck. *Paul Tillich: His Life and Thought.* Vol. I, *Life.* New York: Harper and Row, 1976.

Peukert, Helmut. *Science, Action, and Fundamental Theology: Toward a Theology of Communicative Action.* Cambridge: MIT Press, 1984.

Poggi, Gianfranco. *Calvinism and the Capitalist Spirit: Max Weber's Protestant Ethic.* Amherst: Univ. of Massachusetts Press, 1983.

Post, Seymour C., ed. *Moral Values and the Superego Concept in Psychoanalysis.* New York: International Universities Press, 1972.

Poster, Mark. *Critical Theory and Poststructuralism: In Search of a Context.* Ithaca: Cornell Univ. Press, 1989.

———. *Critical Theory of the Family*. New York: Seabury Press, 1978.

Reich, Wilhelm. *The Invasion of Compulsory Sex-Morality*. New York: Farrar, Strauss, and Giroux, 1970.

———. *The Mass Psychology of Fascism*. New York: Farrar, Strauss, and Giroux, 1970.

Richard, Jean, ed. *Religion et Culture: Actes du Colloque International du Centenaire Paul Tillich*. Quebec: Presses de l'Université Laval, 1987.

Rickman, John, ed. *A General Selection from the Works of Sigmund Freud*. Garden City, N.Y.: Doubleday Anchor, 1957.

Riesman, David. *The Lonely Crowd: A Study of the Changing American Character*. Garden City, N.Y.: Doubleday Anchor Books, 1953.

Robertson, Roland, and Burkart Holzner, eds. *Identity and Authority: Explorations in the Theory of Society*. Oxford: Basil Blackwell, 1980.

Rosenberg, Charles E., ed. *The Family in History*. Philadelphia: Univ. of Pennsylvania Press, 1975.

Rouner, Leroy S., ed. *On Community*. Notre Dame, Ind.: Univ. of Notre Dame Press, 1991.

Ruddick, Sara. *Maternal Thinking: Toward a Politics of Peace*. New York: Ballantine Books, 1989.

Russell, Letty. *Human Liberation in a Feminist Perspective: A Theology*. Philadelphia: Westminster Press, 1974.

Sagan, Eli. *Freud, Women, and Morality*. New York: Basic Books, 1988.

Sahay, Arun, ed. *Max Weber and Modern Sociology*. London: Routledge and Kegan Paul, 1971.

Scaff, Lawrence A. *Fleeing the Iron Cage: Culture, Politics, and Modernity in the Thought of Max Weber*. Berkeley: Univ. of California Press, 1989.

Schaefer, Roy. *A New Language for Psychoanalysis*. New Haven: Yale Univ. Press, 1980.

Scheible, Hartmut. *Theodor W. Adorno*. Hamburg: Rowohlt Taschenbuch Verlag, 1989.

Schluchter, Wolfgang. *The Rise of Western Rationalism: Max Weber's Developmental History*. Berkeley: Univ. of California Press, 1981.

Schroyer, Trent. *The Critique of Domination: The Origins and Development of Critical Theory*. Boston: Beacon Press, 1973.

Sennett, Richard. *Authority*. New York: Vintage Books, 1981.

Siebert, Rudolf J. *From Critical Theory of Society to Theology of Communicative Praxis*. Washington D.C.: Univ. Press of America, 1979.

———. *Horkheimer's Critical Sociology of Religion: The Relative and the Transcendent*. Washington, D.C.: Univ. Press of America, 1979.

———. *Hegel's Concept of Marriage and Family: The Origin of Subjective Freedom*. Washington, D.C.: Univ. Press of America, 1979.

Skolnick, Arlene. *Embattled Paradise: The American Family in an Age of Uncertainty*. New York: Basic Books, 1991.

Slater, Phil. *The Origin and Significance of the Frankfurt School.* London: Routledge and Kegan Paul, 1977.

Soelle, Dorothee. *Beyond Mere Obedience.* New York: Pilgrim Press, 1982.

―――. *Political Theology.* Philadelphia: Fortress Press, 1974.

―――. *The Strength of the Weak: Toward a Christian Feminist Identity.* Philadelphia: Westminster Press, 1984.

Stammer, Otto, ed. *Max Weber and Sociology Today.* New York: Harper and Row, 1971.

Staten, John C. *Conscience and the Reality of God: An Essay on the Experimental Foundations of Religious Knowledge.* New York: Mouton de Gruyter, 1988.

Stein, Edward V. *Fathering: Fact or Fable?* Nashville: Abingdon, 1977.

Stendahl, Krister. *Paul among Jews and Gentiles.* Philadelphia: Fortress Press, 1976.

Stokes, Allison. *Ministry after Freud.* New York: Pilgrim Press, 1985.

Stone, Lawrence. *The Family, Sex, and Marriage in England: 1500–1800.* New York: Harper and Row, 1977.

Stone, Ronald H. *Paul Tillich's Radical Social Thought.* Atlanta: John Knox Press, 1980.

Strouse, Jean. *Women and Analysis: Dialogues on Psychoanalytic Views of Femininity.* New York: Viking Press, 1974.

Stumme, John. *Socialism in Theological Perspective: A Study of Paul Tillich, 1918–1933.* Atlanta: Scholars Press, 1978.

Tennis, Dianne. *Is God the Only Reliable Father?* Philadelphia: Westminster Press, 1985.

Thomas, Laurence. *Living Morally: A Psychology of Moral Character.* Philadelphia: Temple Univ. Press, 1989.

Thompson, John B., and David Held, eds. *Habermas: Critical Debates.* Cambridge: MIT Press, 1982.

Thorne, Barrie, ed. *Rethinking the Family: Some Feminist Questions.* New York: Longman, 1982.

Tillich, Paul. *Fuer und wider den Sozialismus.* Munich: Siebenstern Taschenbuch Verlag, 1969.

―――. *The Meaning of Health.* Edited by Perry LeFevre. Chicago: Exploration Press, 1984.

―――. *Political Expectation.* New York: Harper and Row, 1971.

―――. *The Protestant Era.* London: Nisbet and Co., 1951.

―――. *Der Protestantismus als Kritik und Gestaltung.* Munich: Siebenstern Taschenbuch Verlag, 1966.

―――. *The Religious Situation.* Translated by Franklin Sherman. New York: Meridian Books, 1956.

―――. *The Socialist Decision.* New York: Harper and Row, 1977.

―――. *Systematic Theology.* Vol. 3. Chicago: Univ. of Chicago Press, 1963.

Troeltsch, Ernst. *The Social Teachings of the Christian Churches.* Vols. 1 and 2. London: George Allen and Unwin, Ltd., 1931.

Tucker, Robert, ed. *Marx-Engels Reader.* New York: W. W. Norton and Co., 1972.

Tyson, Phyllis, and Robert Tyson. *Psychoanalytic Theories of Development.* New Haven: Yale Univ. Press, 1990.

Van Herik, Judith. *Freud on Femininity and Faith.* Berkeley: Univ. of California Press, 1982.

Wallwork, Ernest. *Psychoanalysis and Ethics.* New Haven: Yale Univ. Press, 1991.

Walzer, Michael. *The Revolution of the Saints.* Cambridge: Harvard Univ. Press, 1965.

Weber, Max. *Economy and Society.* Berkeley: Univ. of California Press, 1978.

——. *The Protestant Ethic and the Spirit of Capitalism.* 2d ed. New York: Charles Scribner's Sons, 1958.

Weinstein, Fred, and Gerald M. Platt. *The Wish to Be Free.* Berkeley: Univ. of California Press, 1969.

Welter, Barbara. *Dimity Convictions.* Athens: Ohio Univ. Press, 1976.

Werk und Wirken Paul Tillichs: Ein Gedenkbuch. Mit der letzten Rede von Paul Tillich und Beitraegen von: T. W. Adorno, Ernst Bloch, Max Horkheimer, et al. Stuttgart: Evangelisches Verlagswerk, 1967.

Wesel, Uwe. *Der Mythos vom Matriarchat: Ueber Bachofens Mutterrecht und die Stellung von Frauen in fruehen Gesellschaften.* Frankfurt: Suhrkamp Verlag, 1980.

Western Marxism: A Critical Reader. Edited by New Left Review. London: Verso, 1978.

White, Stephen K. *The Recent Work of Juergen Habermas: Reason, Justice, and Modernity.* Cambridge: Cambridge Univ. Press, 1988.

Wilkinson, Rupert. *The Broken Rebel: A Study in Culture, Politics, and Authoritarian Character.* New York: Harper and Row, 1972.

Wren, Thomas E. *Caring about Morality: Philosophical Perspectives in Moral Psychology.* Cambridge: MIT Press, 1991.

Wren, Thomas E., ed. *The Moral Domain: Essays in the Ongoing Discussion between Philosophy and the Social Sciences.* Cambridge: MIT Press, 1990.

Ziff, Larzer. *Puritanism in America: New Culture in a New World.* New York: Viking Press, 1973.

INDEX

Chodorow, Nancy (*cont.*)
    ily, 99–102; and Christopher
    Lasch's critique, 165 n.26; and
    Dinnerstein-Chodorow thesis,
    94–96; and Hans Loewald, 166
    n.4; and Juliet Mitchell, 164 n.6;
    and mother relation, 162 n.21;
    and superego concepts, 100, 106–
    7
Conformism, democratic, 60–61, 68,
    70
Conscience: and critique of its pa-
    thologies, 95, 128, 134, 141, 145;
    definitions of, 1–3; externalized,
    65; Freud's account of, 5, 6, 16–
    19; humanistic, 67, 134, 140; in-
    tersection of psychological, fa-
    milial, and ideological factors in,
    5, 8–9; and intersubjectivity, 152
    n.23; motherly component in,
    54–56, 67–68, 142–43; recovery
    of, 6, 8–10, 134, 145; and its self-
    criticism, 9, 73–75; as superego
    and ego ideal, 126, 137; trans-
    moral, 52–56, 132, 142; as voice
    of ideal self in ideal community,
    9–10, 74, 130, 132–33, 144–45
Consciencelessness, 3, 14, 128
Conscientization, 167 n.24
Critical theorists. *See* Frankfurt
    School, the

Dinnerstein, Dorothy, 8, 124, 134,
    135, 136, 140, 163 n.16; and
    Erich Fromm, 97–98; and gender
    arrangements, 96–99
Dinnerstein-Chodorow thesis, 95,
    100, 107, 110, 161 n.3
Disillusionment, 5, 133, 143
Domination: and its critique, 80–81;
    by ego, 47, 48; by external au-
    thority, 49, 70; internalized, 9,
    23, 30, 32–35, 39–40, 60, 61, 65,
    72–73, 76–77, 104, 128; patri-
    archal, 23, 30, 32, 39, 84; and its
    tenacity, 93–94
Duruz, Nicholas, 164 n.41

Ego: and control of nature, 104; de-
    velopment in men, 100; develop-
    ment in women, 109; psychoana-
    lytic feminists' view of, 104–6;
    and superego, 130–31; *see also*
    Individualization
Ego ideal: combined with superego,
    121–22, 137; as distinguished

from superego, 113–16, 136–37;
    and incest fantasy, 113; and mor-
    ality, 132–33; and mother rela-
    tion, 114–16; pathologies of,
    137; progressive and regressive
    types of, 121–25; and transmoral
    conscience, 115–16
Eliot, Patricia, 163 n.26
Elshtain, Jean Bethke, 92
Engel, Stephanie, 121–22, 132, 137,
    142

Family: as alternative to totalitarian
    state, 64; autonomy of, 42, 77; in
    bourgeois society, 74–77, 81,
    118–20, 125; Erich Fromm's
    view of, 28–29; and father-
    absence, 108–9; feminist cri-
    tique of, 134; Freud's view of, 18,
    28–29, 36, 80–81, 96, 110, 155
    n.26; history of, 7, 36–37, 62, 79–
    80; and ideology of mothering,
    138–39; Mark Poster's view of,
    81–84; Marx's view of, 19–20;
    Max Horkheimer's view of, 36–
    41, 74–75; and patriarchy, 22–
    24, 40–41, 60–61, 93–94, 133–
    34; Peter and Brigitte Berger's
    view of, 84–87; and Protestant-
    ism, 34–35, 38–43, 56–57, 64,
    142–43; as psychological agency
    of society, 28–29, 31, 76–77; and
    superegos of men and women,
    135; and its symmetrical devel-
    opment, 98, 99, 101, 111, 124–
    25, 137; Wilhelm Reich's view
    of, 22–23
Father relation: in Dorothy Dinner-
    stein and Nancy Chodorow, 109;
    in Melanie Klein, 108; progres-
    sive potential of, 113–15; in psy-
    choanalytic feminism, 95–102;
    in Theodor Adorno, 64–65
Feminism, 7, 16, 24, 79, 80, 84, 86–
    87, 93, 128, 129, 134; and cri-
    tique of patriarchy, 117; and vi-
    sion of utopian community, 90
Frankfurt School (Frankfurt Institute
    for Social Research), 7–8, 46, 49,
    64, 79, 80, 83, 86, 128, 141, 142,
    144, 150 n.13, 153 n.35; and
    bourgeois family, 119, 120; and
    Christopher Lasch, 119, 120,
    127; and critique of conscience,
    134; and critique of ego domina-
    tion, 104; Erich Fromm's role in,